The Munro Society

JOURNAL

No. 6 **2022**

THE MUNRO SOCIETY JOURNAL No. 6, 2022

Published by The Munro Society 2022
www.themunrosociety.com

A catalogue record for this book is available from the British Library.

ISBN 978-1-9996293-2-8

Design and typeset by Jeremy Fenton

Printed and bound in Great Britain by Bell & Bain Ltd., Glasgow

Front cover – Sgùrr Fiona, An Teallach (Norman McNab)
Back cover – Ben Loyal from Lochan Hakel (Norman McNab)

SIR HUGH T MUNRO

(©SMC Image Archives)

The **Munro Society**
Office Bearers

The Munro Society Objectives

- To provide an informed and valued body of opinion on matters affecting the Munros and Scotland's mountain landscapes.
- To foster social and cultural exchange between members.
- To maintain archive material on Munros and Munroists.

The views expressed by contributors to the Journal are not necessarily those held by The Munro Society.

CONTENTS

Part 1 – The Munro Society

The Munro Society – the First Twenty Years............ Anne Butler* 1

Part 2 – Rounds, Lists and Completions

A Munro Round .... Donnie Campbell........15

The Corbetts – Time Well Spent.................................... Anne Butler*.................21

Coming Full Circle on Ben Nevis .... Alan Rowan* 29

Munro Musings by an Australian Compleatist .... Ilona Turnbull*.............37

Carless Hills .... Pauline Symaniak 45

Munros and Corbetts by Train................................ Oliver Bartrum* 51

Mullardoch Round.. Mark Gibson* 61

The First Munro Dogs – Storm................................ Hamish Brown* 67

'I've Got a Little List' .... Iain Robertson* 75

A Winter Munro Round .... Kevin Woods...............79

Number Culture .... Alan Dawson* 87

A Posthumous Completion .... Robin Campbell*........93

Part 3 – Going the Distance

Cairngorm Parkrun... Ian Stewart 99

A Journey through Wales – Summer 2005 .... Mike Weedon* 107

The Cape Wrath Trail.. Robin Wallace 117

282 Munros in a Day... Mark Hartree *et al* 126

Coast to Coast... Andrew Fraser* 136

A Wee May Stravaig... Jim McKenna 142

Part 4 – Round the World

The World Ribus Project .... Rob Woodall 151

Life on the Ice.. Fran Pothecary.............159

Captain's Log (Star)Date 1770............................... Alec Mamwell* 165

Karakoram Experience... David Gibson* 175

The Alps.. Stewart Logan* 183

Kayaking in Patagonia.. Will Copestake.............195

The Luck of the Irish.. James Forrest................207

The Red Tartan Shirt.. Elizabeth Mellows........215

Part 5 – Life in the Mountains

Citizen Science – Secret Life of a Chionophile............... Iain Cameron 221

The John Muir Trust .... David Balharry 232

Mountains for All... Lucy Wallace................237

Photographing Mountain Flora .... Bert Barnett* 245

Siren or Sanctuary .... Heather Morning*........250

Part 6 – Reflections

First Munro Compleater – Rev AE Robertson .... John H Robertson........257

John Dow, 1881 – 1972... Robin Campbell* 264

Reflections of an Ancient Hillwalker....................... Norman McNab*..........271

Six Decades on the Whaleback............................... Derek Sime* 281

'Tis 60 Years Since .... Charles Murray*...........293

Three Dogs on my Head .... Alf Barnard* 295

Summit Nights .... Jeremy Fenton* 300

Appendices

Appendix 1 – TMS at Twenty 308

Appendix 2 – The First Twenty Years – A Photographic Essay 313

denotes Munro Society member.

iii

Editorial

The Munro Society has existed now for 20 years, and for our sixth Journal, we have an extra special collection of articles. Inevitably, due to the pandemic affecting all of our lives for much of the last two years, many of the articles reflect this, and how people coped with the restrictions.

Part 1 (The Munro Society) deals with the activities of The Munro Society over the last 20 years, and Part 2 (Rounds, Lists and Completions) is all about people completing rounds or lists of one sort or another, and what it has meant to them.

In Going the Distance (Part 3) we read about the long haul, whether it's running, long distance trails or just doing their own thing, while in Part 4 (Round the World) we head off over the sea to mountainous areas near and far, furth of our shores.

Part 5 (Life in the Mountains) looks at the experience of people who either work in the mountains or have taken up some particular interest in the mountain environment.

Appropriately we end with Reflections (Part 6), starting with a couple of historical items and followed by the authors' personal reflections on the hills they hold in such high esteem. The many photographs throughout the Journal help add colour and context to each article and some will inspire the reader to seek out such places, and the skills to photograph them, for themselves.

The appendices comprise a humorous pair of McGonagallesque 'poems' (stretching the definition somewhat), and a photo-montage of a pot-pourri of Munro Society activities over the last two decades.

Following tradition in our Journals, there is a collection of beautifully illustrated thought-provoking poetry by Stuart B. Campbell, as well as members' writings on The One that Got Away, and Desert Island Hills, and a selection of photographs of Lochs and Lochans.

None of this would be possible of course without the contributions from members and non-members alike, and we thank them all. In addition, special thanks go to Gary Duncan for assembling the Photographic Essay for Appendix 2, to Stewart Logan for assisting with the daunting task of proof reading (although the responsibility for any errors is ours, and ours alone), and to Jeremy Fenton for once again putting the raw text and photos into a layout fit for printing.

We hope you enjoy reading the Society's sixth Journal.

Editorial Team

Oliver Bartrum	Alan Rowan
Anne Butler	Derek Sime
Norman McNab	Bill Wheeler

August 2022

Part One – The Munro Society

The Munro Society – the First Twenty Years

Anne Butler

The inaugural meeting leading to the formation of The Munro Society was held in April 2002 and since then the Society has gone from strength to strength. The idea of an association of Munroists was not new, with our now Honorary President, Robin Campbell, suggesting that it was 'about time that Munroists organised events for themselves'. There was widespread agreement that the new Society would give Munroists the opportunity to 'give something back to the mountains', an ethos that is still pertinent to this day.

What follows is a brief summary of TMS activities and achievements over the last 20 years, and as you can see, we have been very busy!

Honorary President, Robin Campbell

2002

At the inaugural meeting a draft constitution was written and Irvine Butterfield was elected as the Society's first President. An Executive Committee of ten people was formed with a President, Vice President, Hon. Treasurer, Hon. Secretary plus six committee members, with the emphasis very much on member participation.

The initial objectives of The Munro Society were to:

- foster social and cultural exchanges between TMS members,
- encourage research into matters connected with the Munros and the people who have climbed them,
- provide a valued body of opinion on matters affecting Scottish mountains and mountaineering.

Twenty years on, it is good to reflect on how successfully these initial objectives have been achieved and how relevant they still are.

The first edition of the Newsletter was sent out to members in July with a message from the President entitled 'Touching the Gavel'. At the end of the inaugural meeting, wood turner Flora Isles presented the Lindertis Gavel to Irvine Butterfield. The gavel had been made from wood donated by Sir Hugh Munro's great-grandson, Alisdair Hopkinson, from Sir Hugh's Lindertis estate.

The Society's first social event was the Annual Dinner, held at the Grand Hotel in Fort William in November.

2003

The first AGM was held followed by the Munro Lecture given by Sue Harvey of Harvey Maps. John Moore commenced his role as Munro Society Archivist, soon finding a home for the archive at the AK Bell Library in Perth. The archive aims to hold information pertinent to the formation and running of TMS and also records material regarding Munros and Munroists. This includes diaries, logbooks, photographs, maps, journals, interviews and DVDs. Many of these items now have significant historical value.

The first Munro revisit took place on Beinn Dorain, and the Mountain Quality Indicator project (MQI) was launched. The aim of the project was to assess and evaluate environmental changes affecting the Munros. In September, TMS members took part in the Gleouraich Path Maintenance weekend where volunteers received instruction on footpath repair before taking to the hillside to clear ditches and culverts on the popular stalkers' path.

Michael Urquhart was presented with an inscribed plaque to commemorate becoming the 3,000[th] registered Munroist; the plaque was made from wood from Sir Hugh Munro's house at Lindertis. It should be noted that in the following 18 years the number of recorded Munroists has reached over 7,000.

2004

The Annual Dinner was held at the Atholl Arms in Blair Atholl, with Ian Smith, editor of *High* magazine giving the after-dinner speech.

A Munro revisit weekend took place in Torridon in July. TMS hosted an exhibition of photographs and paintings, *A Celebration of Mountains*, at Blair Castle.

Irvine Butterfield (President 2002 – 2004)

Irvine was born in Yorkshire and worked for many years with HM Customs and Excise. He was a talented photographer, producing several books - notably *The High Mountains of Britain and Ireland, The Magic of the Munros* and *The Call of the Corbetts*. He was life president of the Crochallan Mountaineering Club and a Trustee of the John Muir Trust. Irvine served as Secretary of the Mountain Bothies Association, as well as Maintenance Organiser for Dibidil on Rùm. He was awarded a Lifetime Achievement Award by the John Muir Trust at the 2008 Dundee Mountain Film Festival. Irvine died in Dundee on May 12th, 2009, and his ashes were scattered by Loch Clair in Torridon.

First President, Irvine Butterfield

2005

The annual Munro Lecture *Beyond the Munros* was given by Martin Moran. Following successful weekend meets in 2003/04, further weekend meets were held in Kintail and Inchnadamph. The first in the DVD series *The Early Munroists*, produced by Jim Closs, featuring an interview with Jim Cosgrove, was released. Subsequent DVDs featured Nan Rae, Irvine Butterfield and Iain Robertson.

2006

To mark the 150th Anniversary of Sir Hugh Munro's birth, many TMS members climbed a Munro over the weekend of Sir Hugh's birthday and recorded details of the walk in a 'Tribute Book'. TMS members also stationed themselves in a tent at the summit of rather dreich Driesh and asked walkers to sign in at the top. Over 400 tributes were received and placed into the archive.

Jamie Andrew gave the Munro Lecture and Dick Balharry was guest speaker at the Annual Dinner in Fort William.

The first overseas meet took place when members travelled to Ireland to walk in Macgillycuddy's Reeks.

John Burdin (President 2004 – 2006)

John was one of the founder members of the Society and instrumental in setting it up. He became its first Vice President, and then its second President, in 2004.

John was very keen to set up a monitoring system for the Munros to reflect changes in the mountain environment over time and in 2003, he devised the Mountain Quality Indicators. The scheme was launched later that year, and the first MQI was completed at the Munro Society's weekend meet on Beinn Dorain, in November that year. After some refinements, the scheme eventually led to all the Munros being assessed in spring, summer and autumn, and a good many also in winter.

2nd President, John Burdin

2007

The Heightings project was launched in May with the survey of Foinaven carried out by CMCR Ltd., with the results being announced at a press conference the following month. Beinn Dearg was surveyed in August and both hills were confirmed as being below 914.4m and therefore remained as Corbetts.

With the meet weekends becoming increasingly popular, Glen Breaden was appointed as the first Meet Secretary. The annual Munro Lecture was given by Chris Townsend on his continuous Munros and Tops walk. Robin Campbell was appointed as Honorary President and the first Journal was published in October.

2008

The Munro Lecture was given by 'Island Man' Andy Strangeway. Members of TMS completed a round of MQI assessments and former President Irvine Butterfield was awarded a Lifetime Achievement Award by the John Muir Trust.

Iain Robertson (President 2006 – 2008)

Iain can claim to be the person with the longest association with The Munro Society. In 2001 he sent out the letters inviting fellow Munroists to the inaugural meeting. Iain then served as Hon. Secretary before becoming President in 2006.

Iain takes great satisfaction from the way in which the Society has developed. TMS is a group of disparate individuals that has coalesced into a body which is valued by its members and respected by others among the ranks of hill-goers.

Iain has also acted as Heightings Co-ordinator and was instrumental in designing the Mountain Reports format.

3rd President, Iain Robertson

2009

Irvine Butterfield, our first President, died in May after a long illness.

The Heightings Project continued with surveys of borderline Munros and Corbetts. Beinn Teallach and Ben Vane were surveyed by G&J Surveys. Both remained classified as Munros. Sgùrr a' Choire-bheithe was also surveyed and retained its Corbett status. The remeasuring of Sgùrr nan Ceannaichean took place in July and the hill was reclassified as a Corbett, the first change to Munro's Tables since 1997. A website was set up by Angus Campbell.

A Phase 1 MQI report was published after a report had been submitted for every Munro.

The Munro Lecture was given by Cameron McNeish.

2010

Geal-charn, The Fara and Beinn a' Chlèibh were all resurveyed as part of the Heightings Project with no resultant changes to their classification.

The Annual Munro Lecture was renamed the 'Irvine Butterfield Memorial Lecture' and the first talk was given by Jim Crumley.

A memorial stone sculpted by Bruce Walker of Kirriemuir was erected above Loch Scresort on Rùm in honour of Irvine Butterfield.

Journal No.2 was published in the autumn.

Derek Sime (President 2008 – 2010)

Derek Sime joined the Society in 2002 shortly after it was formed and joined the committee in 2004, becoming Vice President in 2006, during which time he took on editing of the Newsletter. He became the fourth President in 2008. He was part of the Heightings team surveying Foinaven and Beinn Dearg in 2007. During his time as President (thanks to the Editor Ann Marie Foot), the Newsletter went from two to three editions per year. Derek has been Editor of all The Munro Society's Journals and in 2014 he took over as Editor of the Newsletter on a temporary basis and has been editing it ever since.

He is the only person to have completed an MQI round.

4th President, Derek Sime

2011

The Heightings Project recommenced in July with surveys of the Fisherfield peaks Beinn a' Chlaidheimh, Ruadh Stac Mòr and Beinn Dearg Mòr. The surveys resulted in the reclassification of Beinn a' Chlaidheimh as a Corbett.

2012

Heightings surveys of Leathad an Taobhain and Beinn Bhreac took place and both remained Corbetts.

The 10th Anniversary Dinner took place in Fort William with guests from the SMC, MCofS and the LSCC; an after-dinner 'McGonagallesque' poem was delivered by Derek Sime (see Appendix 1).

Stewart Logan created a slide show showing ten years of TMS activities; some of these photos are shown again in Appendix 2.

Members were asked to complete an Anthology walk during the anniversary year, ensuring that The Munro Society completed a Munro round in its 10th year.

Glen Breaden (President 2010 – 2012)

Glen had been part of the steering committee involved in the formation of the Society and was the first woman to be elected as President. Glen was instrumental in organising the weekend meet programme which is still well supported to this day. During her term in office Glen focussed on increasing the number of members and encouraging member engagement in the social activities of the Society.

Glen completed the Corbetts in 2005 and is well under way with the Grahams.

5th President, Glen Breaden

2013

The heightings of the Bhàsteir Tooth and Knight's Peak took place alongside members of the SMC. Knight's Peak was shown to be below 914.4m and was removed from the list of Munro Tops.

The first TMS Photographic Competition took place at the Annual Dinner and was won by Derek Sime.

TMS sponsored two Winter Mountain Safety Lectures delivered by the

Mountaineering Council of Scotland, part of our ethos of 'giving something back to the mountains'.

To mark the 10th Anniversary of the Munro Society in 2012, the Anthology was published – a tribute to the Munros by The Munro Society, personal recollections and a members' Munro round.

Robin Campbell donated the effigy of Sir Hugh Munro to TMS. The 'dummy' Sir Hugh completed his Munro round on the Inaccessible Pinnacle in 1992, having taken 113 years to become a Munroist! (See article 'A Posthumous Completion' on page 93). Past Presidents John Burdin and Iain Robertson became Honorary Members.

2014

The MQI project was concluded with all Munros having at least one spring, summer and autumn MQI recorded. Derek Sime completed an MQI round on Ben More (Mull), accompanied by David Batty and Peter Willimott, thereby attaining the remarkable achievement of completing an MQI on every Munro.

TMS members and G&J surveys were interviewed by BBC1's Reporting Scotland and on BBC Radio Scotland concerning the results from the Heightings project.

The Munro Society Facebook page was launched and now boasts over 1,300 members. Journal No.3 was published.

The Irvine Butterfield Memorial Lecture was transferred to the Dundee Mountain Film Festival where it is still held.

Anne Marie Foot edited her last Newsletter in April 2014 and Derek Sime took over the role as interim editor and is still in post today!

The Irvine Butterfield Goblet was presented to TMS by sculptor Bruce Walker of Kirriemuir. David Fraser became the TMS Webmaster.

Eleanore Hunter (President 2012 – 2014)

During her Presidency Eleanore hosted the 10th Anniversary Dinner, an event enjoyed by members and invited guests alike. She also oversaw the start of the Society's sponsorship of some

6th President, Eleanore Hunter

of the Mountaineering Scotland (formally MCofS) Winter Mountain Safety Lectures. These lectures, which the Society still sponsors, are an important part of 'giving something back to the mountains'.

Eleanore was involved with several of the Heightings and continues to be an active hillwalker, the hills providing her with challenge and solace in equal measure.

2015

The new system of Mountain Reports, replacing MQIs, was launched, and copies of all completed MQIs were made available online.

The Heightings project drew to a close with the final survey being performed on Meall Gaineimh, which was not high enough to become a Munro Top.

A German TV film crew worked with Stewart Logan filming a piece about hillwalking, taking part in a mock heighting filmed part way up Beinn Ghlas in very dismal weather (the intention had been to do this on the summit of Ben Lawers, but this proved too ambitious for the rather slow film crew).

Hon. President Robin Campbell was presented with the Scottish Award for Mountain Excellence in Mountain Culture at the Fort William Mountain Film Festival.

On the 159th anniversary of Sir Hugh Munro's birth a plaque was unveiled at the Gateway to the Glens Museum in Kirriemuir. The ceremony was attended by President Peter Willimott, Hon. President Robin Campbell and four Past Presidents.

TMS donated £375 to the Scotways Donald Bennet memorial bridge appeal.

Stewart Logan took over from John Moore as Hon. Archivist.

2016

TMS became an Associate Member of Mountaineering Scotland.

Sir Hugh Munro and the Munros were included in the Great Scottish Tapestry which chronicled significant events and people in Scotland's past. Munro was also nominated in the NTS Great Scot poll for historical heroes whose achievements have had a profound impact on Scotland.

Derek Sime and Hamish Brown became Honorary Members of TMS.

Journal No.4 was published.

A base was made for the glass goblet with Presidents' names engraved on the silver band.

As part of the 'giving something back to the mountains' objective, TMS sponsored a student scrambling weekend to enable university students to learn essential hill skills. The course was delivered by Mountaineering Scotland.

Peter Willimott (President 2014 – 2016)

Originally from Norfolk, Peter was introduced to the hills by Stewart Logan who interviewed him for a job in 1969. Peter did not keep any records of his Munro bagging and it was his wife Heather who eventually worked out he was only seven summits away from completion. He eventually completed just in time to attend the A E Robertson 100th Anniversary Dinner as a Munroist.

7th President, Peter Willimott

TMS membership has introduced Peter to kindred spirits and over the years he has enjoyed many formal and informal events and meets. Peter was involved in the Heightings project and was instrumental in revamping the Society's website.

2017

TMS donated £250 each to the John Muir Trust and Mountaineering Scotland to help with the costs incurred in challenging the Caplich Windfarm development.

TMS honorary member Hamish Brown was presented with the Scottish Award for Excellence in Mountain Culture at the Fort William Mountain Festival.

President Stewart Logan attended a reception at the Scottish Parliament for those involved in mountain safety.

Jim Robertson and Stewart Logan manned the TMS stand at the Mountain Aid 'Skills for the Hills' day in Glasgow.

Following months of redesign by Webmaster David Fraser, the TMS website was relaunched.

2018

Scaling the Heights was published. It provided a detailed account of the Heightings project including technical details and personal reflections from those taking part in the surveying. The first edition sold out and the book was reprinted in 2019. A grant of £2,460 was received from the Scottish Mountaineering Trust towards publication costs.

The Society continued to sponsor some of the Mountaineering Scotland Winter Safety Lectures. Over 400 people have attended the talks in a variety of locations since 2013.

Some TMS members joined the John Muir Trust 'Keep it Wild' demonstration outside the Scottish Parliament.

TMS donated £914.40 to the 'Mend Our Mountains' initiative (914.4m being the metric height of a Munro).

Stewart Logan (President 2016 – 2018)

Stewart was born and brought up in Kirriemuir near the Munro family estate and his interest in the hills was kindled when grouse beating in the Angus glens. After a career working at the Ravenscraig steelworks and raising a family, Stewart was re-introduced to the hills by Peter Willimott after taking time out for family and career.

8th President, Stewart Logan

During his term as President, Stewart led the Editorial Committee involved in the publication of *Scaling the Heights,* the story of the Heightings project.

Stewart has completed ten rounds of Munros and Tops and 1,550+ Marilyns.

David Batty (President 2018)

9th President, David Batty

As soon as he joined the Society in 2007, David became a regular at meets, AGMs and dinners and was involved in the Heightings project, the production of *Scaling the Heights* and Journal No.4. He particularly enjoyed regular trips to the hills with fellow members.

He joined the Executive Committee in 2010 and was elected President in 2018. David was the inspiration and driving force behind the Munro Legacy Exhibition.

David died suddenly on the hill in November 2018 and is sorely missed by his friends and family.

2019

The Munro Legacy Exhibition opened at the AK Bell Library in Perth to mark the centenary of Sir Hugh Munro's death. The exhibition celebrated Munro's life and the legacy he left behind. The exhibition featured on STV, with former President Stewart Logan being interviewed on the day of opening. The exhibition was displayed in Perth for three months and afterwards it was taken on tour to various locations in Scotland including Torridon, Skye, Arrochar, Dundee and Glen Doll. A grant of £1,000 was received from the SMT towards the exhibition costs.

In March 2019, TMS member Liz Smith MSP tabled a motion in the Scottish Parliament to discuss Sir Hugh Munro. The debate was attended by TMS members Stewart Logan, Bill Taylor, Alan Watt, Bill Wheeler and William Munro.

Anne Butler and Derek Sime attended the book launch of the Harvey Maps book *The Munros – the Complete Collection of Maps* at their headquarters in Doune.

TMS sponsored 32 students on a series of night navigation courses delivered by Mountaineering Scotland.

2020

Anne Butler attended a Parliamentary Reception at the Scottish Parliament in January; the reception was held for organisations and individuals involved in mountain safety and recognised The Munro Society's involvement in sponsoring mountain safety training and talks.

Following the Society's involvement in the monitoring of hill tracks, Davie Black, Access & Conservation Officer at Mountaineering Scotland, noted that, 'TMS's recording activities were instrumental in the tightening up of planning conditions with regard to track construction'.

TMS made donations of £500 each to SARDA, Mountain Aid and Trees for Life.

Journal No.5 was published with over 150 copies being sold to non-members. All profits were donated to our nominated charities. The new logo was launched following many months of debate.

The AGM and Annual Dinner both became victims of the Covid lockdown restrictions with the AGM voting being held via email/post and all the Executive Committee meetings were held online via Zoom.

The 50th edition of the Newsletter was published.

2021

With the lockdown restrictions continuing, the AGM was held as a virtual meeting via Zoom. However, as restrictions eased, the summer and autumn meets, and the Annual Dinner, were able to go ahead.

The pull-up display panels from the Munro Legacy Exhibition were updated and replaced following receipt of a grant of £2,500 from the Scottish Mountaineering Trust, and the first post-pandemic showing was held in the Scottish Parliament for three days in October.

Plans were cemented for celebrations to mark The Munro Society's 20th Anniversary in 2022. These include a short film *Scotland's Mountains – The Legacy of Sir Hugh Munro*. The film will be available to clubs and will also be shown at film festivals. The Executive Committee is working with the Knoydart Forest Trust to plant 914 native-species trees as part of the regeneration of the Knoydart peninsula. The tree planting will also coincide with the spring meet in Inverie. We will also be hosting a meet in Torridon in September – 'The Big Birthday Bash' – where members old and new will be able to celebrate one of the Society's founding objectives 'to foster social and cultural exchange between members'.

Anne Butler (President 2018 – 2022)

Anne joined the Executive Committee in 2012 and has served as Hon. Secretary, Vice President and President.

Taking over as President following the unexpected death of David Batty, Anne co-ordinated the Munro Legacy Exhibition during 2019 and has successfully kept the Society's momentum going through the Covid pandemic.

Anne is well known for walking the hills with her dogs Molly and Ralph who have both been regular attendees at Society events. Anne is a prolific hillwalker; she has trashed knees and has been Meet Secretary and Membership Secretary for many years.

10th President, Anne Butler

TMS members are spread throughout the UK with several based overseas in Europe and the USA. Despite this geographical diversity, the meets, Newsletters and Journals have managed to create a sense of identity amongst our members.

Over the last 20 years Munro Society members have been busy on the hills. Multiple rounds of Munros, Munro Tops, Corbetts, Grahams, Donalds and Furths have been completed with several members also completing a Full House.

With thanks to all those who have served on the Executive Committee since 2002:

Alf Barnard, Oliver Bartrum, David Batty, Glen Breaden, John Burdin, Irvine Butterfield, Angus Campbell, Robin Campbell, Michael Cowen, John Donohoe, Alasdair Dutton, Anne Marie Foot, Julian Foot, David Fraser, David Gibson, Keith Grant, David Hand, Eleanore Hunter, Ethel Jessett, Frank Johnstone, Joyce Kettles, Irene Leckie, Stewart Logan, John MacKenzie, Roderick Manson, Walter McArthur, Alan McCaffrey, Alistair Milner, John Moore, Tom Rix, Iain Robertson , Jim Robertson, John Ross, Alan Rowan, Derek Sime, Findlay Swinton, Bill Taylor, Mike Thewlis, Alex Thomson, Michael Urquhart, Fred Ward, Alan Watt, Bill Wheeler, Ann White, Di Williams, Keith Williams, Pete Williams, Peter Willimott.

Part Two – Rounds, Lists and Completions

A Munro Round

Donnie Campbell

June 2019 – I was sitting at the breakfast bar waiting for my wife Rachael to come home from work to tell her about what I had decided on my training run that day. I always do my best thinking when I am running up and down hills. As she walked through the door, I was excited to tell her my plan for next summer! I was finally committing to taking a year off racing to do a self-propelled round of all the Munros. I had always wanted to climb all the Munros in Scotland and for the last few years I had thought about the idea of doing them all in one go in a self-propelled style of kayaking, cycling, running, walking, scrambling or crawling! So May 2020 was going to be it!

Fast-forward to 6th March 2020 – Covid-19 is starting to take hold all around the world and I am on my way to Edinburgh for an MRI on my lower back as I have not been able to run since Christmas Day. Every time I tried to run I got pain in my right groin which felt like a muscle strain but after numerous trips to the physio I was referred for an MRI as the pain was neural, and had not been getting better with all the rehab work (stretching and strengthening) I had been doing since the start of January. The strange thing was I could go ski-touring, cycling or use the stair-master machine in the gym and it would be fine, but as soon as I tried to run it would flare up instantly. Basically, the MRI showed some disk degeneration, but the main problem was L4/L5 bilateral foraminal stenosis which was causing the neural pain in right leg and numbness in left quad. As I was about to be referred for a lumbar epidural to try and calm the inflammation down in the L4/L5 region, Scotland went into lockdown. This meant I was unable to get the injection and also made the Munro round very unlikely to happen at the end of May.

At the same time as the lockdown restrictions came in, the neural pain was starting to ease, and I was slowly able to build up the running. By the beginning of June, I was able to get a good block of training in on my local hill (Dunain Hill, 281m) and was confident that, if the Covid restrictions were lifted in time, I could potentially have a crack at a self-propelled Munro round in August.

August 1st 0600 – I am off! Running up the Landrover track that leads to the path up Ben More on the Isle of Mull, it has finally stopped raining and the clouds are starting to break up, but that is the least of my worries. Full of nervous energy and worried about my support crew, my wife Rachael, missing the ferry to the mainland (there are only two sailings this morning due to Covid-19) I worked harder than I would like for the first Munro of 282. But it felt good to have finally started the Munro round after over 12 months of planning and all the uncertainties of the injury and Covid restrictions. On paper I did not look at this day as a big day but it took me 14.5 hours to climb Ben More, Sgùrr Thuilm, Sgùrr nan Coireachan and Gulvain and get to Glen Nevis. This definitely confirmed my 33-day schedule was very ambitious and to be able to stick to it I was going to need to be on top of my game and require a fair bit of luck with the Scottish weather.

Week 1 was fairly straight-forward big mountain days bashing through bogs, peat hags and slogging up steep heather slopes. The weather was a usual Scottish summer, mixed

Kayaking to Mull
(Donnie Campbell collection)

at best, some okay days, some gale force winds and horizontal rain. Day 7 was when the suffering really began! My right tibial tendon was grumbling big-time and not happy with all the bogs and rough terrain. Day 6 had seen me traverse the Cairngorms from Glen Feshie to the Cairngorm Ski Resort car park with Ally Beaven and Holly Page, so for Day 7 all I had left was Bynack More, Beinn a' Chaorainn, Beinn Bhreac, Beinn a' Bhuird and Ben Avon before finishing the day in Ballater. This however turned out be one of the worst days of the round; every time I had to descend I was in severe pain as every time I put my right foot down I would get a shooting pain through my ankle that would bring a tear to my eye. The eastern Munros turned out to be a very painful experience but by the start of Day 10, which I thought at the time was going to be longest day of the round, 80km with over 5k of ascent from Glen Shee to Blair Atholl, the right ankle was getting more manageable. I had been doing intensive rehab on it when not running, with ice, elevation and compression along with some anti-inflammatories and trying to protect it as much as possible when running by favouring my left side and using poles, which brought the pain down to more of a tolerable level.

At this time Scotland was starting to bask in a mini heat-wave. When I say heat wave, as soon as the thermometer hits double figures it's taps-aff weather for the locals! Day 12 saw me take an afternoon bath in the River Lyon to try and cool down after climbing Meall Ghaordaidh. For about two days bagging the most southerly Munros (Days 14 & 15) I was greeted with almost constant cloud inversion which was spectacular and one of the highlights of the round.

Shortly after that I hit the lowest point of the round – Day 17. I had hit Groundhog Day, so far from the start yet so far from the finish, I felt like I was getting nowhere after putting in some massive days, and I still felt no closer to Ben Hope, the finish. I had lost focus on just taking one day at a time, one Munro at a time and was looking at the big picture. As they say, the straw that broke the camel's back was my left tibia tendon starting to grumble very loudly that it was not happy that day and all I could see ahead of me was daily 12-14 hour days of pain with no real reward.

Aonach Eagach
(Donnie Campbell collection)

With a bit of shuffling the schedule about I managed to clear the Glen Coe and Lochaber area still on my schedule, but it had taken its toll on me by Day 21. I was feeling pretty fatigued after putting in some big days and there was no let up, as Day 21 was the Knoydart Munros (64km with 6,000m of ascent). It is safe to say that Knoydart delivered. The Munros were spectacular, views were amazing (until the weather crapped out about midday) but the terrain was brutal and by the time I got back to my support van after 14 hours I was completely physically broken after battling the weather and relentless steep, rough terrain.

Day 22 – I was meant to do Sgùrr a' Mhaoraich, Gleouraich, Spidean Mialach and the South Shiel ridge, but with the weather being very dreich and windy, and me being very fatigued, I was struggling to stay warm and with big days coming up,

The end of Day 19 – cycling to Kinlochewe
(Donnie Campbell collection)

the realisation was starting to hit me that I was going to have to drop a day, and at the time Day 22 seemed the right time rather than trying to battle through weather and end up even more fatigued. So I finished that day in Cluanie at lunchtime after bagging Sgùrr a' Mhaoraich, Gleouraich and Spidean Mialach, which gave me the opportunity to catch up on sleep and food. With over 12 hours of sleep and a belly full of food I was off again at 4am on Day 23 as I had another timing I could not afford to miss – the 16:00 high tide at Glenelg – miss this and I would have a very long cycle to get to Glen Brittle on Skye. I had 12 hours to bag the South Shiel Ridge, The Saddle and Beinn Sgritheall. With the extra rest and sleep I felt recharged and banged out these Munros in plenty of time, confirming to myself I had made the right decision to cut the previous day short. The next day was the highlight of the round, back home in Skye, and it did not disappoint, with perfect weather conditions, blue skies, sunshine and a cool breeze to keep the notorious Skye midges at bay. The Cuillin Ridge was spectacular, and I was able to share it with John Smith and Jordon Young.

In the planning I had convinced myself that if I made it to Skye, I knew I would make it to Ben Hope; in reality even after Skye there were still some big days left but I was starting to see a glimmer of light at the end of a very long Munro tunnel. Day 29 – I finally got to meet Spyke, the previous Munro Round record holder; he had travelled all the way up to Scotland from the Peak District to run with me. I was enjoying his company so much going up Moruisg that we missed the summit in the clag, and I only realised my mistake when we

Sunday 23rd August – 4am start at Cluanie heading for the South Glen Shiel ridge and The Saddle
(Donnie Campbell collection)

got to the bottom, so we had to do it again! After a fairly easy day bagging the Torridon skyline (28km with 3,000m ascent) on Day 30 I was scheming on how I could make up a day and get back on my 33-day schedule. I decided I would stick with the schedule for Monday, Day 31, then go big on Tuesday with an early start doing the Fannichs, Wyvis and the Ben Dearg six Munros leaving the last four Munros up in Sutherland for the Wednesday.

As I was climbing A' Mhaighdean the weather was turning into a stunning afternoon and I started thinking. I am feeling good, I have just had a solid

12 hours in bed, the weather is good, the weather is going to crap out on Wednesday, should I keep going and do a night raid on the Fannichs.........
Then the call was made as I summited An Teallach; I called Rachael asked her to get my dinner ready for when I came off An Teallach as I was going to carry on and do the Fannichs. The new plan was to try and get as much done before the weather broke on Wednesday. I know when I have trained and tapered, I can go for 48 hours in the mountains without sleep but the question now was could I do it after 30 days of Munro bagging? This is what I was wanting; I wanted to find out how far I could push myself physically and mentally. There was no point in holding back. I had Ben Hope in my sight and now was the time to completely empty the tank!

My heart was thumping louder than had it had for the last 31 days, my legs were screaming, I was red lining, I was chasing a time. With about 400m of ascent left to go on Ben Hope I realised if I could climb it in under 18min I could finish on an hour, the time I was chasing was 31 days 23 hours. I had dropped my friends who had come to climb the last Munro with me and my focus was touching the cairn before 5am. I had no idea where the energy came from, as on the last 100m of the climb I was sprinting through the clag; finally I could see the cairn and a few friends waiting for me at the summit. I touched the cairn and looked at my watch. 'Bugger I missed it by two minutes'; then collapsed to the ground.

The finish on Ben Hope with my wife Rachel (Donnie Campbell collection)

LOCHS and LOCHANS

Above – Sunset on Fionn Loch from Càrn na Paite above Carnmore Lodge, May 2021.

Below – Molly cooling off in Loch an Duin, after the long walk in to the Gaick Corbetts, spring 2009.
Anne Butler

The Corbetts – Time Well Spent

Anne Butler

There's a mountain-top that I'm dreaming of
If you need me, you know where I'll be.
— *George Ezra*

In the middle of July 2021, I completed my second round of Corbetts. The finish was a long time coming, but reaching the end has given me time to take stock and reflect on what the Corbetts have meant to me.

Anybody who refers to Corbetts as 'lesser hills' clearly hasn't climbed many of them. Once upon a time I was one of those people and considered that anything below 3,000ft simply wasn't worth climbing. Most Munro baggers consider the Corbetts as an afterthought, something to be tagged on after the important business of completing a Munro round has been achieved. A Corbett is a hill between 2,500ft (762m) and 3,000ft (914.4m) with a drop of at least 500ft (152.4m) on all sides. It is this drop that not only makes the Corbetts a more physically challenging proposition, but it also makes them a more clearly defined list than the Munros. The summits stand out as individual and distinct hills and it is rare to be able to link more than two Corbetts together in a walk. It is wrong to think that Corbetts offer shorter or easier walks than the Munros; many walks are long, remote and over pathless, demanding terrain. The drop criterion means that there are very few instances where three or four can be combined in long traverses as is the case with Munros.

Like a lot of Munro completers, I was a bit unsure of what to do next. Most people, including me, started their hillwalking careers on the Munros as they comprise an iconic and extremely well-known list of hills; the Munros enabled me to learn and develop my hill skills and where I began to love the time I spent in the mountains. So, after the Munros, the Corbetts seemed to be a natural progression. I had climbed the Munros just before my 40th birthday and when one of my walking companions suggested 'Corbetts by 50, Grahams by 60', like a fool, I immediately took up the challenge (actually, the Corbetts were completed at 44 and the Grahams at 53).

Alfred Wainwright believed that you 'should always have a definitive objective in life, an ambition; a life without ambition is simply aimless wandering' (and who am I to disagree?). I am an extremely focussed and list-driven person. However, over the years I have come to appreciate that being so list-driven can border on obsession. I realised that I was becoming overly fixated on lists and bagging so I now make sure that I take time out each year to climb hills that I 'want' to climb rather than hills I 'need' to climb, something that only a true bagger will fully understand and appreciate!

21

After completing my first round of Corbetts in 2010, I moved my focus back to the Munros and ultimately onto the Full House lists, so many of the Corbetts were not revisited again for many years. The familiarity of climbing the Munros again and again gave a welcome and comforting feeling, but when I returned to the Corbetts it was like climbing a new hill. I felt invigorated. It wasn't the same mountain, and I was not the same person. On the map it looked like the same hill, but my approach was different. I may have been climbing the same hill again but personal (and to a certain degree, environmental) variables made each ascent a unique experience.

Let's face it, size isn't everything (despite what the Munro baggers would have us believe) and even with the massive increase in the popularity of hillwalking, Corbetts are still less well-known and still feel untamed. On many of the Munros you will be crushed in the stampede to get to the summit for a selfie, but on a Corbett a long leisurely lunch at the cairn is nearly always possible.

The Corbetts present a rugged challenge to anybody who is prepared to put in the time to get to know them. Apart from a few obvious exceptions like The Cobbler and Ben Ledi, most Corbetts are relatively unfrequented and will reward those willing to put a little bit more effort into their bagging. The Corbetts feel wilder and there is a lot more up and down. Both the planning and completion of the rounds felt much more complex; there were few guidebooks or websites with dedicated Corbett routes. For me, planning a walk forms part of the overall enjoyment of the hill and enhances the whole

Arran (Anne Butler)

bagging experience. I learned to take them in bite-sized chunks. A list of 222 hills can seem daunting at first but split it into sections and smaller goals and suddenly it becomes much more manageable.

Navigation can be challenging without the security of a well-worn path to the summit. Corbetts may be smaller, but they are certainly not easier; they are mentally stimulating, many are remote and require lengthy or demanding approaches, often walking for hours without seeing another person.

A Corbett round involves a lot more travel and allows the hillwalker to explore areas of Scotland that the Munro bagger would probably never visit. To complete the Corbetts, trips to the Munro-free zones of the Borders, Galloway, Ardgour and Moidart are needed, plus visits to Rùm, Harris, Arran and Jura, which quite frankly are never a hardship. There is the rugged exposure of the Ardgour peninsula; there are gems such as Garbh Bheinn, Beinn Dearg Mòr and Beinn Làir and at the other end of the scale, the much-maligned summits of Brown Cow Hill and Carn na Fhreiceadain. Don't write these hills off; on a blue-sky winter's day, walking across their vast featureless slopes below never-ending skies is an enlightening experience.

Corbetts have more than their fair share of wildlife, both the good and bad variety. I have seen foxes, pine martens and more types of frustratingly unidentifiable birds on Corbetts than any other group of hills. Unfortunately, the lack of foot traffic means that ticks and clegs are hungry for a meal and latch on to the unsuspecting Corbett bagger. Just remember, size isn't everything!

Key to my enjoyment of the Corbetts has been sharing the journey with

Ralph on Buidhe Bheinn (Anne Butler)

23

Anne & Molly on A' Chir (Anne Butler)

my dogs Molly and Ralph; to me, hillwalking without them is an empty experience. Dogs live in the moment; the sights and smells of the hills invigorate them. They may not appreciate the views in the same way that we do and they do not worry about what has passed before or what lies ahead. Maybe we should learn to 'be more dog'.

Like any round of hills there have been highs and lows – easily won summits and those that require physical and mental fortitude to climb. For most people, The Cobbler is the most difficult Corbett to climb, requiring a short, exposed scramble to the top, but watching Andy lead Molly up to the top of the summit block was far more nerve-racking than threading the needle myself. And then there was the A' Chir ridge on Arran which was probably, with hindsight, not an ideal place to take a Border Collie! Two abseils and a lot of tricky scrambling later I almost kissed the ground with relief as the rock gave way to heather and we rejoined the easy walkers' path. Needless to say, second time around we ambled along the bypass path on the easy terrain below the ridge.

As anyone who spends a lot of time in the hills will testify, extremes of weather will feature heavily. There may be a particularly good or bad weather experience which will make a day on the hill stay in the memory for all eternity. My most unforgettable bad weather day was on the Glenfinnan Corbetts Sgùrr Ghiubhsachain and Sgorr Craobh a' Chaorainn. I was still recovering from a virulent stomach bug and it rained biblically for six hours. We summitted the

Beinn Làir (Anne Butler)

first hill in the dry and then suddenly the weather deteriorated with a speed I had never seen before. The paths turned into rivers and Andy had to carry dogs and rucksacks across swollen burns. Luckily a large fallen pine tree provided the only safe way across the final burn, with dogs carried around Andy's neck like a mediaeval ruff and me shuffling across à cheval. After that every wet weather day is rated in comparison to the Glenfinnan Corbetts. Thankfully we can laugh about it now.

Weather also features in visits to Fisherfield but thankfully it was heat rather than rain on this occasion. Andy, Molly, Meg and I cycled from Poolewe as far as my rudimentary cycling ability would allow, dumping our bikes in the heather above the Fionn Loch before continuing up onto the vast plateau of Beinn Làir. It seemed to get hotter as we gained height and the wind at the summit was similar to opening the oven door whilst baking a cake; we collapsed in the meagre shade offered by the huge summit cairn.

On the way back to the loch we walked around the rim of the massive cliffs, grateful for the cooler air that was rising up from the crags. We spent an age sitting at the causeway submerged in the water to freshen up and then continued to Carnmore for a fitful night of mercifully midge-free 'sleep'. Eventually we gave up on our attempts at sleep and arrived at the summit of Beinn a' Chàisgein Mòr as the early morning mists were swirling around the tops; the air was fresh and all the sweaty suffering of the previous day was forgotten.

Then there was an 'experimental' bike and hike route to Sgùrr an Fhuarain from the north. On paper (we still used paper maps in those days), it seemed like a good idea but it wasn't. The track through the forest ended at an exceptionally boggy ATV track and it took an inordinate amount of time to get to the foot of the ridge. We made it to the top of the Corbett and Sgùrr Mòr looked so tantalisingly close we decided to climb it as well, conveniently forgetting how slow our progress along the boggy track back to the bikes would be. When we got back to the bikes it was rapidly getting dark and we discovered that one of the team had forgotten her headtorch. So there were two people, two bikes, one dog, one headtorch and endless miles of forest tracks between us and the car. What could possibly go wrong? Well, I spent a lot of time falling off and Andy spent a lot of time helping me out of ditches! Note to self - always carry a spare headtorch.

Ben Aden (Anne Butler)

We travelled by boat – not just the obvious ferries to the islands but kayaking to Ben Aden. Ben Aden is difficult to reach from any direction and summitting it will involve a lot of effort. I needed to climb Ben Aden again for my second round and in a moment of extreme madness we decided to paddle in again. This time it was a bigger and heavier Canadian canoe and getting it onto the roof of the car would have provided a good training session for an Olympic weightlifter. (Molly had sat on my lap and spent the whole journey trembling with fear, and it took me ages to get enough sensation back in my legs to climb out of the kayak.) In the canoe, Ralph went rigid with fright, and it took two of us to lift him into the boat. Collies are clearly not water dogs!

The Rùm Cuillin have also been kind with perfect conditions on both of our ridge traverses. After being traumatised by a ferocious midging on our first visit we upgraded to a luxurious camping pod. It was a perfect trip; we ate well, we slept in comfort, the midges were barely noticeable and despite the heat and struggle to find water on the ridge (we drew the line at drinking out of the muddy puddles favoured by Ralph and Ally), we had views and were pleasantly surprised to find that despite being 11 years older, we managed the traverse in 12 hours, exactly the same time as on our previous visit in 2010.

There have been disappointments along the way. Two trips to the Rois Bheinn group and no view. I am sure Rùm was out there somewhere, but we didn't see it; both visits were spent walking in cloud and drizzle. Third time lucky I suppose.

500th Corbett (Anne Butler)

We were saving a blue-sky day for the ascent of Meall a' Bhuachaille, my 500th Corbett. MWIS and the Met Office were promising high pressure and crisp clear winter conditions. But like many of my plans for 2021 it wasn't to be. It started snowing as we reached the bothy and stopped about an hour after we got home, our summit picnic abandoned in favour of a hot chocolate in front of the wood burner!

Having climbed them all before there was really no excuse to leave a clutch of the hardest and remotest hills until the end, despite all my good intentions not to. I was down into single figures, but I still had the Rùm Cuillin, Glamaig on Skye, Streap and Bidein a' Chabair at the far end of Glen Dessarry to climb.

Hardly the easiest summits to reach and not exactly the ideal choice for a completion party either. I kept chipping away until eventually only Streap remained. I waited until my husband Bill and friends Andy and Heather were available and we went for it. Luckily, we picked the only cool day in the long

Bidein a' Chabair (Anne Butler)

hot heatwave of July 2021 and tackled the brutal slopes of Streap from Glen Dubh Lighe. I was told in no uncertain terms that next time I would be on my own unless I picked something a lot easier to finish on!

I approached the Corbetts with a different mindset to the Munros which resulted in a far greater sense of achievement once I had completed them, and I look back fondly on the challenge that both Corbett rounds have presented. I savoured the Corbetts and took time to study their character and enjoy the solitude. They weren't rushed and reaching the end of each round felt like time to press the reset button and start again rather than the end of something.

I found the Corbett round much harder than the Munros and the second round was far harder than the first. Maybe that was because I was older and my knees are well and truly trashed.

Streap completion (Anne Butler)

All the years and all the miles have been worth it; the Corbetts really were time well spent.

Coming Full Circle on Ben Nevis

Alan Rowan

I suppose there was a certain inevitability that Nevis would be the venue for the compleation of my Full House. My mountain life had started with an ascent of the Ben so it was fitting that the latest chapter came to its conclusion here. A combination of fate, but only latterly, design, had left Carn Dearg South-west, that outlying Munro Top, as the final piece in the jigsaw of the six lists – Munros, Munro Tops, Furths, Corbetts, Grahams, Donalds (including the Donald Tops of course) – that make up the Full House.

I've been on the Ben many times, but had never made it out to this summit, and a few years back I decided to keep it just for this moment. It meant the Munro Tops remained unfinished for what seemed an eternity, but I reckoned it would be worth the wait.

When it comes to the mountains, I've never been one for planning far ahead. It's a case of opportunity over order; the first choice is to go where the weather is best and if that means turning my back on a required tick on a list for a bit longer, so be it. It doesn't always work out – mostly on the Donalds to be fair – but this is Scotland, where the weather gods seem to revel in being contrary.

My compleation Munros have been random. I admire/am suspicious of anyone who can make a choice of a final peak at the beginning of any round. My planning is only put into motion when there are ten or so to go. Occasionally, I have a notion of a peak I would like to finish on, but that turns out to be fleeting. For instance, about halfway through my first round, I reckoned it would be nice to finish on one of my Gaelic namesakes. There are three Chaorainns on the list, but I then proceeded to climb them all in the space of a couple of weeks. It was perhaps a subconscious reaction to the thought that I had suddenly become organised.

I doubt that anyone starting out on the hills has done so with the intention of doing a Full House. For a start, most walkers have never even heard the term. The majority want to complete the Munros, and only then, possibly, the Corbetts, and that's often enough for one lifetime. The percentage who start dabbling in other lists is far smaller.

My tipping point came about five years ago. Having finished the Munros three times, plus the Corbetts and Furths, my only target was to wrap up the few outstanding Munro Tops. I had started climbing Grahams a few years earlier as an option during harsh winter days when the high tops seemed too hostile. There was never an intention of doing them all. Then the bagger inside takes over. And when you get into Corbetts and Grahams, the Donalds start becoming entangled as well. The early Grahams mostly fell into two categories: local or classic. The final 50 or so produced some spectacular outings. It was the middle bit that was the problem.

I remember accompanying a friend in the final stages of her round with a 13-hour day on the Arkaig Munros. We were in the eye of a storm: the day before had seen monsoon conditions, and this was the relative calm before a resumption of hostilities the next. Water was running everywhere; the streams were swollen, the vegetation was soaking, the rock was slippy. Yet this still seemed like a holiday compared to the previous few outings on the Grahams. As I bemoaned my lot, my friend asked: 'Well, if you're not enjoying them, why are you still doing them?' A reasonable question, but equally, to my ears, it sounded the most idiotic one ever. My reply was simple but obvious: 'I've started, so I'll finish.' I'm certainly no mastermind, but I had become the Magnus Magnusson of the hills. From that point forward, I started to embrace and enjoy the Grahams.

Fast forward a couple of years, and I am closing in on a triple finish. For once, a plan was coming together: three completions in a week. First, it would be a midweek Borders raid for the remaining Donald, Hudderstone, then a trip to Mull for the final Graham, Beinn Fhada, before the grand finale, Glen Nevis and the last Munro Top.

Windfarm Central – a view from Hudderstone (Alan Rowan)

My previous completions had been low-key – five finishes, only six people in total attending. Two of these walks were just little old me. It's not a deliberate policy, though I admit I'm not particularly fond of big summit parties: it's more to do with the scattergun approach of my hill-going and the lack of forward planning. Difficult to round up a posse if they are only told the night before that you are completing on a mountain 400 miles away.

The scenario this time was completely different. The trip to Mull was in tandem with a Munro Society meet, and the Nevis finale with a Grampian Club weekend. Unless I decided to sneak away alone under cover of darkness (and, of course, I would never consider that), there would be people. And just as well. Otherwise, I would never have managed to experience passing through the traditional archway of walking poles to reach the summit cairn of Beinn Fhada. This is nigh impossible if you are on your own.

Waiting at the cairn were celebratory bottles of fizz. There were handshakes and kisses, and, equally importantly, a selection of cakes and other goodies. And in another break with tradition, there were also blue skies and sunshine. Often these final days are masked by mist and coated in a degree of wetness ranging from drizzle to heavy, pounding rain.

It wasn't all sweetness and light. There was a strong wind, so strong, in fact, that when the gathered forces of The Munro Society arrived on the shores of Loch na Keal it was hard to avoid being shunted sideways. It drove directly into our faces on the initial march over boggy ground to gain the slope ahead. The grasses were waving in synchronicity like a driven sea, the loch filled with herds of white horses thundering across the blue.

Doubts started to surface about the plan to do the full circuit onward from Beinn Fhada over A' Chioch and round to Ben More. If the wind was demonstrating such power at this low level, what will it be like high on the ridge? I had been thwarted from sampling this classic on three previous occasions, once by naïvety-stroke-ignorance in my early days, twice later by the weather. A memorable springtime ascent came to an abrupt halt at the top of Ben More when we gazed down at intimidating ice-coated slopes, the other simply by the misery of the 'normal' lack of clarity brought about by mist and rain.

Beinn Fhada, the long mountain, is well named. Once on the ridge, there is a succession of rises and dips, culminating in a steep final push to a rocky rampart with some minor handwork needed. This was all done to the accompaniment of superb vistas; Loch na Keal and its captive isle of Eorsa behind, the dark shadow of Ben More's skyline to the right, the rugged, scree-ravaged walls of the impressive Beinn a' Ghraig on the left.

With all the elements coming together at the right time, Beinn Fhada turned out to be an inspired choice for the finish of a list of smaller hills that proved far more challenging than mere height would suggest. A round that had started almost by default and was in danger at one point of being abandoned. I'm glad I stuck with it: I came to admire and even love these hills, and the run-in provided many moments to match outings on bigger rivals.

We regrouped before the last push, then formed up for the celebration. It seemed unlikely, but the wind was less ferocious here than it had been down below. Suddenly, the Ben More circuit was back on the agenda. Sunbathing

The group on Beinn Fhada (Derek Sime)

and celebrations fulfilled, the party split, and seven of us dropped south for the steady climb to the dark, pointed peak of A' Chioch. There was a rough path weaving its way through outcrops and crags, but as the angle steepened just below the summit it was simply a case of putting hand to rock and hauling ourselves up to the final platform.

Depending on the direction of light, the volcanic rock of Ben More's

A' Chioch and Beinn Fhada from the final climb to Ben More (Alan Rowan)

north-east ridge can take on an almost flawless blackness, a dark beast with a hypnotic, enticing beauty. Resistance is useless – the only way is straight up.

The wind perked up again at the col, reminding us of its potential, but once over the gap and clinking our way along the shattered path, it was soon forgotten. A cairn provided a marker for a steep clamber up a long, broken chimney which gained height quickly. We emerged on a small platform for some respite, or, as it is more often put, a chance to admire the views. And what views.

The eyes were drawn down the jagged edge of the ridgeline to A' Chioch with unknown drops into a dark void, but the whole of the island was laid out under our feet. Loch Scridain was a shining, silver slash, the sun radiating from it with nuclear intensity, Iona a distant smudge. The Paps of Jura rose on the horizon, their ruggedness masked in pale blue, the flatlands of Islay to their left. We wandered down the easier route to the road, the wind growing stronger the lower we got, a strange end to a momentous day.

It was in complete contrast to four days earlier, for my farewell to the Donalds. I did manage to drag one friend along for the ascent of the rounded lump of Hudderstone, but she lived just a few miles away and it was a lovely day. To be fair, I didn't expect a rush of volunteers for a hill which translates as 'stone in the heather' and whose summit delivers exactly that. And no, we didn't attempt a pole archway. Anyway, she had forgotten to bring hers along, so I left mine in the car as a show of solidarity.

Now here I was, in the shadow of Ben Nevis, having come full circle. Some 40 years earlier, I had been part of a group who had made an ascent by the tourist track. It was late spring, but the snow cover still held sway on the top third of the mountain. We were naïve, we were ill-equipped, and although conditions were clear, looking back we were probably fortunate there were so many others on the hill to make sure we didn't stray.

Our gear was something else, too. I had boots and waterproofs, but underneath was a jacket from an army surplus store and many cotton layers, each in disproportionate levels of wetness. One of our group was wearing a sports jacket. No, it wasn't Arthur Montford.

There are many factors to take into account when planning an ascent of the country's highest mountain – not wearing a sports jacket being one – not least of which is the sheer number of walkers heading up. This seemed likely to be a particularly busy one. The glen was buzzing, several big charity events simultaneously colliding with a promise of decent weather conditions.

The Carn Mòr Dearg Arête was one way to avoid the crowds, but I always fancied a climb from the south by the waterslide above Glen Nevis. This route rises some 900 metres in just over two kilometres, a continuous push in two steep sections. The scenery was dramatic all the way, the perception of depth from such a precipitous gradient immense. An added attraction was that it avoided any need for the huge drop and subsequent re-ascent required from other directions.

The initial forecast had been gloomy, but it continued to improve in the countdown to the big day, and as we left our base the mist was burning off to reveal a mountain which had been invisible only an hour or so earlier. By the time we were ready to start, a bit of neck craning provided views up to the col from which the waters of the Allt Coire Eòghainn tumbled forcefully down the polished, obsidian bedrock of the chute.

Shifting cloud during the ascent from Glen Nevis (Alan Rowan)

The steepness began immediately on a rough path through the trees. We were being filmed for a BBC Alba news slot by a friend, and she had hinted we may have to do a couple of takes. A thumbs-up from below suggested we had got it right first time, much to the relief of some of the party. As one said: 'Good, if she thinks we're going back down there ...'

Once we fought through some deep vegetation and hidden boulders, we found a path, sometimes obvious, sometimes ambiguous, but it kept us to the right of the water so there were no unexpected problems.

The banks of languid cloud which hung around at various levels enhanced the vistas up the glen and over the Mamores. These are big mountains, yet with our accentuated height gain, they appeared to shrink with every footstep. The plunging waters of Steall Falls started as a long lace of silver and reduced to a sliver, then a teardrop, always glistening amongst the dark claustrophobia

The waterslide route (Alan Rowan)

of their surroundings. Our constant companion had been the waterslide, thundering waters hypnotic at times, but it would have been foolhardy to be tempted into any crossing. At one point, there was a cairn in the midst of the deluge, a curious marker with no obvious purpose.

Once safely over the water above the col, we began the second steep push, this time vanishing into the mist to reach the cairns on my final summit. Three hours, and we had not encountered another soul, but the push to the final heights of the Ben changed all that. We could make out shapes shuffling along ahead in the mist, a conveyor belt of ghostly figures determined to keep

The final summit – Carn Dearg South-west Top
(Alan Rowan)

35

going. The roof of Scotland was jammed, and there was a queue to get a summit picture. It was a timely reminder of why I often prefer to walk at night.

There were topless walkers (male), near topless walkers (female). There was happiness, there was misery, there was pain. There was a Roman centurion – Summus Maximus, I presume – and his dog, Thor. And, inevitably, there was lots of rubbish. We picked up bottles and cans, and continued to do so on the way down, but it was a token gesture. You would need a skip to make any real impact.

You have to walk a narrow line to avoid sounding like a mountain snob. The vast majority of these walkers were doing it for admirable reasons, and it would be a real achievement for many, but some were lacking in outdoor etiquette and I wonder whether we should show the mountain a little charity of its own sometimes and give it a break.

As the day drew to a close, the mountain gave us a final, unexpected salute, courtesy of the retreating sun, the slopes turning a burnt umber for a few minutes as though they had caught fire. It was a fitting finale to a long journey.

—TMS—

The One that Got Away: An Cliseam – Graham Thompson

After some past bad days on the Munros I had to forgo any attempt on An Cliseam despite the summit being visible and readily attainable from the road north out of Tarbert. I did not favour another buffeting on the highest point of the Outer Hebrides so An Cliseam stays forever in my memory. Sad to relate it is the unclimbed hill that missed me when valour deserted me and age claimed me. Eighty years plus is as good an excuse as any for my failure – common sense ruled – so I will have to rely on the sight of the summit in my memory bank. The hill remains forever and the years flash by as I am not the man of yesterday's young years. And yet there are still hill books and maps for recall plus imagination and wistfulness. Some day one may lead me up to the summit where the weather gods may have a welcome.

Munro Musings by an Australian Compleatist

Ilona Turnbull

Reading Norman MacCaig's poems draws me straight into a world of Scottish hills and landscapes – a liminal world, an awe-inspiring world, an ephemeral world, a world that is my world.

Out in the hills, I'm Munro Compleatist 6840. But I have a name too, not just a number – Ilona Turnbull. During the months of post-Christmas lockdown in 2021, I was missing the hills and looking through pictures of my hikes during 2018-2020. I started sketching a picture of Corrour Bothy and then turned my pen to some Munro musings. That unsophisticated list seemed to strike a chord with hillwalkers on social media, and so this is an expanded version of those musings.

I know I'm inevitably mentioning things that those who are more erudite have more eloquently described, but all are truisms arising from my experiences.

A bit about my hillwalking background: I grew up in that country of extreme weather conditions, Australia. My brothers and I were taken camping and walking by our parents from a young age. Avoiding dehydration, sunburn, sandflies and eight of the ten most deadly snakes in the world (the 'Danger: Adders' signs I've seen in Scotland still make me laugh) was par for the course. Flash flooding and cars stuck in bogs also featured – perhaps inadvertently preparing me for the conditions Scotland can throw at you. I moved to London in 2006 and to Edinburgh in 2010.

I was lucky enough to have friends who introduced me to the concept of Munro-bagging when I lived in London and I climbed four during my time there. Ben Vorlich and Stùc a' Chroin at Loch Earn were my first two, climbed on 7th April, 2007 on a bluebird day.

Next were Spidean Mialach and Gleouraich in late March 2008. First lesson learned. Despite being only two weeks' difference between my first bag and second bags, the weather was completely different – from windless, cobalt-blue sunny conditions, to albescent, morphing into a blank canvas of sky-to-cornice-loch whiteness. A descent mired in sensory deprivation, then benighted and castigated by the hotel owner on return are my abiding memories.

Since that early experience, I've always carried additional warm kit and food, a head torch with spare batteries and told someone when I would be likely to return. I've been in situations where I've needed the kit, food and torch but happily, I've always returned safely.

Following a promising start and my move to Edinburgh meaning I'd

*Looking back on the An Teallach pinnacles
(Ilona Turnbull)*

bagged 83 Munros, I suffered badly from depression and bipolar disorder which led me to drop out of Munro-bagging by the end of 2017. After some significant life decisions and events, I re-started hillwalking on 5th June, 2018 with the Glen Lyon four. For my own mental health and to keep the black dog at bay, it became part of my weekly must do, as important for me as having breakfast or a Matryoshka doll-like nest of rucksacks of varying shape, size and colour.

During 2018, I climbed 82 new Munros and one repeat. In 2019, I did 85 new and 16 repeats and during the *annus horribilis maximus* of 2020, I compleated on Ben Hope in 'fair is foul and foul is fair' weather on 11th October in a Black Watch dress with my Aussie flag, becoming the first Australian woman to compleat, so far as the Clerk of the List is aware.

I've had the most marvellous time wandering the hills, in all sorts of weather (but luckily no deadly beasties), and I've met lifelong friends on and off the hills even though I've climbed many on my own. I've discovered wonderful writers and poets, explored large parts of Scotland, lost at least ten woolly hats, become a member of the Kilmarnock Mountaineering Club (and I really recommend joining a club) and I'm now a director of Mountaineering Scotland.

I'm passionate about hillwalking and want to encourage others to try it or re-start it. Whilst I'd hiked growing up in Oz, hillwalking in Scotland's a different story but it doesn't mean you can't do it just because you didn't grow up in Scotland or you haven't hiked in a while.

One quick note – I mention some brands by name – I'm relatively brand agnostic but these are standouts from my own experience (and I'm not being paid to endorse them). Without further ado, here are my musings.

1.   Physically and mentally, you get so much more contentment and achieve a greater sense of purpose than you ever thought possible. When I'm out there, my emotions range from butterflies of anticipation, then grumbles during the first 30 minutes in, to just smiling, clearing my mind and feeling utterly serene. Time becomes meaningless, hearing becomes attuned, smells are amplified, eyesight is more acute,

Compleation (Ilona Turnbull)

breathing vacillating between stertorous and metronomic. Muscles draw on memories of hills gone past. A suffusion of senses. I feel complete – and that feeling lasts for days and sustains me in my normal life. I can also scoff as many Scotch eggs and pies without fear of never walking them off.

2.   Breaking down groups of hills and starting with 'easier' hills, preferably in good weather, makes it less intimidating and doable. I remember first picking up Cameron McNeish's guide to the Munros and feeling overwhelmed by the descriptions. I honestly didn't think I'd be up to it. Breaking my Munro virginity was easier than I thought though; advice on which hills were good starter hills, choosing high-pressure systems to walk in, companions who can push you out of any 'I'm not good enough' internal rhetoric – but safely – all contribute to a more self-confident mindset. I'll say it again: clubs are brilliant supports.

3.   On difficult stretches, counting 100 steps at a time helps push you onwards/upwards/downwards (and sometimes sideways – definitely not regarded as a slip, of course). I'm rubbish at maths, so literally decimating steps in groups of 10 and giving thanks to the hiking formula demi-god of Naismith to work out that 10 minutes knocks off 100 metres of ascent just works. Better than counting sheep which don't tend to flock in groups of 10s.

On the South Glen Shiel ridge (Ilona Turnbull)

4. Estée Lauder Double Wear mascara survives hail/rain/snow/sleet/sweat/ the Fisherfield round. Seriously, this is the best. I don't need to say any more on this.

5. Sun cream mixed with Smidge doesn't taste great. Two essential items for summer hikes but that kind of seasonal hiking also lends itself to sweating like a Scotland supporter in the last eight minutes of overtime in the final Six Nations match of 2021 or Odysseus having discovered there's a wood shortage around Troy. The equation of sun cream + Smidge + sweat = acidic, oily, salty mouthfuls of grimness which would make you reach for an over-ripe banana which has been mushed into a paste at the bottom of your rucksack to alleviate the taste.

6. Chocolate and dry socks immediately make you feel better. Hiking's an unsophisticated thing at its heart. Wet socks send a literal chill through your body. Dry socks are a beacon of warmness in a frigid environment. Chocolate gives you that happy sugar high which never fails to lift flagging spirits or quells any hunger pangs left over post-Scotch egg consumption.

7. Toenails can fall off if you hike a lot. You can also bruise toes which can turn a kaleidoscope of colours. Dark nail polish can cover this up. For those who don't paint their toenails, you'll have to accept nude nailbeds as an alternative.

8. You end up with a better grasp of Gaelic vocabulary, particularly colours and topographical features (see 'Stùc' above) – russet ruaidh, buttercup buidhe, gentian gorm, UFO green or ghostly geal can illuminate landscapes of spiky stùcs, craggy carns, lustrous lochs and monolithic mealls.

9. There's a lot of wonderful Scottish poets/authors and poetry/books about the hills out there to discover. I've started this piece with a reference to the poems of Norman MacCaig. It means I can dip into hill descriptions, conjure up mesmerising memories and learn more about the Scottish environment and history.

10. Curiosity about maps grows exponentially. Paper ones unfold with pleasing crispness when new, then fold into a welcome embrace of well-used creases with time. Names of topographical features are fascinating – looking at a map of the Cairngorms right now records mellifluous names such as Sgùrr an Lochan Uaine, Coire an t-Sneachda, Lagganauld, Carn na Craoibhe Seileich, and, rather jarringly, Brown Cow Hill. Those names alone tell of different patterns of human settlements over time though the features are literally sometimes as old as the hills.

Taking a breather on the Aonach Eagach (Ilona Turnbull)

11. The Twitter hillwalking community is really helpful and encouraging. If you want to know which bridges are still extant, which are the worst peat bogs, where the snowline is, where the best loos are on the A9 (House of Bruar) or simply, what's an easy-ish six-hour hike near Pitlochry, Twitter can help. Some of my now closest friends were those I made via Twitter.

12. If asked repeatedly on a hike of the Braeriach traverse if female hikers can do it solo, in one day and under 11 hours, the answer is yes. I came across this sort of query quite a few times – I don't know if it's a perception thing that I was out of my depth potentially because I was a solo female walker in remote

areas, or it was a safety question or type-casting but solo female hikers do exist. We're pretty sensible and happily, we're growing in number, albeit we still struggle to crack 25% of compleatists per year even over the last ten years. I have confidence this will change.

13. Completing tricky sections of walks is adrenaline-producing and incredibly satisfying (even if it involves lots of swearing). 'Tricky' is, of course, subjective. Sometimes it is because it's a very long hike, or because there are precipitous bits, or the weather is down. The buzz is there though, albeit it usually follows the swearing.

14. Day 2 is more painful than Days 1 and 3. Day 4 sometimes bites you in the backside though. Not sure why, it just does.

15. Not enough female hiking trousers have an appropriate number of useful pockets. Given hikers, regardless of gender, carry the same kit into the hills, why do so many clothing companies skimp on numbers and position of pockets? This remains a mystery to me.

16. Red Mountain Equipment waterproofs are superb, and I've not (yet) met an unhappy hillwalker wearing one. I'm not sure if red goes faster but you can also be spotted easily if you need rescuing, and whilst we may have to watch out for crepuscular suicidal deer, wild bulls aren't around to take us on in red waterproofs. I can't imagine they're top of the list for re-introduction either.

17. Hiking poles are transformative (I have now pole-induced biceps – short of World's Strongest Man-worthy but decent) and are not just for the over-80s. There's a reason so many guides use them. They're excellent at testing the depths of peat bogs too.

18. Always buy a comfortable pair of good quality hiking boots, even if it means trying on every pair of boots in both Edinburgh Tiso shops. Be kind to your feet and it pays off.

19. OS maps / Viewranger / Walkhighlands / MWIS and Mountaineering Scotland give you great support, the right amount of confidence, an increased chance of a safe walk and excitement and eagerness of trying a new route.

20. 'Wow, what an amazing view' and 'Aw crap, I've just fallen into another peat bog' are phrases which can be used interchangeably on the same hike. The first can also immediately be followed by 'I don't remember the summit boulder field being this long/wide/so full of boulders coming up here'. Ben More Assynt/Conival and Schiehallion, I mean you.

21. I'm happiest in the hills when I'm alone but I'm not lonely.

22. Tunnock's caramel wafers are more structurally sound than Tunnock's tea cakes. I discovered this on my compleation when I tried to make a cairn of Aussie and Scottish treats. Marshmallow isn't a good cairn base. It's decent as a lodestone though.

23. Compeed is your friend and it's worth the extra money to buy that brand.

24. There is a large array of serial killing/murder podcasts available to listen to when travelling to or walking on the hills. Disclosing this to new friends who have agreed to go hiking with me can be a little unsettling apparently.

25. Merino pants/undies are worth the extra money; chances of numb bum decrease when wearing them. I'll not go into any more detail but suffice to say, they are happily less fragrant than normal pants at the end of a hike too.

26. It is possible to have contacts blown out of your eyes and get cold hives which land you in A&E (damn you Ben Wyvis in December).

27. You can only ever reach the summit under your own steam and your own determination and no one can take that away from you. Even if you're a billionaire, you'll see awe-inspiring places that those with all the money in the world will never see. Scotland may never be the Maldives, and certainly not if the Jetstream moves, but it's all the better for it.

28. Scotland is astonishingly beautiful, and I'm constantly delighted by new discoveries in my peregrinations around this lovely country.

Why 28? Because there are 282 extant Munros so there's a musing for 1 in 10 Munros or thereabouts. Back to my fondness for multiples of 10.

I think the word 'joyful' is under-used but that is probably the feeling I get when I'm on a hill. And it's a feeling that lasts. I seek it out actively almost every weekend and I surround myself with similarly minded folk, poetry, writings.

I've been smiling whilst I've been writing this, recalling peat bogs of note, sublime views, historical events, and an ancient landscape. I may have grown up in the Lucky Country – as Australia's often referred to – but Scotland, and its hills, is where I feel so lucky (with apologies to Kylie).

Winter conditions on The Saddle
(Ilona Turnbull)

—TMs—

Bothy

Candle Light
   at the window;
      the green flame,
the red flame.
   Warming and
      rising sap:
fire; a fist
   -full of amber
      liquid; ice
melting
   inside; outside:
      the long breath
of the Caledonian
   wood
      -wind.

Stuart B. Campbell

Image: N. McNab

Carless Hills

Pauline Symaniak

E ight hours after leaving home, I got off the Skye bus at the Cluanie Inn and took the old road south, the route used by walkers for the east to west traverse of the seven Munros of the South Shiel Ridge. This was not my target, however.

I was heading to Knoydart – and I had a long way to go. I skirted the shoulder of Creag a' Mhàim to pick up the path running west for eight kilometres to Glen Quoich. Then I turned south on the track along the loch shore which leads down to the road, before following it to its end at Kinloch Hourn and the start of the Barrisdale path.

Most Munro baggers looking to use this access point for Ladhar Bheinn, Luinne Bheinn and Meall Buidhe will drive to Kinloch Hourn. But I don't have a car. Never owned one, in fact. All my hill journeys are made using public transport and pedal power.

It means a lot of planning and a lot of travelling, but I have never regretted my decision to go carless. Not having a car means getting to explore so much more of the wild country. My walk into Knoydart, for instance, may have started the day before those who drove to Kinloch Hourn but they will have to retrace their steps along the Barrisdale path while I can make a stunning traverse of the area by walking out via Glenfinnan to catch a train home. Going without a car is not something everyone can do. I'm aware I'm in a privileged position to be able to make that choice.

I chose to live in a big city in central Scotland to ensure I could live without a car. It's a hub for trains and buses, plus I can easily cycle to work. It also means it's easy to jump on a train on a Friday after work and get somewhere nice, then back home at the end of the weekend.

Cars generate pollution which contributes to climate change and impacts health. The increased number of cars on our roads is the reason often quoted by folk for not cycling or using other active travel. Congestion causes business billions and, as well as noise pollution, greatly reduces the quality of life in urban areas. Of course, hillwalking is great for health but when it adds so many vehicles to the roads, it has a negative impact on population health.

The other reason I don't have a car is that I find using public transport to get to the hills so much more fun, albeit there are significant challenges. You have to be creative, but it's more rewarding. Travelling by bus or train means you never have to consider where you'll leave a car, and you don't have to plan a route that ends up back where you parked. The train is so relaxing after a weekend or a week in the hills. You can sit back and relax, enjoy the scenery, kick off your boots and treat yourself to refreshments from the trolley. You'll rub shoulders with people from all over the world, and there is a camaraderie amongst the passengers. You can have a blether and sometimes there have been guitars and a musical accompaniment on the Sunday evening train from Fort William. Using trains, buses and rural buses also helps these services survive for those who really need them. I prefer the train, but I also use buses where the train doesn't go. You'll often find that bus drivers on more rural routes will drop you at the start of a walk if it's closer than the bus stop.

I think not having a car adds an extra layer of excitement to hillwalking trips. If you have a car at the bottom of the hill, it provides a relatively easy escape, and you can be tucked up in your own bed that evening. This option is not always available with public transport. For instance, it's a Saturday night, a storm is moving in but there's no Sunday bus service where you are. You have to plan ahead more.

I'm doing the Munros at a leisurely pace, but I just do whatever takes my fancy. There's no rush. I rarely do day walks, only if I was staying local, somewhere like the Pentlands. It's not that I can't do lots of hills within a day timetable – for example, many folk will be familiar with fitting in Beinn na Lap at Corrour between the morning and evening trains – but if I'm spending

Corrour Station (Pauline Symaniak)

a few hours travelling and a fair bit on a ticket I want to get value for money, so my Munros would always be done as part of a weekend away with an overnight wild camp. Being without a car really slows life down. It forces you to spend longer in the hills and immerse yourself in the experience for longer.

For most folk Ben Venue would be a quick, half-day excursion. I took the bus into the city, a train to Stirling then a bus to Aberfoyle. I followed the track round the south shore of Loch Ard to reach Ledard, so it was 1.30pm by the time I got to the 'start' of the walk. But as it was mid-winter and relatively late, it was quiet, and the sun was sinking. I was able to walk out a different way next day to Callander.

It doesn't always have to involve epic journeys. A traverse of the Lomond Hills saw me taking a train to Markinch and then walking through the housing estates of Glenrothes – an unusual start to a hillwalking trip. That took me to the bottom of the path at Pitcairn that goes up East Lomond. After a wild camp, I came off Benarty Hill at Loch Leven to pick up a train home from Lochgelly.

I also use public transport to start cycling trips further afield and to go kayaking. I have inflatables so I can get them on the bus or train. A folding bike is a great ally because it doesn't need to be booked on the train in advance and you can take it on buses.

When I did the Glen Lyon Munros, I took the folding bike on the train to Dunkeld, then on the local bus to Aberfeldy, cycled to Invervar and left it in the woods. It's my cheapest bike so I don't worry about leaving it! I also did the Strathfarrar hills that way, cycling in on a folding bike from the train station at Beauly.

Camp in Glen Strathfarrar (Pauline Symaniak)

One of the tricky things about using public transport is that you have to decide while still at home what kit to take, e.g., crampons and ice axe, only to discover later you don't need it after carrying it all that way. With a car, you would just chuck everything in the boot and then make a decision about what to actually

47

carry when you reach your destination.

So many trips involve taking the Friday evening Fort William or Inverness trains to reach some amazing places in the West Highlands, the Perthshire hills or the Cairngorms. On other occasions, I'd leave the house at 5.30am on a Saturday to get a bus to the city centre and then a train somewhere nice like Corrour, camp overnight, then return on the Sunday evening train, getting home about 11pm. That often means carrying a Sunday evening meal and cooking it on the platform.

Recently, I managed to switch to a nine-day working fortnight so I can have every second Monday off, a great result as it means I can get three days out of any train ticket; also, public transport for returning is much better on a Monday than a Sunday.

I've a vague radius of what's do-able by public transport in a weekend or long weekend; the Great Glen is probably the imaginary boundary. Other areas beyond that I save for holidays. For example, I'd never go to Torridon for a weekend: if you get off the train at Achnashellach, you still have to cross the mountains on the south side of the glen before you can get to those on the north such as Beinn Eighe. So the likes of Knoydart, Glen Shiel, Skye, Fisherfield and the Fannaichs are only tackled on holidays.

My most creative approach was for a trip to the Loch Lochy hills and Gulvain. I got off the train at Banavie, just after Fort William on the Caledonian Canal, and as I'd only be cycling seven miles or so to the road-end, it didn't seem worth taking a bike. This is when I first got a kick scooter. I scooted from Banavie up the canal to just beyond

Achnashellach Station (Pauline Symaniak)

Gairlochy, hid the scooter under a bush, then set out on foot along the shore track and up to Sròn a' Choire Ghairbh. I then walked out to do Gulvain with a couple of nights' wild camping. I'd enjoyed the adventure with the scooter so much that I didn't climb Meall na Teanga so that I had an excuse to do the canal scoot again another time!

The scooter (Pauline Symaniak)

After Gulvain, which is a long walk in from that side, I retrieved the scooter and scooted back all the way to Fort William for a train home. The scooter is more comfortable than a bike when wearing a heavy, multi-day pack as you are in a more upright position, more like walking. Speed wise, it's between walking and cycling. Effort-wise, it's harder than both!

If I had to pick a favourite area it would be between Knoydart and Glen Shiel. I also love all the options for routes when you get off the train at Corrour – so many trails, so many hills and no long walk in!

But there's always that slightly unnerving moment at Corrour when you wonder if the evening train home will show up. One time I was stranded when it couldn't get through heavy snow. I had to call ScotRail from the information phone on the platform and get them to tell my flatmate not to call mountain rescue when I didn't return home that night.

Beinn Sgritheall was a stunning day out and a good example of how using public transport makes you more creative with routes and provides rich rewards. Most folk drive to Arnisdale, but I started further away by getting off the Skye bus at Shiel Bridge. It's a long but beautiful walk in from there; through the mountain pass below The Saddle, a long remote stretch that passes Suardalan Bothy, then a long pull up the north side of the hill into Coire Min. This side is so wild and rugged, and I never saw another soul. I pitched the tent below the corrie so by the time I pulled up onto the ridge, there was nobody on the summit and the sun was sinking beyond Skye. Of course, a long walk in means it's a long walk out too!

Getting off the Skye bus at the Cluanie Inn gives you a few options. One of my favourite trips from Cluanie was doing the South Glen Shiel ridge, setting up the tent at the far end for the night, then walking back to the bus at Cluanie over the Brothers ridge on the other side of the glen. Another great cross-country traverse is from Attadale on the Kyle of Lochalsh rail line to Tomich and a bus to Inverness. It's a stunning route that takes in Glen Elchaig, Bealach an Sgàirne with Beinn Fhada and the Glen Affric hills.

Sometimes things don't go to plan. On my way to the Fisherfield hills, walking in via Loch a' Bhraoin, the Inverness train got in four hours late after a breakdown and rail replacement bus chaos and I missed the last Ullapool bus. I had planned to get off at Braemore Junction and walk a few miles along the road. As there was no other bus, ScotRail paid for a taxi just for me and told the driver to go to Ullapool but I diverted him up the Dundonnell road instead and got dropped right at the start of my walk, missing out all the road miles.

On another occasion, when I was planning to camp on the Trotternish ridge with a friend, the bus saved the day. The first day was beautiful and it was a good forecast for the next one. During the night, unexpected storm force winds piled through and we evacuated our spot about 4am as the tents were flattened. We wandered down to the Uig road which was deserted as it was winter. We didn't know the nearest bus stop or the bus times but as we walked towards Uig, the Citylink bus stopped for us and took us into Portree. I don't think he charged us either!

If we are going to convince more people to switch away from cars, we need major investment in convenient and affordable public transport and a massive overhaul of our transport system so it's not biased towards cars.

I'd like to see active travel infrastructure vastly improved all over the country so it's safe to get on to your destination if the bus or train doesn't go all the way there. Think about Glen Coe: how do you move safely through the glen on foot or bicycle when the bus only drops you at either end or your nearest train is miles away along a busy road.

We could really do with bringing back club coaches and local rambler services. For example, the Angus Glens are a nightmare to get to on foot because the nearest bus or train is so far away. And these need to be year-round services, not just summer. Many places don't have a Sunday bus service, one of the two most likely days in the week when people want to travel for leisure.

Education is also important, to help people understand the impact of using cars and what the carbon footprint of the average Munro round must be for someone living in the central belt. We can't keep ignoring the impact the excessive use of cars is having. Yes, they are convenient, but we have to make compromises in our lifestyles for the sake of the planet.

As told to Alan Rowan.

—TMs—

Munros and Corbetts by Train

Oliver Bartrum

I have made frequent short trips by train to Scotland to climb the Munros over a fifteen-year period (1996-2011) and, all being well, it will be slightly less for the Corbetts (2011-2022), since I am no longer working full time in London and, recently, have been more intent on their completion.

It is easy to overlook how much travelling is required within Scotland to cover the Munros, and more in the case of the Corbetts. Driving to Glasgow is often only half-way. For me, a better option has been the train, especially the sleeper service from London to Inverness or Fort William. Many hills can be covered on three-day camping trips starting or finishing at Blair Atholl, Dalwhinnie, Kingussie, Aviemore, Arrochar, Crianlarich, Tyndrum, Bridge of Orchy, Rannoch, Corrour, Tulloch, Spean Bridge and Fort William. The lines out to Mallaig from Fort William and to Kyle of Lochalsh from Inverness present further opportunities, and if a taxi drop-off or pick-up and/or a boat are included in the planning, a week-end break can take you to the remotest places. Leaving the office in the City of London at 7.00pm on a Thursday evening, we would be in the hills 12 hours later. I have averaged 20 Munros and Corbetts a year in this manner. This article reminisces on some of these trips and the attractions of the sleeper service. The arrival of 'new' sleeper carriages in 2017-18 and, more recently, the effects of Covid-19, have enforced changes, not all of them for the good.

There was no better place to meet after work before boarding the sleeper at Euston than the Bree Louise pub, in Euston Street. The pub, known as 'Euston's best kept secret', was renowned for its range of real ales, cider and pies. Sadly, the pub was compulsorily purchased in January 2018 for the HS2 railway project. The sleeper experience has

Arrival (Oliver Bartrum)

not been the same since. Early boarding of the train and access to the lounge carriage were restricted when the Caledonian Sleeper was taken over by Serco. Gone are the days when we would be well into a game of cards as we passed Watford Junction and the forfeits for the loser, typically a circuit of the lounge carriage without touching the floor, have been strictly off limits since the new carriages were introduced. Covid travel arrangements led to the closure of the lounge bar and recent services have been beset by delays and cancellations. It feels as if it will be some time before normal service is resumed.

The downside with this sort of travel arrangement can be the weather. Knowing the return transport was in three days' time was a bit of a shock as we stood on the platform at Blair Atholl one cold morning in April 2006. It was freezing, the sky was black, and snow had started to fall. We were heading for the Munros Carn Liath, Bràigh Coire Chruinn-bhalgain, and Carn nan Gabhar. It was not long before we were battling our way in near white-out conditions. Occasional clear patches helped with orientation. We were very relieved to arrive eventually at the 'Tarf Hotel' bothy and enjoyed better conditions on An Sgarsoch and Carn an Fhidleir the next day. On day three, heavy snow hampered our return to Blair Atholl by way of Carn a' Chlamain. We were delighted to be able to wait for our return train in the Bothy Bar of the Atholl Arms Hotel.

Somewhere near Carn nan Gabhar, April 2006 (Oliver Bartrum)

An Sgarsoch, April 2006 (Oliver Bartrum)

On a similar trip in better conditions in April 2008, we caught the train to Inverness from where we got a taxi to the power station in Strathfarrar. We traversed the four Munros Sgùrr na Ruaidhe, Carn nan Gobhar, Sgùrr a' Choire Ghlais and Sgùrr Fuar-thuill in excellent conditions and descended to Loch Monar to camp near Monar Lodge.

From Loch Monar we headed east over Maoile Lunndaidh and down to an overnight camp near Glenuaig Lodge. Our last day was over Bidean an Eòin Deirg, Sgùrr a' Chaorachain and Sgùrr Choinnich and then down to Craig and a train from Achnashellach back to Inverness.

Combining the sleeper service with a car can lead to difficulties as I found in July 2004. I had organised a trip for a party of six from London. We had traversed the Grey Corries from the car park at the top of Glen Nevis. After finishing on Stob Bàn and heading back towards the car, I realised that we had left it too late for one member of the party to get to Fort William in time for the overnight sleeper. He had to be in London the next day for a potential business deal. We offloaded his kit and urged him to make best speed to get to the car park; encouraged by another team member who was a Royal Marine reservist and well up to a bit of double time. As they disappeared out of view, I realised that I had the car keys. All their efforts would be in vain if they could

Outside Achnashellach Station (Oliver Bartrum)

53

not get to the station. Turning to another younger and fitter member of the party, I said that 'one of us has to do better than best speed to catch up with the other two and it's not me!'. To his great credit, he caught up and handed over the keys. Sadly, no deal was struck in London the next day. The Royal Marines had the last laugh when I was invited to join a sea-kayaking 40th birthday party on Barra in September 2012. The wind was up, we never made it to Mingalay and I capsized. We did have a memorable overnight camp on Vatersay, though I wondered if I'd ever make it back to Castlebay. I did – just.

Barra (Oliver Bartrum)

The Cairngorms is an excellent area for rail-borne expeditions. On the first trip from Aviemore in July 2006, we got a lift to Glenmore Lodge and then headed over Bynack More to the Fords of Avon refuge from where, the next day, we made a circuit of Beinn a' Chaorainn, Beinn a' Bhuird (South and North) and Ben Avon, descending north for a return via Glen Avon where we met a rather bedraggled DofE party heading the same way. We reassured them that the refuge was not far away. Day three took us past Loch Avon and over Ben Macdui and down to Corrour bothy. Two Glaswegians were settling in for the night and not best pleased to share space with Sassenachs unless, as a minimum, we took up their challenge of a dominoes match. We did and the Glaswegians lost but a bottle of whisky restored spirits and honour all round. The final day was a traverse in superb conditions over the Devil's Point, Cairn Toul and Braeraich, returning to Aviemore via the Lairig Ghru and Rothiemurchus Forest.

On our second trip in early November 2008 we encountered unexpectedly heavy snow that made us abandon an attempt to cross the high plateau of the Mòine Mhòr to get to Monadh Mòr in favour of a traverse over Sgor Gaoith, and its northern tops. We returned in November 2009 from the Braemar side. Walking in from Linn of Dee, we left kit at Derry Lodge and detoured to Beinn Bhreac, before continuing to Corrour bothy. It was so full that there was a 15-minute rotation for the available sitting space. We had a better night in our tents. The next day we made a fine circuit of Angel's Peak (Sgor an Lochain

Uaine), Monadh Mòr and Beinn Bhrotain, returning for a second night at the bothy. We returned to Aviemore via Cairn Toul and Braeraich again.

Starting and finishing at Fort William, I attempted a three-day traverse of Knoydart in October 2017. A taxi took three of us to the end of Loch Cuaich and the start of an ascent of Gairich, from where we descended southwest to Kinbreack bothy, crossing the River Kingie proving quite an ordeal after a very wet day.

The plan to continue west over Sgùrr nan Coireachan, Garbh Chioch Mhòr and Sgùrr na Ciche was abandoned due to poor weather, in favour of a long, wet, walk up Glen Dessarry to Sourlies bothy. We enjoyed the company of a large herd of deer outside the bothy that night as well as a cloud, colony or cauldron of bats roosting in the walls of the bothy. After an early start on the final day, we climbed the length of Beinn Bhuidhe (Corbett) from Màm Meadail before descending to Inverie; the old bridge over the Carnach was washed away later that week. Our schedule meant that we had to catch the 4.30pm ferry to Mallaig. We arrived on the quayside in Inverie as the ropes were being slipped and without having to break stride, stepped aboard. Seldom have I cut the timings so fine.

The furthest north I have got for a weekend in the hills by train (plus taxi and boat) from London is Fisherfield in April 2013. We crossed Loch Maree to a point east of Letterewe and headed north to Carnmore via Beinn Làir (Corbett) and Meall Mhèinnidh (Graham). After a very wet night we made a traverse of the Fisherfield Corbetts: Beinn Dearg Mòr, Beinn Dearg Bheag and Beinn a' Chàisgein Mòr before a boat pick-up on the shore of Loch Maree on the third day.

Other train/taxi camping trips based near Kinlochewe led to superb days on Beinn Alligin and Beinn Eighe, a circuit of the Flowerdale Corbetts Beinn an Eòin and Baosbheinn, and the Torridon Corbetts Beinn Dearg, Sgùrr Dubh and Sgorr nan Lochan Uaine.

Based at the campsite in Torridon in July 2017, an old climbing friend joined me to make a

Beinn Làir, April 2013 (Oliver Bartrum)

Sgùrr Bàn, Beinn Eighe, April 2008 (Oliver Bartrum)

Near Mullach an Rathain, July 2015 (Oliver Bartrum)

long-overdue west to east traverse of Liathach from the Northern Pinnacles to Stùc a' Choire Dhuibh Bhig. It was worth the wait for good conditions for such a fine route.

The station from where the most hills can be done is possibly Upper Tyndrum though heavy snow in November 2012 prevented us from completing what the SMC guide calls the 'unique hand': five Corbetts in one day. On an earlier bad weather trip, Tyndrum had been the starting point for a traverse of the Munros Beinn Challuim, Creag Mhòr, Meall Glas and Sgiath Chùil with an overnight stop at Batavaime bothy. It rained solidly for two days. Fortunately, conditions were better for the final day: a circuit of Stob Binnein and Ben More from Glen Dochart. We caught the train back from Crianlarich.

Bad weather forced me to revise plans for a trip that was to have started from Dalwhinnie in April 2009. Despite high hopes of being able to catch a bus from a place that is twinned with Las Vegas, this was not the place to try combining road and rail. I discovered that bus timetables, especially online ones, are no more than a guide, that advertised routes are likely to be cancelled or changed at no notice and that bus shelters are placed in some of the most inhospitable places possible: a seatless, unprotected shelter on the A9, over a mile from the station and not far short of the Drumochter Pass. A kindly driver (DofE instructor) took pity and stopped to pick me up. He said: 'you must be from England'. He added: 'nobody around here waits at that bus stop!'. Inexplicably, it seems to be impossible to get from Fort William to Inverness by bus or coach on a Sunday – or I have been incredibly unlucky on the two occasions I tried.

Bad planning meant that my last two Munros were the remote pair Bidein a' Choire Sheasgaich and Lurg Mhòr. To make a three-day trip of it, we got the train to Strathcarron and climbed the Corbett An Ruadh-Stac before walking in to the bothy at Bendronaig Lodge for the two Munros. The weather could not have been worse – so bad that we managed to head 180 degrees in the wrong direction from the top of Lurg Mhòr, an error we put down to the summit celebrations.

We returned to Achnashellach via Sgùrr na Feartaig (Corbett) on the final day. It was rather fitting that this trip combined my last Munros with some of my first Corbetts, a round of which was greatly encouraged and assisted by the late David Batty – until his untimely death in November 2018 during his term as President of TMS.

I was delighted to contribute towards the Society's compleation of David's Third Round of Munros[1], by train of course, in April 2019. Starting from Rannoch station, I headed to Carn Dearg (Loch Ossian) where I scraped a message in the sandy summit: 'OPB was here 11.00am. CU later'. This was not meant as a message for David! It was for a friend who was arriving on

Lurg Mhòr, October 2011 (Oliver Bartrum)

a later train and would be following me, and my phone battery was almost flat. He told me later that he had seen the message. Our route continued over Sgor Coinnich, and Beinn a' Chumhainn before heading down to Benalder Cottage for the night. We were joined by two mountain bikers who had come from Dalwhinnie via Culra and the Bealach Breabag, one of whom wasn't too happy about the terrain. They were heading for Fort William. Given the weight of their bikes and the distance, we were not surprised to find out later that they caught a train from Corrour. Our second day took in Ben Alder, Beinn Eibhinn, Aonach Beag, Geal-Chàrn and Sgòr Iutharn; that night the wind got up rattling the door in a manner befitting the haunted reputation of the Cottage. Our last day was a walk out over Beinn Eibhinn's westerly Tops (David's Third Round included the Tops) to Corrour station where the waiting room/restaurant must rate among the best in the British Isles.

I have now climbed most of the Corbetts that are reasonably accessible from the rail network so, as with the last of the Munros, I have hired a campervan from Inverness to get to the most distant hills and mountains. My wife, Catherine, joined me on a circuitous trip in April taking in three Corbetts in Strathconon, Meall Dubh north of Loch Garry, and An Cliseam plus its three tops on Harris. We enjoyed fine but cold conditions and took time to explore more of North Harris.

For me, access to the Scottish hills through train and tent started out of a need to minimise travelling time and became more attractive with the passing

Luskentyre (Oliver Bartrum)

of time and desire to complete my hill rounds. I still enjoy the planning and preparation for these trips; the research of train and boat timetables, the possibility of combining hills into one trip, identifying good camping spots and the company of old friends and family who, for one reason or another, still agree to accompany me. It has been a very worthwhile pastime for more than twenty years and I look forward to many more days in the hills – and the train journeys getting there.

[1] The subject of an article in TMS Journal No. 5

The One that Got Away:
Mullach Fraoch-choire – Rebecca Ricketts

Mullach Fraoch-choire is best climbed as a pair with A' Chràileag unless, of course, the weather has other ideas. My first attempt was brought to an abrupt halt by spring snowstorms which left an impassable wall of white at the summit of A' Chràileag. I retreated to the Cluanie Inn, in March of the Penguins-style, my walking companions in tow. Despite making better progress on my second bid, reaching Stob Coire na Cràileag, snow once again brought us to a complete standstill on the bypass path round the back of the pinnacles. According to Cameron McNeish, in snowy conditions this ridge can be 'extremely tricky.' I was taking his word for it! For me, it was a case of third time lucky, relieved to finally reach the summit of Mullach Fraoch-choire in 2017.

LOCHS and LOCHANS

Above – Loch Avon and the Shelter Stone from the foot of Coire Raibert, staying local after lockdown ended.

Below – Loch Mallachie in Abernethy Forest on a misty autumnal dog walk.

Anne Butler

Mullardoch Round

Mark Gibson

I f you've ever been inspired by an article or conversation, then this account of how I came to be humping a large pack over some of the wild hills in Scotland in the depths of February will mean something to you. A long time ago I'd read Richard Gilbert and Ken Wilson's book, *Classic Walks*. Although the book's format is a bit coffee-table-ish, it was responsible for planting the seed of an idea in both my, and my friend Martin's, heads that we ought to have a crack at this classic winter outing. Despite the publication of the SMC's hugely successful *The Munros* book and Irvine Butterfield's *The High Mountains*, getting more detailed accounts of traversing these hills in winter proved difficult. I guess there might have been accounts in the SMC journals but actually laying hands on anything relevant wasn't easy. It was the plan to hire a car, but a friend offered to lend his, an offer we took up. We both lived in Hebden Bridge, aka the Hampstead of the north, back then, and it was our routine to drive up overnight, have some sleep in the car, and start walking at first light. This is pretty much what we did, and in the cold grey light of a February morning we set off from the bleak surroundings of the Mullardoch Dam with provisions for three nights plus a little extra for contingencies.

It was deeply cold as we set off. Taking the shortest possibly route, we summited Carn nan Gobhar, our first Munro of the round. All the way up the ground was frozen and once above the snowline crampons were donned and were to remain on for most of the day. Visibility was variable with the clouds swirling about us but very little wind to bother us on our generally westward course. Staying close together we made excellent progress on the big pull up Sgùrr na Lapaich. But it took its toll. We'd forgotten to fill our water bottles and with no prospect of finding any, we were going to be increasingly thirsty in the coming hours. Some compass work saw us safely along the ridge with only one minor problem – the dog-leg route off An Riabhachan, which coincided with the cloud being at its thickest. This proved quite a challenge as we found ourselves on steep ground with no obvious easy way off. A short period of front-pointing meant we made our way crab-like to easier slopes and the correct ridge down to Bealach Bholla. The lack of water was becoming a trial. Finding the trig point on An Socach was a relief.

Heading off An Socach we made for the nearest running water. Our mouths were parched. We drank our fill of brain-chilling water from the burn which flows out of Coire Lungard. Cutting across the hillside, we descended to make camp on the north side of glen, setting up the next day's route nicely.

For this trip we used Martin's single-skin Gore-Tex tunnel tent. At the time

61

this was being touted as the future, issues with condensation being the main problem. The Trangia was soon humming away, the sky darkened, and the long night was upon us. It was a tight fit in the tent. I cooked up some curried lentils and rice whilst half hanging out of my sleeping bag with a down jacket on. It can take a while to get all the food cooked and pans cleaned for the next meal. With plenty of brew-ups and subsequent trips outside for a pee, a few hours passed; there's not much else to do.

Camp, looking towards Carn Eighe and Màm Sodhail (Mark Gibson)

It was a cold night, but we were warm enough. A warming sun woke us, and we wriggled out of our sleeping bags to have breakfast *al fresco* in the still air of the glen. I don't remember there being any difficulty crossing the river in the middle of the glen. With everything packed we made our way across the frozen bog towards the mouth of Gleann Sithidh. Today we didn't repeat our error of the day before - we filled our water bottles in a burn at the beginning of the day. A steep slog up frozen turf and we emerged into the sunshine at Creag a' Choir' Aird. Taking the path on the eastern side of the glen we covered a bit of ground before forsaking it and striking up the steep slopes towards Munro number five of the trip, Mullach na Dheiragain. This was warm work and before we reached the top we drank as much as we could from a burn, not expecting to find any running water for the next few hours.

To the east, the twins of Màm Sodhail and Carn Eighe glinted with the strong sun behind them. They seemed so close, but we knew that we wouldn't reach them that day. Ahead lay three Munros and several hard miles of snow and ice. The grass gave way to hard snow during the next 300 meters of climbing up to Mullach Sithidh. The crampons were put on and stayed on for the rest of the day. We crested our first Munro of the day, Mullach na Dheiragain, and took a break on its summit. We were hot from the effort, and with no breeze to chill us sat about without our jackets.

We were feeling good and we quickly moved off southward towards the distant Sgùrr nan Ceathramhnan. The hill shimmered in the bright sun as we progressed along the narrowing ridge towards the summit. The two downs and two ups passed in a blur. The narrow section of the ridge up to Sgùrr nan Ceathramhnan caused us to waken out of our trance to apply just enough focus on our foot placing either side of the arête. At the summit we had a nip of whisky whilst I mused on the possibility that the peak further to our west might just be higher. Martin put me right on the matter and no more was said about my rash flight of fancy.

It was nearly 2pm when we left Sgùrr nan Ceathramhnan. The sun was noticeably at our backs as we worked our way down the steep eastern slopes. With a few miles to cover on a February afternoon we were keenly aware that we had to get a move on or risk benightment and struggle to locate a suitable pitch for the night. On the map Bealach Coire Ghàidheil looked promising

Sgùrr nan Ceathramhnan from SH1108 on Màm Sodhail (Norman McNab)

and that's where we aimed for as we rolled along the easy-going ridge. The Munro An Socach barely registered our attention as we moved easily over the frozen snow and down into the col as the light started to fade. On its north side we descended for a few minutes until we found a convenient grassy ledge for the tent with a nearby water supply. Another long night was broken up by numerous cups of tea, food, the odd dram and watching the stars on a cold clear night. It was a memorable night's camp. Late in the evening a plane flew westward at a similar height to us. We dimmed our torches to avoid drawing attention. That night we slept with our down jackets plus everything else we had. It was cold on the north side of the ridge.

Carn Eighe (Derek Sime)

Before first light we were wriggling out of our sleeping bags. The water bottles (we'd kept them between us in the tent) had miraculously not frozen. Porridge, dried fruit and tea constituted our standard breakfast. With chilled fingers we forced our feet into cold boots and attached crampons. Our pitch was no place for a slip. The pull back onto the ridge soon had us warmed up. Despite the cold, near the top, we found a spring running. Hmm, shame we hadn't spotted it the previous evening. Up and over the hulking twins of Màm Sodhail and Carn Eighe we went. Early on cloud obscured the view much of the time. It cleared just enough for us to identify our route off Carn Eighe. Taking a prolonged break beside the large cairn we weighed up our options. We both wanted to claim Beinn Fhionnlaidh but did we want to haul our gear down and back up the 350m to where we now sat? Leaving all our

The author on Carn Eighe (Mark Gibson)

Beinn Fhionnlaidh from Carn Eighe (Derek Sime)

gear on top of a 1,183m mountain in winter whilst we were off peak bagging seemed a bit rash, even by our 'it'll be rite' standards.

So, we trudged our way down into the Bealach Beag and dumped them there, and carried on to Beinn Fhionnlaidh. Through gaps in the rising mist we caught the view down Loch Mullardoch.

The 350-meter climb back up the highest hill north of the Great Glen wasn't the greatest of experiences but we did it in one steady haul. Moving off again we navigated our way over the 1,147m Top in poor visibility.

Heading north-east, we couldn't see much at all. Knowing there were cliffs to our right concentrated our minds as we searching for any clue to where we should swing round to the south-east. We both had our doubts when I got distracted by a map falling out of Martin's rucksack's top pocket. I was too late to save it but at the same time the cloud peeled away to reveal the Dhomhnuill pinnacles. We were off track by about two hundred meters. With that error righted we approached the verglassed pinnacles. Interest in photography was waning and time was getting on. We shimmied a way through the rocky formations and at one spot Martin had to release my Karrimat which had become wedged in a tight gap.

Once again our thoughts turned to finding a camping spot, preferably with water. After the Munro Top An Leth-chreag we cramponed down the hard snow into Coire Mhic Fhearchair. Here we could see depressions in the snow of what looked like water courses. We were too done-in to look elsewhere by this stage and the light was all but gone. A flat enough patch of ground was selected, and we threw the tent up. Taking axes and water bottles we hacked away at a likely looking depression in the snow. Digging down a couple feet we found running water – brilliant! We fashioned a few steps in the snow to make it easier and safer to get to and we retired to the tent for the long night. This was our third night in the tent, and I guess we'd got into something of a routine. The kit we didn't need was stashed until the morning and I got on with cooking up some grub. The earlier shenanigans had caused Martin's hands to get cold and he was having a bad bout of chilblains whilst his circulation rediscovered his white fingers. Hot drinks and as much lentil dahl he could manage saw him restored.

It was a slow start to the last morning, around 10.30. Martin was away before me. Heading for the low point on the ridge north-east of An Leth-chreag and pt. 1,032m, he broke through a small cornice to reach the ridge. I followed a short time later. A little bit of compass work saw us reach the 11th and penultimate Munro of the trip, Tom a' Chòinnich. Misty conditions continued, and with no signs of previous passage evident we took a bearing down into the Bealach Toll Easa and the briefest of stops to down some oatcakes, cheese and water.

Tom a' Chòinnich (Derek Sime)

We soon reached Toll Creagach, but the cloud was thick, so no views. We paced out our dog-legged line off the Munro to head down to Creag a' Bhaca. Below 500m the snow and ice thinned out and so we removed the crampons for the final time. The woods above the loch seemed like a comparative riot of colour after our time in the monochrome world of the high mountains. By early afternoon we were back at the car and on our way home. I'm sure there must have been a chip shop involved somewhere. I think we'd run out of film for the camera, hence no photos of the final day.

The First Munro Dogs – Storm

Hamish M Brown

C hance was to bring me a second Shetland Collie – Storm. I'd had a few years without a dog and wanted one badly. I was returning home (from Morocco) in my camper van and had diverted to visit Rosslyn Chapel (pre-Dan Brown effect luckily). Heading off again I passed a lady walking two Kitchy look-alikes, proper Shelties, not the brainless powder puffs they were becoming, so I stopped to ask where she'd obtained them. The breeder, contacted, said she'd let me know when pups were available. Weeks later I rang only to be told 'the bitch had missed' but, she did have a two-year old dog they could part with, because it was 'a bit too big for the show ring'. Super-trained, medically pampered, wow! Yes, I was interested.[1]

A year later (1979) Storm would go walkies with me from John o' Groats to Land's End, within which markers we made the first ever foot-link of the four highest summits: Ben Nevis, Scafell, Snowdon and Carrauntoohill, and doing the Furths again while at it. (Ben Lomond, en passant, completed a then unique sixth round of the Munros.) The cover of *Hamish's Groats End Walk* had Storm posing with Snowdon behind and when the lady who'd sold me Storm

Hamish and Storm test gear for the Groats End walk (Hamish Brown)

saw it and what he'd done, she turned to a friend to exclaim, 'You'd never guess he'd a broken leg when a year old would you?' Ah ha! So that was the real reason why Storm was sold. I had noticed he walked with a slight twist of a back leg and that of course would have been no good for winning prizes in the show ring! Storm came with the pedigree name Ellenyorn Spider's Web. Imagine shouting that on the top of Snowdon!

Munro-baggers I'm sure keep to simpler names. Three of us, who had just walked coast to coast across Scotland in what is today's TGO Challenge, met up with our dogs at the end and took them down for a walk on the sands at Montrose. When we turned for home and called out for our mutts, we shouted for Storm (Sheltie), Misty (Alsatian) and Cloud (Spaniel).

Storm became quite well known as he was often posing as useful foreground in photos I took to illustrate articles. He really did pose and, because I took colour and black and white photos, he would stay still 'till there had been two clicks of the shutter. We climbed Am Bàsteir one spring when snow still edged the ridge (which I once saw described as being 'sheer on one side and vertical on the other') and Storm thought it would be pleasant to roll on the snow. More than my nerves could take he went on belay (on the lead) and we continued. I was praying we wouldn't meet anyone who would probably think only a nana would be taking a dog for a walk in such a place. So of course, we did meet someone. However, his reaction was an enthusiastic 'Is that Storm?' Acknowledged. 'Oh, do you think I could take his picture, please?' So Storm was posed, then the man glanced up and waved, 'And do you mind getting out the picture please'. At least he said 'Please'.

On two other occasions something similar occurred. We met someone on the hill and I was asked, 'Are you Hamish Brown?' Well, yes; then came the put-down. 'Thought so. I recognised the dog.' (Storm was difficult to live up to.) I was his human as much as he my dog. He could read my thoughts I felt, was biddable and quick to learn any new game. Because he came from that (to me) prison background he had much to learn. He had to learn about sheep for instance.

So one of his first outings was to the Borders, a night in my camper van above Loch Talla. In the morning we jumped out to water some rushes. Sheep grazed nearby and the curious dog went to investigate. The sheep backed off. The dog advanced. The sheep ran. As the dog made to follow, I bellowed, 'No!' and at the same moment a shepherd in a Land Rover arrived. He stopped. But my gabbled explanations were hardly necessary. 'If he obeys like that, you'll have no bother with him.' Storm soon learned that whenever we encountered sheep he would automatically walk to heel.

We'd been on the Graham Stob Breac, south across the valley from Stob Binnein, and were descending when we saw the local shepherd coming the other way off the hill. He was known as very anti-dog. The body language said as much. We walked down the top field full of sheep and when we met, he let out a guffaw. 'I was going to give you hell not having your dog on a lead, but...' Storm was at my heels and, nose-to-tail following him, was a line of thirty ewes.

We once had an odd encounter on top of Brandon, that magical mountain in the extreme south-west of Ireland. It has a long crest, cut away on one side into a vast corrie with steep, cliff-eaten headwalls. Sheep were always falling down the cliffs I was told by the shepherd who I met staggering along under a load of stobs (fence posts). He was going to fence off the cliff edge, an astonishing work for every post and coil of wire had to be carried up on his back from sea level to 3,000ft.

While he was talking, Storm – the most placid and friendly of dogs –

Storm on the east ridge of Mount Brandon (Hamish Brown)

was receiving a bit too much attention from the shepherd's two collies. In the end he turned on them and, in seconds, routed both. Before I could open my mouth there was an awed, 'Do you see that now? That's some dog you have there. You wouldn't be for selling him at all?'

Storm was the most unaggressive of dogs. With the exception of bothy mice and bonxies he liked whatever he met. Once, after sleeping out on a hill with the dog tucked in behind my knees as usual, time came to rise. Usually Storm would leap up but on this occasion he continued to lie still; puzzling, till I saw, snuggled into him, was a gawky curlew chick he did not want to disturb.

Hares regularly gave fun and games. I had one laugh-aloud moment. Storm and I were sitting at a reef of granite boulders, the only landmark in a sea of heather moor, when a hare came trolloping along, hare and us in full view of each other. The dog tensed with excitement as the beast came nearer and nearer and finally ran (still at full tilt) straight into him. With mutual looks of astonishment, the hare disentangled and shot off only to take another header over my outstretched legs. It then set off again, looking back (with pardonable anthropomorphism I'd say it was mouthing curses at us) – and promptly ran straight into another big boulder.

The most magical wildlife moment of all with Storm had to follow another sleeping out on a heather knoll near Rubha an Dùnain at the mouth of Loch Brittle. We went down to the Loch na h-Airde for breakfast and were sitting there when an otter arrived. It splashed about and then landed and, seeing Storm, began to advance, as did curiosity Storm. They met nose to nose then the otter simply turned back and Storm returned to my side. I breathed again. But minutes later it, or a mate, landed again, this time with two kits who danced about demanding to be fed, for the otter had a writhing eel in its jaws. This was swung this way and that to avoid their opportuning. A sandpiper had been bobbing on a rock beyond this pantomime when one of the swings of the eel knocked the bird into the water. It flew off noisily complaining and I'm afraid I laughed. In an instant there were no otters.

This incident happened near the end of April 1985 when I was wardening the hut in Glenbrittle. We had a strange month with good snow conditions for Storm to climb seven of Skye's Munros – then it turned atrociously wet, on and on. A few days of that and cabin-fever saw us driven out when conditions just eased slightly. We just set off up the nearest slope and so ended on Sgùrr Dearg. The In Pin loomed in the wind and wet, water running down under what had been its icy armour. I didn't even consider climbing it. But astonishingly (questionably) there were 'young soldiers' being put through their paces and being heaved up to abseil off with much crossing of ropes and military language. Talking to the sergeant in charge, the story of Kitchy came out and then Storm's nearing completion. Suggesting I climb it there and then my response was, 'Not in these conditions, not with a dog in my rucksack!' So the sergeant said I could have a top rope! Was I to put my trust in some squaddie belaying me I wondered, but I couldn't resist, could I? The short side, wet, icy, slobbered with mud from all the abseiling, was not very enjoyable. There is one out-of-balance move high up that I've never liked, even in summer, and on it I was teetering on the edge of adhesion, the weight of Storm almost pulling me off. He, at that point, leaned forward and gave my ear an encouraging lick.

The weather then turned hot, like blazing summer so I went off with Storm on bivouacs, high or low, including the one when we had our otters encounter.

Storm went on many canoe trips. For the 1988 Boots Across Scotland attempt at doing all the Munros in a day our chosen peak was Beinn Bheòil, next to Ben Alder, so a nephew and I, plus Storm, canoed down for a few days at Ben Alder cottage. We had brilliant weather – except for the Boots day. Nephew Colin thought that day diabolical. (A canoe was a real asset in ticking off Corbett Stob an Aonaich Mhòir across Loch Ericht from the bothy.)

The last canoe trip Storm and I made together had an ironic twist to it. We'd bag Munros along Loch Mullardoch by canoe! (As a teenager a sortie north had been stopped abruptly by finding the hydro had joined Loch Lungard

Storm in his element – Hogmanay glory looking to Beinn Sgritheall (Hamish Brown)

and Loch Mullardoch. With my pre-war map I'd planned to walk between them.) Launching the canoe was not easy. The tide was out and what looked like firm sand was just a surface skin on top of bottomless black peat mud. A slaistery start. Then halfway along, horror of horrors, the long drought had re-created two lochs and between lay the barrier of a rushing rocky river!

Storm coincided with years when I was trying to do as many winter Munros as possible on skis. To begin with, the dog found the downhill skiing a frustration. I'd shoot off in one direction and he would follow, only for me to suddenly swoop round in the opposite direction and repeat, repeat. Who says dogs don't think? He soon let me go off and just sit and watch until I reached the bottom, then he'd just trot down.

Once, wanting to cross a stream, I managed by hopping stone to stone, a route beyond the dog's abilities. He ran up and down the bank a bit and then plunged in to make a perfect ferry glide to land on a spit of sand he'd seen.

For the Groats End Walk we had been given packets of Frolic, a dehydrated dog food which he liked. (Even if lighter than tins I still had to carry it.) So cartons of this were sent to Kinghorn, Sheffield, Dublin and Holyhead to restock on the way. But they sent packs four times larger than the try-out packets. He was still eating Frolic a year later.

Storm would steal food given half a chance. At a BFMC meet, camping at

Strontian, I took a photo of him, rump in the air, tail waving with pleasure. His head was invisible as it was through under the flysheet of a tent. Yelled at to 'come', he withdrew and trotted up, trailing a string of sausages behind him.

A friend, Ben the Burner (he worked at the local crematorium), told me a story about Storm at one of our Hogmanay meets at Suardalin bothy which the Braes o' Fife then maintained. Most of us had gone for a day on Beinn Sgritheall, leaving behind a dirty array of supper and breakfast dishes and pans. Storm and I arrived back first and, while I went off to fetch water, Storm set about licking all the dirty dishes. Ben, who had not been on the hill, said Storm made an excellent job of cleaning the pans and when the others returned, they thanked him for washing all their stuff. Ben hadn't the heart to inform them of the truth.

It was about this time I received a letter forwarded from a newspaper which I thought might have been a spoof from some of my friends (spelt minus the r) but eventually decided it was genuine as the hand indicated somebody elderly:

7-8-78

Dear Sir

I was appalled to read in The Sunday Post, 6-8-78, about your dog Storm who is to climb mountains with you.

Don't you think this is cruel? The poor animal could be frightened out of his wits and terrified at the heights he has to climb. Please don't be hard on him; he looks such a beautiful dog.

Yours sincerely

One who cares for Animals.

We had a great snowy day on the hills all round Culra Bothy in January 1985 when Storm compleated on Beinn Eibhinn, north-west over the Bealach Dubh from Ben Alder. He's climbed 459 Munros in all, and 127 Corbetts and goodness knows what else.

Sadly, Storm slowly began to feel his age. His last Munros filled another splendid winter round of the Coire Làir hills above Achnashellach. In August 1990 we went up Cockleroy, (now there is a good test name. Do you ken where it is?) and the dog was really struggling. With views from Arran, the sweep of the Highland Line, to Arthur's Seat, the wee hill has a mighty view. A few days later, while walking through the Union Canal's tunnel, Storm staggered and fell into the water. The garden sufficed thereafter till one night he had a final massive heart attack. All I could do was hold him and comfort as I could, a lick on my nose quite breaking me, as I lifted him from our second-home camper van to go in to the vet's.

During the Groats End Walk, at the end of traversing the Irish Galtymore range, I picked up a parcel at Mitchellstown (the next maps, film, Storm's Frolic etc.) and sat on a bench to sort things out. A gypsy mother and daughter came along and we chatted. The mother then explained the girl was blind and could she 'feel the lovely dog?' The girl ran her hands over Storm, received a lick and turned to me with a smile. 'Sure, and he's a gorgeous fella.' He was indeed.

[1] See also 'The First Munro Dogs: Kitchy' by Hamish Brown, TMS Journal No. 5, 2020.

Storm on Sgùrr nan Ceathreamhnan (Hamish Brown)

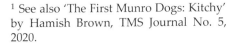

The One that Got Away: Beinn Damh – Julian Foot

Stephen, one of the most brilliant minds I ever encountered, always ribbed me over our single-minded pursuit of hills over 3,000ft. He could see no reason for excluding lower mountains. Although we both worked and lived in London, he loved Torridon and especially Beinn Damh. When we went there to tick off the Munros, he was insistent we include it and, foolishly, we didn't. I promised him we would climb it together when our round was over. Sadly, Stephen died suddenly in 2021. We never made the climb together, but I went up Beinn Damh this summer with Stephen in my mind and held some prayer flags for him on the summit cairn.

LOCHS and LOCHANS

Above – Leum Uilleim from Loch Coir' a' Bhric Beag, on a fine April morning after an overnight stay at Corrour.

Below – Loch Etchachan and Cairngorm during a July heatwave, taken from where my tent was pitched for the night.   ***Derek Sime***

'I've Got a Little List'

Iain A. Robertson

Not another list!, I hear you say.
Your implication being that there are already sufficient lists, not least, those involving Scottish hills. In addition, the comment might imply disillusion with the growth of ever-more complicated criteria for list-inclusion. But I claim mitigation, for this is not a newly devised list; it is merely recognition of a list which has been in the public domain since 1948. And which, moreover, has one clear and unambiguous criterion for hills that should be included.

Readers may not immediately recognise the group of hills being written of, and before revealing all, I will give information to allow you to test your deductive abilities. On this list there is a total of 85 hills, of which 21 are Munros, 10 are Corbetts, 6 are Grahams, with the remainder not in any of the SMC classifications – an eclectic selection to suit all tastes. The highest hill on the list is 4,241ft (in 1948 terms) and the lowest is 555ft. All are contained within a circular area of 7,539 square miles with a circumference of 308 miles. The centre of the circle is at Lat. 56°23' 20" and Long. 3° 23' 12". It is a relatively compact group though, given the Highland road network, some are more accessible than others. Full marks if you have already guessed the nature of the list.

I will now give another clue which should make identification of the list easier; it has to do with Covid-19 and Lockdown (hasn't everything these days?). With the onset of Lockdown, Jen and I had decided that we would continue to go to the hills to the extent that the restrictions allowed. Being based in Perth, this meant Perth & Kinross, Angus and Fife, depending on how the restrictions varied. The local hills beckoned, and very attractive they are, but why not have a plan. I recalled having seen 'the list' in the past and had retained a copy. As we had both climbed all the Munros, Corbetts and Grahams listed, we decided to go for all the remaining 48 hills, of which we had previously climbed a surprisingly small number.

Think of sections of the Highland Boundary Fault, of the Ochil Hills, of the Sidlaw Hills, of the Fife Hills and of other bumps (none lower than 555ft). There is so much beauty and interest on one's doorstep. How many of you have heard of, never mind climbed, Finbracks, Glenduckie Hill or Drumcarrow Craig? Some, like the Fife Lomonds, are well-trodden, but on the more obscure hills the bracken and the brambles can be formidable. That many of them were seldom visited fitted in with the requirements of Lockdown and we infrequently met other walkers after leaving the car, which encouraged the thought that a slightly longer journey in the car might have no consequences in terms of the number of people met.

There are two Meall Reamhars on the list; one is a Graham above Amulree, the other is nearby above the Newton Brig in the Sma' Glen on the north side of the River Almond. We headed for the latter towards the end of May. The sun shone and the grass was fresh green on the lower slopes. The hill barely exceeds 2,000ft, but the upper slopes are steep and rocky and one has to work to earn the height gained. Many of us have driven through the Sma' Glen many times, going or coming from higher hills. It is a glen of character and images of the steep-sided valley remain in memory, but in a car, it is but a few minutes before one is out on the broad moorland heading for Aberfeldy or for Crieff. On that day, however, time was plentiful; the floor of the glen gradually revealed itself as we ascended. The River Almond meanders, but not the lazy meandering of lowland rivers with little or no gradient, but the urgent rush of water over a stony bed, hell-bent on losing height and re-joining the ocean from whence it came. Yet higher, the tops of the ridges that walled-in the glen became apparent, defining the Sma' Glen as a distinct part of the much longer Glen Almond. And creating also an almost perfect example of a U-shaped valley. Higher still, and on the south side of the glen, another almost perfect topographical example became apparent. The Coire Cruinn of Meall Dubh is a fine example of a hanging corrie, scooped from the hillside by some ancient glacier, with a burn tumbling down from its lip to the glen below. On that day (30th May) a last vestige of the winter snow was tucked into a sunless corner of the upper corrie. At the summit, the hill is surrounded by higher ground on three sides, but down the Sma' Glen there were glimpses of Strathearn with the Ochil Hills beyond.

The 2nd of July 2020 was a Thursday, Lockdown restrictions had been eased and we drove to Glen Lednock expecting to share the glen with a few more cars. We counted 39 cars parked at Invergeldie, and there could well have been more! Clearly, the relaxation of restrictions had released a pent-up urge to return to the hills. My friend Willie told me that on a subsequent weekend, there had been over 100 cars parked over a stretch of two miles down from Invergeldie.

But we were not bound for Ben Chonzie. Eagle Crag – Creag na h-Iolaire – has a romantic, indeed, dramatic ring to it, and we were not disappointed; moreover, we had it entirely to ourselves. It is indeed a prominent crag, with some rock, but rather more heather. It commands a view over the lower reaches of Glen Lednock, with Meall nan Tarmachan prominent to the north-west. On reaching a summit on a clear day, I take great pleasure in identifying the surrounding hills; recognising old friends as it were. But the pleasure is enhanced if the viewpoint differs, albeit marginally, from previous viewings. Such was the case on Creag na h-Iolaire; there were old friends all about, as we both agreed, but there was resort to the map to settle which old friend was which. As will become apparent, the list is largely made up of single hills and so one hill per expedition was our usual. At 1,783 ft, we devoted an afternoon to Creag na h-Iolaire, enjoying a leisurely walk amidst some of Perthshire's finest scenery.

So, you've worked it out? Oh well, never mind, not everyone can live in Perthshire. The list is that on the mountain indicator on top of Kinnoull Hill, 729 ft, which hill now belongs to the citizens of Perth. The inscription on the indicator reads: 'Kinnoull Hill, 1948, Erected by John L. Anderson Esq., a citizen of Perth, to commemorate Lord Dewar's (White Label Whisky) munificence in gifting this beautiful hill to his native city in 1923'. The unambiguous criterion for inclusion on the list is that the hill in question

Coire Cruinn of Meall Dubh
(Iain Robertson)

can be seen from Kinnoull Hill. Experience suggests that Kinnoull Hill is quite difficult to distinguish from a distance, but one must accept that the reciprocal must be so. The information on the indicator is the name of the hill, the height in feet, the distance from Kinnoull Hill, and an adjoining reference point; thus: Ardnadave Hill, 2,332ft, 36 miles, west side of Loch Lubnaig. The most distant hill is Cairn Toul at 49 miles, which gave a radius for the circle described above. In the absence of any information to the contrary, and with great originality, we have decided to call the hills on the list 'Kinnoulls' [1].

It would make a satisfactory conclusion to say that we had climbed all the Kinnoulls, but that is not so. Restrictions in March 2021 (at time of writing) required that we remained inside Perth & Kinross, and some nine Kinnoulls, mostly in the Glen Clova area, remained to be climbed, but we are raring to go.

I have considered making available a copy of the Kinnoulls List, but on reflection, I have decided that I would be doing no one a favour. You should not be deprived of the experience of climbing Kinnoull Hill on a clear day, viewing a panorama of 85 hills rising above Strathmore, Strathearn and the Carse of Gowrie, and then taking a photograph of the mountain indicator. Do it and you will know that I am right.

[1] A much more comprehensive account, but with a similar approach, is Kellan MacInnes's: *Caleb's List*, Luath press, 2013, which involves the hills visible from Arthur's Seat.

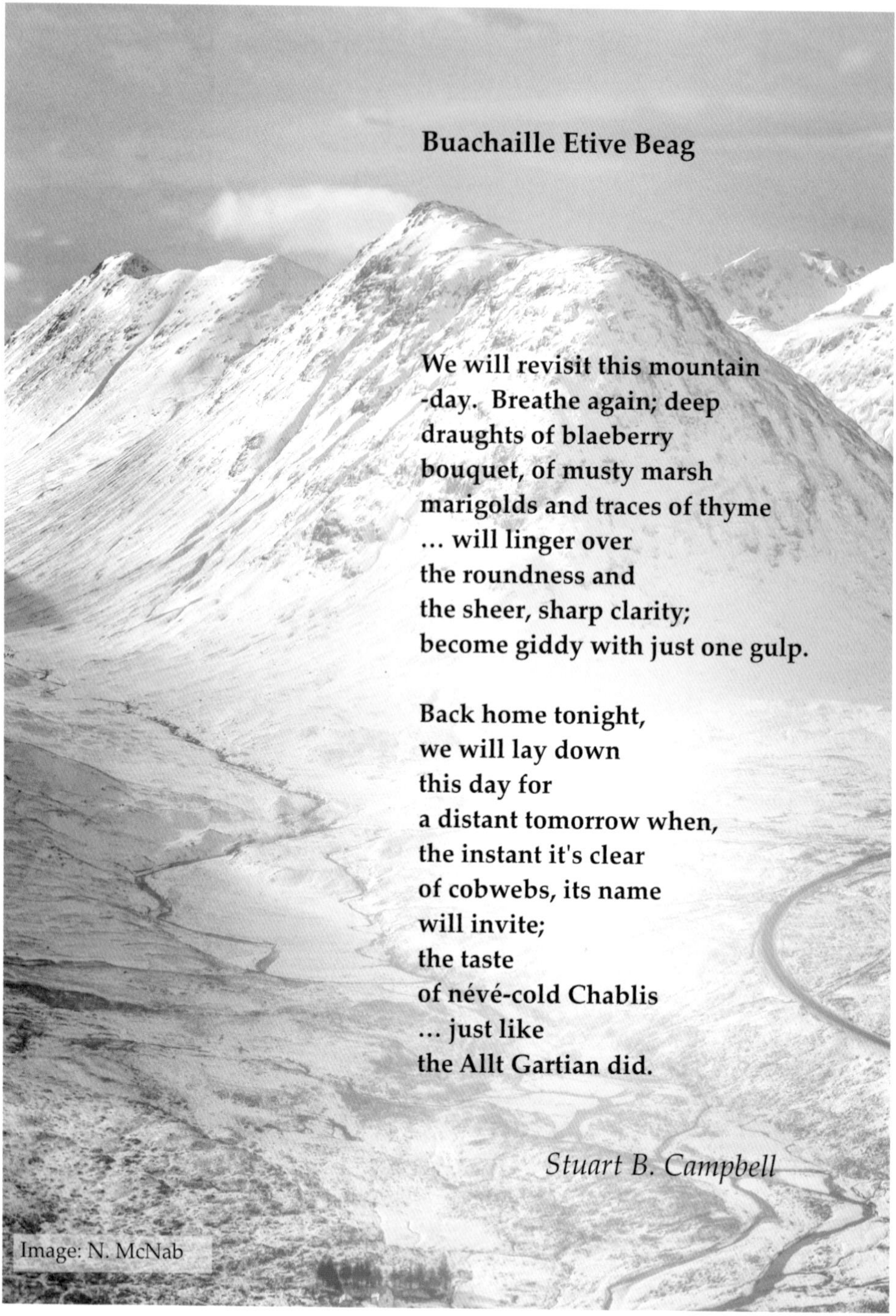

Buachaille Etive Beag

We will revisit this mountain
-day. Breathe again; deep
draughts of blaeberry
bouquet, of musty marsh
marigolds and traces of thyme
… will linger over
the roundness and
the sheer, sharp clarity;
become giddy with just one gulp.

Back home tonight,
we will lay down
this day for
a distant tomorrow when,
the instant it's clear
of cobwebs, its name
will invite;
the taste
of névé-cold Chablis
… just like
the Allt Gartian did.

Stuart B. Campbell

A Winter Munro Round

Kevin Woods

I was drawn to the Munros almost as soon as I'd heard of them. They are visually impressive, they throw down a superb physical challenge and they've provided me with a lifelong passion.

In the summer of 2013, I did a round of the Munros in three months from May to August. That was a life-changing summer; it cemented a love for the Scottish hills and it massively expanded my sense of the possibilities. It was tough; I learned a lot. That summer squeezed out inexperience. By the end of that summer I was moving around massively better than I had when I started. The first few weeks gave incessant heavy rain, occasional snow and a very steep learning curve. In that time I'd had more of a pounding than I could stomach, but conditions eventually cleared to calm and dry. Great blue summer skies dominated the rest of the summer season - confidence and fitness climbed and my tactics sharpened up. The rest of the summer went by without a hitch and I finished on Ben Hope.

Over the following few years I spent a lot of time on the hills. Casually I was working on a third Munro round, but often doing a lot more rock climbing. Somewhere along the way I began to entertain the idea of the Munros in winter - and there was something! That would be a hard challenge. I didn't think seriously about it for a long time. A winter Munro round was well beyond my level, though if I'd learned anything from mountain trips it was that strands of experience can be nurtured and brought together in powerful ways.

The preparation for the winter Munros was easily as engaging as the resultant winter and it lasted a period well in excess: a pooling of thought, drive and motivation gathered across years. Though in the first instance, I wondered how best to engage with it. It did seem clear that the plan would hang on weather, therefore it was most important that I understood winter conditions. I also just wanted to get better at moving in the mountains but in time I couldn't deny it was all driving toward a winter round.

I split the variables apart to try to understand them. I already had experience of three months in the hills from 2013. This alone subtracted an enormous unknown, though the remaining variables were vast. I recorded winter weather statistics and forecasts. Then, comparing these against personal experience on the hills, I could set boundaries based on facts. The question asked - where is the upper limit? How far do you have to go before it becomes too much?

Across multiple winters, I found that conditions that looked shocking on paper were often quite tolerable. In winter, we focus on the extreme events: the great storms and the blizzards. They cloud our imagination such that they disguise reality. The truth is that these life-threatening events occupy an extreme minority of any winter season. The bar was a lot higher than I first anticipated and it started to seem that the reality was not so unpalatable after all.

I'd been winter climbing across several seasons which helped fluidity on steep ground - after all strength and coordinated movement is a form of safety. I'd often been worried about avalanche and snow stability, but a good grounding in the theory gave strategies for moving around the hills. Winter climbing also assisted this education, because interacting with steep ground forces one to observe the more subtle interactions between snow and terrain.

It took some time to get life circumstances and work into a place that I could go for the Winter Munros. A crucial late decision was to make the trip van-based. Backpacking might give a more intense experience, although it seemed not without considerable downsides. It meant relying on accommodation at a time when the Highland establishments are generally closed for business. Without accommodation, the burden may lie with family and friends who would have to meet me with food and fuel before I disappeared into the hills again. It didn't seem to stack up. By contrast the van offered self-sufficiency, an ability to move to the tune of conditions and importantly would give the benefit of a good, steady diet.

The Winter Munros were starting to drive me mad. It was so clearly a great idea and I was pretty sure I knew how to do it. I was also awed by the scale of it. But better to go for something that matters, than suffer having never done it when you knew you could have. In the first half of 2019 I took the plunge, utterly committed to the following winter, not without some fear, and set all sights on that coming December.

The clock started on the Isle of Mull on the solstice; 22nd December. I hadn't any set plans. Doing so would be futile, a sure way to fail. The only plan was to reach the end in the most effective way possible. I got off to a strong start and the hills around Ben Cruachan and Bridge of Orchy occupied the opening days. On Christmas Day I was on Ben More and Stob Binnein. Walking down the former, my ankle rolled – something that had never happened before. Although considerably sore, it never came to anything else and I spent the New Year period progressing through Glen Coe and Glen Etive. Hogmanay was a stunning day of crystal-clear blue skies and a golden sunset on Bidean nam Bian. Otherwise, the days were wet, stormy and very dark. Momentum was climbing and daily ascents were cranking up.

I also started to trim my tactics to the best of the weather. Among the fronts, intense lows would be interspersed with ridges of calmer conditions. It seemed massively inconvenient to be on the summits in really bad weather - forecasts were routinely suggesting gusts beyond 100mph. On the other hand, walking in the dark in better weather was no big problem, so I started to walk to the tune of weather rather than daylight. As I moved into the region around Loch Tay and Breadalbane the Moon started to appear, leading to some magical nights on the tops of the mountains. Beinn Sheasgarnaich, Meall Ghaordaidh, Schiehallion and Meall nan Tarmachan were all climbed after dark.

As mountain areas were finished off, the enticing question would arise as to where to go next. In three

Ben Lawers (Kevin Woods)

weeks, the weather had only given westerlies, so I continued to the eastern Highlands. The hills of Glen Shee offered shorter days in soaking conditions and blizzards. The desire for this trip was far greater than any inclement weather, so it didn't seem to matter even if I returned to the road drenched.

Momentum was maintained and soon I was straight into the Cairngorms. Helen Rennard joined me for this section – a four-day east to west traverse taking in the Munros. This area had always been in my thoughts. Their bulk is so great that they are better crossed in one go. The first two days on the Cairngorms gave crisp, wintry conditions but on the latter two days, the warm fronts swept in to clear the mountains of their snow. Drizzle replaced the snow; incessant and cold. The thawing conditions were challenging in their own way; we crossed the Mòine Mhòr to Glen Feshie when it was loaded with water-saturated snow, sinking into potholes and standing pools of meltwater. However, the summits themselves were stripped bare for quicker progress. At dusk on the fourth day, I dropped into Glen Feshie. The sense of progress was pronounced; it was the end of one region and the beginning of a new one.

While the westerly fronts continued to pile in, I remained in the east. But crossing the Cairngorms had been a great boost. For a few days at the end of January, the weather swayed in gentle indecision, sun breaking and the mountains snowless for the most part. Things rapidly changed again, and I crossed the Tarf hills in deep, fresh snow – as wild a place as you'll get in mid-winter.

My momentum continually climbed; I'd finally made it to Lochaber. The Creag Meagaidh hills were crossed on a brutal day of torrential rain and hard wind. The following day, a late start on the Loch Treig hills avoided the worst of the rain and gave me the Easains by headtorch, under clear skies and with a Moon. The following morning, I slipped out of Lairig bothy and onto the Grey Corries. The crest was solid névé, the dawn grey and muted. As the light returned, I passed my half-way summit – 141 on Stob Choire Claurigh. The Aonachs and Ben Nevis appeared through the gloom of another incoming weather front, and the snow commenced on Aonach Beag. Carn Mòr Dearg was dramatic through the falling snow and on the top of Ben Nevis, I met Helen who had walked up to meet me.

The momentum continued. I walked from Glen Finnan and over the summits to Gulvain, a rare day of bright skies and settled weather. The following morning, I was out early for the Mamores. Weather gave me relentless drizzle; I saw nothing. For all the ridge-running enjoyment of the central section, I was flattened with tiredness later that night. In the upcoming forecast there were two consecutive days of good weather - the first time that had happened in seven weeks. In spite of deep fatigue, I had to be out on the hill, so in the morning I was off to Corrour station and the Ben Alder hills, They were my last summits south of the Great Glen besides Ben Lomond, which was left for the very end. In contrast to the tiredness, I was just eating up the miles, feeling very fit and moving well. That night was clear. Ben Alder's plateau was snow-covered, and a cool wind made the icy crystals sing on the surface. The sun died out in the west to leave a sparkling moonlit world and here I was, alone in the heart of the Highlands, yet deeply connected to the world - alone in winter, on top of Ben Alder at the end of a fantastic day.

These would be the last big miles for a while. The weather was due to break down dramatically. The following afternoon I completed my last Lochaber summits and in an afternoon, everything changed.

The North Atlantic became swallowed by low pressure systems just as I got started in the North-west Highlands. They would sit and rotate in the Atlantic without actually moving, to feed a conveyor belt of snow and high winds with no easy options and no end in sight. Pulling a tactical lever, I went to the Far North for some respite; it may have worked, but the bleakest of Highland landscapes coincided with the worst weather of the winter, while at the same time a virus put me flat on my back on Beinn Klibreck. It became perhaps the lowest point of the winter, although I could rationalise the circumstances and not be too bothered by a lack of progress. It was an unfortunate convergence of circumstances.

The remainder of February resulted in one of the wettest months in recent years. The Glen Shiel ridges were a low-commitment option to ride out the worst of the weather; even still they were touch and go. Days were often on the verge of not happening and occasionally nothing did happen. Every day brought the same charged showers, high winds, sometimes thunder and lightning. I was chipping against the coal face now: up until Lochaber I'd been on an 80-day schedule, but progress was dramatically stalling.

Skye Ridge (Kevin Woods)

TD Gap, Skye (Kevin Woods)

Into the end of February, things gently improved. I had some outstanding days. I crossed the southern Cuillin and led the Inaccessible Pinnacle on a rare calm afternoon in excellent winter conditions. Into the beginning of March, daylight and conditions opened out a little more. I crossed Liathach and Beinn Eighe in an afternoon. Calm weather allowed a good crossing of the pinnacles, yet snowstorms and incredible winds raged on Beinn Eighe - high drama on these most stunning of mountains. I finished that day with profound satisfaction and deep joy from the crossing. The northern and central Cuillin made an outstanding finale to the technically difficult sections of the winter. Leaving the Cuillin behind was an incredible boost; they are intense of atmosphere and difficulty. Completing them also gave the first glimmers that I was looking down the finish line.

In the middle of March, the hills became buried in deep powder. The avalanche hazard suddenly went to High. The Affric hills were some mitigation against the hazard, but it still took four days to cross a set of hills that I have run across in an afternoon. The lack of any weather but westerlies was biting, but it didn't really matter to me; I'd only do what I could do, without being reckless with risk.

Throughout March, a new problem emerged which defined the end of the round. The pandemic finally made it to our shores while everyone grasped the gravity of what was happening. For three months I'd been in a routine, but Covid grew like an unwelcome intrusion that would not go away. To finish the round, I had a broad swathe of the North-west Highlands to complete. The weather finally settled in the last week of the round – just enough time

Fisherfield (Kevin Woods)

Sgùrr nan Ceathramhnan (Kevin Woods)

to race around Mullardoch, Monar, Fisherfield and the Fannaichs. Things couldn't have been tighter: I was getting blown off my feet in a corrie under the Strathfarrars, profoundly stressed because I could not afford to return. These summits had to be done at this moment and no other.

With a handful of summits left, the world finally stopped. I knew what had been building, but I felt wedged between my need to finish the winter and the fact that for the first time in many years, going to the hills was forbidden. I went out to Seana Bhraigh on a day of eerie silence. A ceiling of cloud drained the colour from the land and on this, my penultimate Munro, I was low and getting lower. I'd left Ben Lomond for my last – a symmetry to my first ever Munro in 2001. But now it seemed difficult to justify that.

Many people had much larger problems than I in my self-imposed predicament. I never wanted the hillwalking to be anything but enjoyment for myself, but there was no denying it had gone well beyond that. I was thinking of the loss of the Winter Munros one summit short of the final. It was not good for the head. I had to finish even just for myself: nobody needed to know, but I had to know. A couple of days later, I headed out just before dawn and finished my winter on top of Ben Lomond, there just myself with the mist. And what else to do than go home, enjoy the spring sun and head out on the bike? And how satisfying to be done and to complete something that had started many years previously.

—TMs—

LOCHS and LOCHANS

Above – 23rd September 2002, just below the summit of Sgùrr Alasdair. Minutes later a thick mist developed, and Loch Coir' a' Ghrunnda disappeared completely from view.
Norman McNab

Below – En route to a cloudless day in mid-August on Beinn Stacath: early morning mist on Loch Voil from near Balquhidder.
Oliver Bartrum

Number Culture

Alan Dawson

We live in a world of data. Numbers keep us informed about our age, weight, body mass index, blood pressure, time of appointments and so on. On a global level, numbers keep us informed about distances, speeds, temperatures, infections, fatalities, population trends, wildlife numbers, the scale of the universe, the size of atoms and so on. All these data help us to understand the world around us. Yet in the Munro Society Newsletter, the President wrote 'most hillwalkers have an unhealthy fascination with numbers'. This casual comment reflected a commonly held viewpoint, but why should an interest in numbers be regarded as unhealthy? It sounds like a guilty secret that most hill baggers share but few are prepared to acknowledge in a public forum.

Let's imagine how The Munro Society would work without an interest in numbers. It would be a society for people who think they have probably climbed all the hills in Scotland that are fairly high, however many that may be. Or let's imagine sport without numbers, a world in which St Johnstone and Dundee United played an entertaining football match lasting quite a while in which both sides scored some goals and the attendance seemed to be reasonably high. A world where a young British woman won the US Open by playing tennis better than her opponents, in the opinion of the judges, and the Ryder Cup was shared because no-one recorded the number of strokes played.

Numbers are essential for economics, finance, medicine, science, technology and most aspects of the modern world. Most books have numbered pages and music has a numeric time signature. It is hard to think of any logical reason why anyone should regard an interest in numbers as unhealthy. Psychologists regard it as healthier for people to acknowledge and accept their own interests and inclinations than to hide them or feel guilty about them. Interests only tend to be become unhealthy when they are so obsessive that they have an adverse effect on other people or on other aspects of life, such as eating nothing but carrots or filling every room in a house with teddy bears or old socks.

No-one would refer to hillwalkers having an unhealthy interest in wildlife, photography, poetry or history, but numbers are culturally regarded as less worthy of attention. Outdoor writers in mainstream magazines reinforce this view. They do not express any interest in numbers in case it is seen to dilute their enthusiasm for the hills, wildlife and wild places. Yet there is no conflict between numbers and the natural world if you are not killing or spoiling anything. Few people are more passionate about wildlife than Chris Packham, yet he is honest enough to express an enthusiasm for data because it keeps him informed and entertained.

It is of course possible to enjoy hillwalking without being concerned with the heights of hills, but hill bagging requires paying attention to heights and keeping count of hills climbed. The consequence is a greater incentive to get out and experience all aspects of walking in the hills in all sorts of conditions.

In recent years, satellite technology has enabled us to obtain far more accurate data about the topography of the landscape than ever before. Not everyone approves of paying such close attention to the heights of hills, as though it somehow detracts from the simple practice of walking up and down hills. However, my own experience has been that the process of obtaining more accurate data through hill surveying has greatly enhanced my days in the hills. It has encouraged me to get out more often, to climb new hills, to choose new routes, to see more sights and to appreciate more aspects of the landscape. It has helped me to keep mind and body healthy and it has encouraged me to analyse in more detail the qualities that make walking in the hills particularly enjoyable. This analysis led me to abandon dependence on round numbers such as 3,000 feet, 900 metres or 30 metres and to choose a definition that in my opinion better captures the landscape and the best walking that is available on higher ground. Such detailed analysis had never been possible before because the data were not accurate enough. This has enabled me to produce a complete catalogue of the high hills for the first time, without having to rely on the vagaries of historical data and inconsistent mapping.

When I felt ready to publish my survey data and the accompanying stories, I was intending to call the book *The High Hills of Britain*, but shortly before printing I decided to make it more precise by inserting a number into the title, so it became *The 1033 High Hills of Britain*[1]. The title embraces the numerical aspect of hill bagging, with seven other numbers on the cover to reinforce the point. This is deliberately unfashionable and counter-cultural. I have acknowledged the simple truth that numbers are an important aspect of hill bagging.

The cover photograph shows four summits over 3,000 feet high. One of them is Bidein a' Ghlas Thuill, the highest point of An Teallach. The other three rocky summits are on the superb east ridge of this magnificent mountain, which stakes a good claim to be the finest in the land. Yet none of these lower summits was listed by Hugh Munro and they have never appeared in subsequent revisions to his work. Why is this? It may have been an oversight that was never rectified. Only three of the four summits qualify as High Hills using my precise definition, which shows that whatever criteria are used, there will always be other points that do not qualify. The Far East Top is 1,002.4m high and rises 19.7m above the col connecting it to the East Top. If I had used a strict definition of 20 metres of prominence then this summit would not have qualified, so I adjusted the definition to include it and 26 other summits with less than 20m prominence, such as Ben Macdui North Top and Bidean nam Bian West Top. This illustrates the principle of fitting the definition to the landscape rather than the other way round. Paying closer attention to the landscape has revealed several other summits that have never featured in any editions of Munro's work, including 25 summits with over 20m drop:

Name	Metres	Drop	Grid ref	Map
Meall Dearg East Top (Aonach Eagach)	922.9	27.3	NN162582	41
Beinn Bhrotain East Top	1109.8	27.2	NN962923	43
Glas Mheall Mòr West Top (An Teallach)	917.8	26.5	NH069849	19
Ceum na h-Aon-choise (Beinn Fhada)	924.9	26.1	NG995201	33
Ben Oss North Top	941.3	25.5	NN290258	50
Ben More Assynt West Top	973.8	25.4	NC315201	15
Beinn a' Chlachair East Top	973.2	24.1	NN486790	42
Beinn Sheasgarnaich North Top	948.9	23.4	NN421391	51
Bidein a' Ghlas Thuill East Top (An Teallach)	1042.8	23.3	NH069843	19
Beinn an Dothaidh West Top	999.7	23.0	NN326409	50
Meall na Aighean West Top	974.5	22.6	NN690494	51
Mullach Clach a' Bhlàir North Top	953.1	22.6	NN891944	36,43
Ciste Dhubh East Top (Màm Sodhail)	1062.9	22.4	NH122243	25
Clach Choutsaich (Ben Avon)	1121.2	21.7	NJ143018	36
Slioch South Top	932.1	21.7	NH007685	19
Stob a' Choire Bhig (Sgurr na Lapaich)	962.7	21.7	NH157330	25
Mullach an Rathain East Top (Liathach)	974.1	21.4	NG915576	25
Ciste Dhubh South Top	932.9	21.2	NH062163	33
Sròn Bealach Beithe (Ben Alder)	1104	21	NN499707	42
Carn nan Gabhar North Top (Beinn a' Ghlo)	947.0	20.9	NN974745	43
Sàil Liath West Top (An Teallach)	918.7	20.7	NH070825	19
Carn Sasunnaich (Beinn Dòrain)	1064.7	20.6	NN325382	50
Ceum na h-Aon-choise South Top (Beinn Fhada)	922.1	20.6	NG996197	33
Sgùrr nan Coireachan South Top	926.9	20.5	NM933955	33,40
Spidean Mialach West Top	977.6	20.4	NH062044	33

Watching this set of hills emerge from the mists of obscurity has felt like filling in the missing pieces in a jigsaw, seeing the landscape as it really is rather than our previous patchy representation of it. Clach Choutsaich is a stunningly fine tor that is more often avoided than climbed. Carn Sasunnaich and Spidean Mialach West Top are well-known cairned summits that have caused many walkers to think they were at the highest point in thick mist. The summits on Aonach Eagach, Liathach, An Teallach and elsewhere are bypassed by paths and not often climbed.

There is of course no strict drop criterion for hills in Munro's list, which is why there are currently several summits listed as Munro Tops that have less than 20 metres of prominence:

Name	Metres	Drop	Grid ref	Map
Meall Gorm South-east Top (Fannich)	922.4	19.4	NH232691	20
Creag an Fhithich (Ben Lawers)	1045.7	19.1	NN635422	51
Stob Coire Cath na Sine (Grey Corries)	1082.4	18.9	NN252730	41
Beinn na Socaich (Grey Corries)	1009.2	18.7	NN236734	41
Druim Mòr (Cairn of Claise)	962.0	17.9	NO189772	43
Carn Dearg South-east Top (Monadhliath)	923.7	17.5	NH637017	35
Stob Coire Bhealaich (Aonach Beag)	1101.0	17.1	NN201708	41
Eagle's Rock (Lochnagar)	1049.2	16.5	NO237838	44
Fafernie (Cairn Bannoch)	998.8	16.1	NO215823	44
Sgùrr a' Ghreadaidh South Top (Cuillin)	969.9	16.0	NG445229	32
Meall Odhar (Glas Maol)	922	16	NO155773	43
Creag a' Ghlas-uillt (Lochnagar)	1066.9	15.8	NO242842	44
Cnap Coire na Spreidhe (Cairn Gorm)	1151.5	15.3	NJ013049	36
An Cabar (Ben Wyvis)	946	15	NH450665	20
Stob Coire Dheirg (Ben Starav)	1027.7	15	NN131426	50
Stob a' Choire Leith (Grey Corries)	1107.6	14.5	NN256736	41
Sròn a' Ghearrain (Stob Ghabhar)	990	14	NN221456	50
Carn nam Fiaclan (Creag Toll a' Choin) [2]	995	13	NH123455	25
An Riabhachan South-west Top (Mullardoch)	1086	13	NH122336	25
Tom a' Chòinnich Beag (Glen Affric)	1032	13	NH157272	25

Having climbed both these sets of hills, my view is that the 25 unlisted hills compare very favourably with the listed 20. That would be irrelevant if the current list reflected Munro's own judgement but that is far from the case, as lots of hills of greater prominence have been removed from recent editions of his work for no apparent reason, so it is inaccurate historically as well as scientifically. My research findings have left me with even more respect for the work of Munro, as discussed in Journal No. 5 ('How Accurate Was Munro?' [3]). This encouraged me to republish his own final work in the *High Hills* book, with as few updates as necessary to bring the 1921 Tables up to date.

Extending close attention to the hills below 3,000 feet has revealed an even greater trove of previously unlisted riches in the Highlands that have been overlooked by most hill baggers. Full details are given in the book, but here is a handful of the most prominent lesser-known summits:

Name	Metres	Drop	Grid ref	Map
Beinn Gharbh	895.3	149.6	NM882876	40
Càrn Gorm-loch	908.9	146.1	NH318800	20
Beinn a' Chumhainn	901.9	145.3	NN462710	42
Meall a' Choire Bhuidhe	868.3	143.5	NO061710	43
Sgùrr Beag	890	143	NM959970	33,40
Carn an Fhidhleir Lorgaidh	848.6	142.1	NN856874	43
Aonach Sgoilte	848.4	141.6	NG840027	33
Hill of Strone	847.5	141.5	NO287729	44
Sgùrr a' Choire-rainich	846.9	139.5	NH247569	25
A' Chailleach	901.9	137.9	NN189579	41
Beinn Chorranach	887.6	137.7	NN254095	56
Sgùrr na Mòraich	875.6	137.5	NG965193	33
Meall Daill	874.7	132.1	NN411434	51
Sgùrr Thuilm	880.1	131.4	NG438242	32
Sgùrr na Muice	890	130	NH226418	25

Most of these names will be unfamiliar to most hillwalkers yet they are just a few of the many high and prominent hills that have been overlooked in the past. There are few paths on most of these summits and none is needed, because the terrain is excellent for walking almost everywhere above 838 metres (2,750 feet).

The set of 1033 High Hills can be listed in ten pages, but the book is over 400 pages long because the accurate data are merely the framework on which numerous rich experiences have been built. These are reflected in all the stories, themes, photographs and satellite maps that form the bulk of the book. Most of the content is therefore verbal or visual, not numerical. The data form a relatively small component but are vital to provide the structure and context for the rest of the content. This is true of most sources of data. A football result determines the points won but it tells you nothing about the ebb and flow of the match, the incidents and individual performances, the intense highlights and the periods when not much happens. All are needed to appreciate the sport in full.

In general, good journalism covers the data, the interpretation and impact of the figures and some of the personal stories from people involved. All are connected and all are important. There is no apparent reason why climbing and bagging hills should be any different. All the elements that hillwalkers experience are connected, including the visual, physical, mental, meteorological and numerical aspects. Some people are not particularly interested in fine details such as the names of moths or mosses, but they can still appreciate seeing them and do not regard it as unhealthy to be well informed about such matters. Perhaps it is time for those who appreciate the finer details of topography and who keep count of hills climbed to regard these as healthy interests, to accept all aspects of our enthusiasm without being concerned about what other people think.

If you are going to count or measure something then it is important to have a clear definition of what that thing is, so you know what counts and what does not. The problem with Munro's list now is that it does not have either a historic or a scientific definition and so the question of what should count has become contentious. In the 1033 High Hills book I have separated the historic list produced and revised by the man himself from the more comprehensive and topographically accurate list that has a precise definition. This has entailed correcting the heights of many of the hills that are shown on maps and in other books.

Renumbering is not as fashionable as rewilding, but perhaps it is time for some rethinking about numbers. After all, how will it be possible to assess the progress of rewilding initiatives if no-one knows how many trees have been planted or how many birds and wild animals there are in different areas. Accurate data are important for most outdoor initiatives and so it seems time for an update to number culture and to refrain from regarding an interest in numbers as unhealthy.

[1] *The 1033 High Hills of Britain* published by Pedantic Press, 2021, price £20. ISBN 9 781916 366220.

[2] Creag Toll a' Choin is the unratified highest point of the Munro previously given as Maoile Lunndaidh.

[3] The Munro Society Journal No.5 (2020).

—TMS—

A Posthumous Completion[1]

Robin N. Campbell

As noted in my recent article about Munro[2], Sir Hugh died with three Tops to go: Carn an Fhidhleir (Feshie), Carn Cloich-Mhuilinn and the Inaccessible Pinnacle, the first two Tops being Munros in the 1891 list. When carrying out the research for this article I formed the opinion that something should be done about this regrettable state of affairs. Light-hearted and tasteless discussions with friends explored the possibilities and eventually arrived at the goal of constructing an effigy of Munro and transporting the object to the three missing Tops. I believe it was my friend Paul Brian who made this ingenious proposal, but he may well wish to deny this now.

In 1991 I found myself in the position of having to address the great gathering of Munro-baggers[3] on November 23rd with little to say, so I resolved to set the effigy project in motion. It was late October before I managed to acquire a kilt (Hunting Fraser) and Glengarry bonnet at affordable (Oxfam) prices. The Munro tartan is a red and yellow abomination which would put the most somnolent deer to startled flight. I cannot imagine that Sir Hugh would have worn it on the hill; surely, he would have preferred the douce and furtive hues of the Hunting Fraser. Once these essential items had been obtained, construction of the effigy could proceed with some confidence that it would be completed. However, I took the precaution of paying a visit to the grave at Lindertis – to seek permission, as it were. No ominous event occurred, so I thought it safe to proceed.

I fashioned a mask for the head, using gauze strips loaded with plaster over a clay mould of Sir Hugh's face, and painted it with tempera-based colours. Latex hands were found in a joke shop: rival manufacturers of these curious products

Munro ready for Carn an Fhidhleir
(Robin Campbell collection)

93

obligingly offered different hands. Ears were fashioned from Fimo clay. Limbs and head were made from stuffed tubular bandages, fixed to a trunk of supernumerary pillows and reinforced with coat hanger wire. A visit to the barber provided hair for wig and whiskers, and amusement for the staff. The effigy, when finally assembled in early November, weighed 30 lbs., stood about 5ft. tall and had cost about £100. If I say so myself, it bore a tolerable resemblance to Munro and was sufficiently life-like – or death-like – to frighten visitors to my house severely. It was too bulky to fit in a rucksack but, protected by plastic bags and folded in Z, it could be strapped to a packframe. We were ready.

On Sunday 10th November, we left Forest Lodge in Glen Tilt, accompanied by my colleague Dr Helen Ross, in darkness and steady rain, at 7.30am. The approach to Carn an Fhidhleir involves climbing over a shoulder of Carn a' Chlamain to the Tarf Bothy, which we reached around 10am. The weather meantime worsened considerably, the rain turning to sleet and a lively westerly beginning to blow. Dr Ross gave it up about a mile beyond the bothy and Munro and I proceeded alone. On the final ascent to the summit the winds were so strong that at times, furnished as I was with a kind of sail, I dared not move for fear of being whisked away. Much snow had fallen, and this became a whirling mass of icy spindrift in the fiercest gusts. We reached the cairn about 1pm. Since there was plainly to be no photo-opportunity, Sir Hugh declined to leave his cocoon, and so we immediately began to descend in the teeth of the gale. When we reached the Allt a' Chaorainn the winds eased and it began to snow heavily. I have a decrepit left knee which acts up worse than usual in heavy winds and it was now providing me with a good deal of discomfort. We collected Dr Ross at the Bothy and left for the final leg around 3.30. Our progress was slow and painful, so much so that we were engulfed by darkness at the top of the pass. By the time we reached the edge of Glen Tilt our torches were more or less done for: the descent path could not be found and we slid down to the Tilt, for the most part on our backs. Parts of poor Munro extruded through the plastic bags in protest. As I limped towards Forest Lodge, I fancied I heard him murmur 'Even worse than 1908', recalling his previous attempt to climb this troublesome mountain, which had foundered in thick darkness and torrential rain.

Although I had originally planned posthumous ascents of all three Tops, this unexpected onset of winter ruled out the Inaccessible Pinnacle, so we had to be content with an ascent of Carn Cloich-mhuilinn on the following Sunday. This was uneventful and, although the mountain was snow-bound and conditions at the cairn were far from ideal, Munro dismounted, and I was able to take a number of photographs. Due to an oversight, we were obliged to celebrate his posthumous completion of the Munros with coffee. I remarked that since his earliest recorded Munro had been Ben Lawers in 1879,

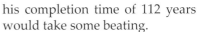

The last Munro
(Robin Campbell collection)

his completion time of 112 years would take some beating.

Since he was now qualified to attend his own Dinner, I smuggled him into the Roxburghe Hotel on the following Saturday[3]. He occupied a table on his own and remained modestly shrouded by a dust cloth until I exposed him to the assembled baggers at the conclusion of my speech. Despite the atrocious bad taste of this outlandish stunt, it received a generous reception from the gathering. It was perhaps fortunate that no member of the Munro family had attended ...

Sir Hugh remains intact and patiently awaits his visit to the Inaccessible Pinnacle, to be celebrated in early June, this time with champagne. In the meantime, I have not neglected his spiritual welfare: I offer him readings from the early Journals, usually taken from his own work, and an occasional verse of the Club Song. I trust that members will realise that although this posthumous completion served less worthy purposes at the Roxburghe Hotel, my motive in bringing it

Munro at the 1991 Dinner tolerating the company of Richard
Gilbert and Irvine Butterfield
(Robin Campbell collection)

about has been to delight the Shade of Munro and to honour his memory.

Later . . .

Sir Hugh Munro, in the form of a full-sized effigy, completed his round of the Tops on Wednesday 10th July 1992 with an ascent of the Inaccessible Pinnacle of Sgùrr Dearg. An attempt had been made on Tuesday 9th in the company of Robin Campbell, Derek Pyper and Helen Ross, but unexpected bad weather sent the party back to the Hut. Wednesday offered better conditions and in the early afternoon Campbell, Munro and Ross set off for the summit. A passing climber, Mr. James Kenyon of Accrington, was roped in for the final attack. Campbell, Kenyon and Munro ascended the Pinnacle by its East Ridge, while Ross remained below in order to take photographs. After descending, the party enjoyed a bottle of champagne before returning to Glen Brittle. Sir Hugh's traverse of the 538 Tops of his 1891 Tables was begun in May 1879 with an ascent of Ben Lawers. At the time of his death in 1919, 535 Tops had been visited. Carn an Fhidleir (Feshie) and Carn Cloich-mhuilinn were ascended last year, leaving only the Inaccessible Pinnacle to be accounted for. His round has therefore occupied a period of 113 years and must be considered as a strong candidate for the Slowest Completion of the Tops.

Bagging Munro
(Robin Campbell collection)

Assisting HTM to the Top Block
(Robin Campbell collection)

Postscript 2021

In the years following his Completion, Sir Hugh made token appearances at various Club events. Perhaps the most auspicious of these was his attendance at John Cromartie's 50th birthday celebrations on the Cioch pinnacle of Sròn na Ciche, Skye on 12th June 1998. The Countess, resplendent in a yellow ball gown, served the nervous company, who were in the main quite unaccustomed to such precarious dining rooms, a four-course meal with matching wines.

Robin (and Sir Hugh Munro?)

The Earl and Countess of Cromartie
request the pleasure of your company
at a Luncheon to celebrate
the Earl's 50th birthday
on Friday, 12th June
on the Cioch, Sron na Ciche 1998

Black Tie   *R.S.V.P. 01997 421337*

Lunch Invitation (Robin Campbell collection)

[1]   Originally published as SMCJ 1992, XXXV, 121-122, and 1993, XXXV, 304.

[2]   'Munro and the Salvationist Tendency', reproduced in *The Munroist's Companion* as Chapter 1.7.

[3]   This well-attended and popular event took the form of a dinner in the Roxburghe Hotel, Edinburgh. It was organized by Bill Brooker, the Keeper of the List, with the purpose of celebrating the Centenary of the Tables, and all recorded extant Completers were invited. It is likely that a similar event will be organized to celebrate the Centenary of Robertson's Round in 2001. On this future occasion the Roxburghe Hotel will hardly suffice: perhaps the multitude might just squeeze into Murrayfield or Hampden Park!

This Article is reprinted with permission from 'The Munroist's Companion', by Robin Campbell, 1999, Scottish Mountaineering Trust. Copyright © 1999 by Robin N. Campbell.

Amongst Woodland

Cruel faerie dust ice crystals in the last light
flicker their brittle laughter, then fade.
Night comes, cold comes, dread comes, strength goes.

Let me break a trail through the snow with my skis.
Follow my path; one track will be better for us both.
Do not let me lose you, call out my name; I will wait.

Forest troll hoar frost wants to feed upon our marrow and
elflin soft snow whispers fall behind, 'See them, see them,
see them in the wood, deep in the dark, dark wood!'

If we really have to we can always find some shelter,
wrap ourselves together; arms and legs entwined, keep each other
warm; though we've never had a need like this at any time before.

There was a kelpie in the lochan, which we passed without
disturbing; the ice stayed like a mirror, though I thought
I saw its shadow stir beneath the starlight on the surface.

Listen to my right boot's binding... creeark: a beat like our hearts'
beat, lazy after love; listening for your langlauf ski soles: schifiss...
soft as a swan; gliding like an arctic snow-goose homeward.

Timber dwarf limbs strike out to blind us, given half a chance,
Big-foot roots will try to trip us; the forest has so many traps:
a fork! A false road; that leads straight to nowhere.

But we have a map to share between us and a route that
we've decided and we shall come out from this forest and reach
across the snow bed; making sure that we're not dreaming.

Stuart B. Campbell

Image: Composite; Morning/McNab

Part 3 – Going the Distance

Cairngorm Parkrun

Ian Stewart

In July 2020 I completed the Cairngorm Parkrun, a continuous journey over the 58 Munros in the Cairngorms National Park. The route totalled 419km with 20,559m of ascent over 141 hours and 54 minutes.

For the last couple of years, my main goal for the summer has been a big expedition race – the Cape Wrath Ultra in 2018 and the Berghaus Dragon's Back Race in 2019. In 2020, rather than signing up for an adventure race, I wanted to create my own and help to raise some funds to help support my friend Dave, who suffered a stroke after a skiing accident in 2018.

Inspired by the idea of the Wainwrights round in the Lake District, I was drawn to a round of my own local hills. The Rigby Round is the established 24-hour challenge in the Cairngorms, but I wanted something bigger. A chance conversation with a local hill runner planted the seed – how long would it take to run all the Munros within the National Park?

There are 58 Munros in the Cairngorms National Park; technically, according to the OS map, the summit of Geal Charn (917m) in Drumochter is 100m outside the Park boundary, but it was obvious that this should be included in the total. As far as I could tell, no-one had ever done this round before.

As soon as I started planning, I knew that this was going to be a monster, with the Park including several groups of hills away from the more obvious Cairngorm and Glenshee massifs. With Mount Keen out on its own to the east, and the Monadhliath hills to the west, getting the route right was going to be crucial. I attempted to work out a schedule, splitting the route into legs with an average speed for each leg, 5km/h for most of the route, dropping to 4km/h on the sections with more climbing. As soon as the Covid travel restrictions were lifted and there was a weather window, we were off!

Day 1: *14 Munros, 86km, 4,058m ascent, 17.5 hours*

With plans in place, we set off up Mount Keen at 06.00 on Friday 10th July, easing into the round with a steady walk up the big track leading onto the moor. The summit was shrouded in cloud and we didn't hang around. Laura, my wife, returned to the van and I headed off west into the mist, one Munro down, 57 to go! Any hopes of this round being an easy trail run were however quickly dashed. I would be linking hills together in a way that the normal Munro bagger wouldn't consider; travelling between the hills was going to be harder than climbing them! There were a few sections that I knew were going to be rough, and this first bit, heading west towards Loch Muick, looked particularly bad: 6km of deep heather and peat hags, energy sapping and time consuming.

The previous two days had been a whirlwind of organisation, sorting kit and plans, cooking food and getting a support team in place. I felt stressed thinking about the route and the massive few days ahead. Climbing Lochnagar, my legs were feeling tired already; a mountain biker overtook me, carrying his bike, the weather was turning and I was feeling anxious. This was definitely not fun!

Once up on the plateau behind Lochnagar, the Munros came quickly. This circuit gives some of the best high level trail running in Scotland and despite some annoying knee pain I was soon ahead of schedule. Hobbling down into Glen Esk my mood was low; this pain had come out of nowhere and felt like the kind of thing that only gets worse. I wasn't expecting to get through six days without a few sore bits, but this was too much, too early.

The first support point in Glen Clova came and went; a big pasta meal, clean clothes and a painful session with the foam roller drew some strange looks. I set off again up the Kilbo path towards Driesh and Mayar, 40 minutes ahead of my schedule. Full of fuel I felt stronger as I pushed up the long climb, my knee not hurting at all.

Exactly what triggered the change I don't know, but at last my head was in the right place. I focussed on the next kilometre and was able to calmly accept the task and just get on with it. Hours poring over maps and aerial images paid off and I was able to make the most of stalkers' tracks across the high moor and find a relatively efficient route around the plateau. It was just getting dark as I summited Creag Leacach, my final Munro of the day, before descending through the ski area to my first proper rest stop in Glenshee.

Enjoying a rare section of path (Ian Stewart)

Day 2: *11 Munros, 51.2km, 3,487m ascent, 12 hours 41 minutes, 6 hours' sleep*

As the alarm went off to start Day 2, Joe, my support runner for the day arrived. It was a relief for me to lighten my load and a good chat got me over the first few hills. 30km shorter than Day 1, but with only 500m less ascent, Day 2 was all about the up and down. At Glas Tulaichean Joe headed back to Glenshee and I was on my own for the final section of the day over Beinn a' Ghlo. Slogging up steep heather above the imaginatively named Loch Loch I wondered if anyone had ever taken that route before.

More mentally fatigued than physically, I was ready for the day to end as I ticked off my last summit. I ignored the path down towards the carpark and headed north, down an unlikely looking descent on the north flank of the mountain. A final steep grassy descent took me to the River Tilt and my support point for the night where a slice of take-away pizza and a dip in the river represented pure luxury!

Day 3: *7 Munros, 72.8km, 3,791m ascent, 17 hours 59 minutes, 5 hours' sleep*

On multi-day events, I always find the morning of Day 3 is the hardest; after that you don't ever really feel much worse. As I crawled out of my sleeping bag and set off up the hill, I didn't feel too bad – tired, but without any real injury concerns. With 18 hours scheduled to do only seven Munros, the third day presented the hardest terrain of the round over remote and disconnected summits. I crossed the wilds of the upper Tarf twice to get out to the two Munros normally accessed from Glen Feshie and then back again to Beinn Dearg. Peat hags, deep heather and bottomless bogs made for slow going. Reaching An Sgarsoch, the second summit of the day gave great views of the Lairig Ghru and Cairngorm.

Many hours passed between Munro numbers 4 and 5, dropping into Glen Bruar, then crossing into the Gaick pass and a welcome support point. The sun was low and the drizzle rolled in for my last descent of the day.

Day 4: *8 Munros, 94.7km, 2,718m ascent, 20 hours 27 minutes, 5 hours' sleep*

I had it in my mind that Day 4 was going to be a relatively easy day – starting on smoother terrain on the four hills west of the Drumochter, then 20km on the road before the Monadhliath traverse and forest tracks into Glen Feshie. I couldn't have been more wrong!

Waking to rain hammering on the van roof, a quick check showed the hills were hidden under menacing low cloud. I dressed with extra warm layers, and added a few more spares into my pack. The 4am start didn't help my mood as I slogged up the hill for a sweaty few hours, cursing the extra weight on my back.

By the time I hit Dalwhinnie the weather had improved. Fresh dry shoes for the road section, no need to carry any kit and fresh coffee all helped my mood. A short piece of estate track along the Spey brought another surprise – a kilometre of original cobbles on a section of General Wade's Military Road, a hidden piece of history and a welcome distraction.

Arriving at the next support point, my days of solitude came to an end just at the right time. As I sat in the sun filling up on food and sorting my feet it felt great to have company all round me. Four of us set off into the Monadhliath. This section was supposed to be fairly straightforward – but I should have known better, having been this way before. I had totally underestimated how rough the ground was and the complaints from my shin were getting louder. Tendonitis building at the front of my ankle was limiting range of motion and starting to affect my ability to descend or run comfortably. We dropped down into the glen as darkness fell, all that was left was 10km along the road and then forest tracks into Glen Feshie, where the van was waiting. Try as I might, I couldn't get any real pace going as I hobbled up to the van to find my dinner and my bed waiting. I was empty. 94km in 20.5 hours; how was that a rest day?

Day 5: *8 Munros, 49.4km, 2,444m ascent, 13 hours 41 minutes, 7 hours' sleep*

When I woke up, I was not in a good way. I was in pain; I was deeply tired and generally feeling pretty rough. I spent the next hour in a pit of despair, feeling sorry for myself and desperately trying to come up with a good excuse to quit. I could drive home in 20 minutes and enjoy a nice warm bath and a few days in bed. The idea of another 110km and 6,500 meters of climbing just seemed impossible. At this point I could easily have quit; however, I had three key thoughts that overrode any desire to sulk off home:

1. The 'unfinished business' that I knew would haunt me if I quit now. Could/should I have kept going? Could/should I have another attempt? The idea of having to re-do the previous four days was unbearable; much better to suffer for two days now, than six at some point in the future.

2. From all the messages of support I was getting as I ran along, I knew that a lot of people were watching my attempt and to quit would let them all down.

3. Most importantly, the focus of my challenge was to raise funds to help out Dave and support his rehab after he suffered a stroke following a skiing accident two years ago. I visited Dave last year and watched him in one of his physio sessions, learning how to stand up again. Dave is making these efforts every day, without any certain outcome of where his efforts will get him; one day he may walk again, but he may not. He has no easy option of quitting. If he can endure that with determination and good humour, another two days of walking slowly round the hills for me should be a piece of cake. I'm sure that Dave would give anything to have that opportunity again, and the least I

could do would be to take mine.

It took a while to organise these thoughts, but once I had, I knew that nothing could stop me. As long as it took, I was getting to Cairngorm.

We had one big day planned to get us into the Lairig Ghru, then the final day would be split into three parts, with two breaks near the Fords of Avon. This meant that I needed to have enough food and kit with me for a 24-hour push, including kit for a very basic camp.

To have done this section solo may well have broken me. To an outsider, these big runs look like an individual achievement, but I couldn't have got to this point without support. I was trotting along on the sections of easy running, but watching Mark walk along beside me as I was flat out, showed how much my pace had slowed. The real challenges were the sections of rocky ground; my right ankle had lost any range of motion, I was peg-legged and hobbling down steps like a 90-year-old and for the first time the schedule dropped away.

Running through the night (Ian Stewart)

Day 6: *10 Munros, 64.9km, 4,061m ascent, 22 hours 41 minutes, 3 hours' sleep*

After just three hours' sleep the alarm went off. The Parkrun was split into 13 legs and I still had three legs, 10 Munros and an awful lot of climbing and descending before the finish. The leg with the most climbing per kilometre lay ahead, starting with the monster double climb out of the Lairig Ghru, over

103

Carn a' Mhaim and then up to Ben Macdui, nearly 1,100 meters in just 9km.

A damp midge morning wasn't great for motivation, but there was no point delaying the inevitable; today was going to be long and slow enough as it was.

Despite my tiredness and immobile right foot I found a reasonable line up the steep flank of Carn a' Mhaim. As we started the slog up the boulder field towards Ben Macdui I saw a figure descending through the mist; at first I wondered about stories of weary walkers seeing the ephemeral 'Big Grey Man of Ben Macdui' but I had never heard mention of him having a spaniel with him! Luckily it was the arrival of another support runner. I was starting to worry that he had arrived empty-handed until the first round of veggie sausage sarnies appeared. After a few hundred kilometres fuelled mostly by dry bars, nuts and a few precious cheese and avocado wraps, I was desperate for some different food. Still warm, these exotic fresh treats were little tin foil bundles of motivation.

Inspired by Dave – motivation to keep going (Ian Stewart)

The mountain feast continued as we arrived at our next support point, just south of the Fords of Avon. Here Dave was waiting with enough supplies to stock an entire marathon aid station. In the feeding frenzy that followed we polished of a massive tray of fresh fruit, a pot of rice pudding, several flapjacks, a bag of jam donuts and a huge flask of coffee. Suitably caffeine and sugar fuelled we raced up the next hill, just six to go, and the sun was back out.

By this point, time had started doing strange things; the hills were coming in rapid succession and it felt like we were moving at a decent pace, yet somehow the day was racing away from us. 2 o'clock quickly became 9 o'clock and we were nearly 17 hours into the day by the time we made it back to the Fords of Avon where our final supporters were waiting. The sensible choice would have been to stop and get some food and sleep but I could see the finish line and any delay now was unthinkable. I had had enough, I just wanted it all to be over!

It is hard to describe how the next five hours running in darkness, low cloud, drizzle and blustery winds felt. My world shrunk down to the size of my head torch beam, a 2 metre treadmill of heather, rocks and bog, uphill, downhill, uphill and repeat in endless purgatory. The support team did an amazing job of trying to keep me engaged in chat, but I could tell that everyone wished that I could just move a bit quicker and get us all off this cold wet hillside!

As we trudged towards Cairngorm, the final summit of the challenge, I was waiting for the surge of adrenaline that would sweep me on to a sprint finish. In previous big events I have been amazed to find my body discovering miraculous freshness once the end is in sight, proof that our limitations are mostly mental rather than physical. On this night, as much as I willed it on, the finishing rush never came. I was empty.

Truly empty in a way that I had never experienced before. Emotionally there was no reward for the effort, no sense of achievement and no elation. I just wanted to go home. I went through the motions of summit photos and tried to look appreciative of the bottle of fizz that Laura had carried all day.

I knew I was still a long way from done; I still had 600 meters of descent to do back to the carpark before I could give in to fatigue, and it was 90 pitiful minutes before I collapsed into the back seat of the car.

D   o   n   e   !   .

In every sense of the word!

—TMS—

My Desert Island Mountains and why – Bill Wheeler

My choice of mountains in my 'paradise' is governed by enjoyment given, the challenge accepted and their place in my journey through Scotland to complete my Munros in a journey which took four decades.

My choice is Ben Nevis, Sgùrr Mòr, Creag Meagaidh, Ben Alder, An Riabhachan, Cairn Toul and Ben Klibreck. Journey's end.

The other item I would take to my desert island is a watercolour of Ben Klibreck, it being my final Munro.

LOCHS and LOCHANS

Above - Early morning, 27th March 2007, an ascent of Baosbheinn via Drochaid a' Ghorm-locha from Poca Buidhe bothy, we passed this lochan with two boulders which echoed the Beinn Alligin tops.

Below – Ben Loyal from Lochan Hakel as the tops clear after a stormy winter shower. 23rd February 2016.   *Norman McNab*

A Journey through Wales – Summer 2005

Mike Weedon

'This summer I've decided I'm going to do a continuous long-distance walk from South to North Wales,' announced Ruth. And there was I thinking she was telling me where she was going for her local walk. 'I reckon it'll take me three and a half weeks,' she continued. 'I'll stay with family and friends where I can and otherwise in B & Bs.'

'So, where have you got this idea from?' I queried, scrambling to get on the appropriate wavelength.

'Well,' she said, 'when my brother and I were in our late teens, we walked and hitch-hiked from South to North Wales, and I'd like to repeat it. Only this time I'll walk it all the way, taking in as much high ground and as many mountains as I can.'

'And are you going to do it with anyone else?' I asked.

'Yes, of course I'll be happy for any family and friends to accompany me wherever they can.'

Then she added what seemed like an afterthought: 'You could join me on the weekend legs. In fact, come to think of it, why don't you take a week's leave and join me for my final week in Snowdonia?' Naturally I agreed.

That spring Ruth studied the Cambrian Way guide which describes a route from the south to north coasts. Drawing on that she devised her own route taking in the particular mountains and high ground she wanted to climb as well as the availability of overnight accommodation stops. From the outset it was clear that the nature and level of challenge of different sections was going to vary considerably. Growing up in Caerphilly she was familiar with most of the ground to be covered during her first week, and there was the additional convenience of being able to stay overnight with family and friends. She had also climbed almost all the mountains in Snowdonia included in her route. It was the hills and valleys of mid-Wales she had the least first-hand experience of, so we decided to spend several weekends reconnoitring a route through areas we didn't know or had only visited many years ago.

On the first of these we tackled the final section of the ridge extending northwards from the Rhinogs that was new to both of us. What a miserable scene it was when we set off in heavy rain from Cefn Clawdd with low cloud covering the hills. At the col beneath Diffwys we found paths heading up the steep hillside either side of a high drystone wall. Of course, the one we chose soon faded out into deep heather, and some undignified combined tactics were required to get back over the wall to join the true path. At least it had stopped raining by the time we passed the summit of Diffwys and arrived at the next top, Foel Penolau. This turned out to be quite rocky, and it had a nasty surprise in store for us when we set off again. Almost immediately we found ourselves perched above a small cliff that appeared to girdle the little summit plateau, and in the poor visibility it took us a bit of time to find a weakness and scramble down it. The ridge then carried on its undulating way past a couple of llyns (lochans); up and down, up and down it went, some of these being steep little crags which we had to circumvent. Then, as we were approaching Clip, the day's final top, the cloud suddenly began to break up, the sun came out, and there was Tremadog Bay laid out in front of us. We ended our traverse of what's a remarkable but little-known ridge walking back down to the car in sunshine, a rewarding contrast to the conditions we'd set off in.

Other days we spent reconnoitring a route through this part of Wales took in Cadair Idris, Rhinog Fawr, and a traverse of Rhinog Fach, Y Llethr, and Diffwys. Then there was a final weekend further south staying at the remote Ty'n Cornel Hostel from which we explored the afforested hinterland east of Tregaron and the area around the Pools of Teifi.

Rhinog Fawr and Rhinog Fach from ascending Yr Llethr (Ruth Weedon)

Two weeks later Ruth began her walk at Castell Coch, Cardiff's fairy-tale castle, and by the following weekend she had reached the Brecon Beacons where she was joined by some friends and me. On the Saturday cloud was covering the tops as we set off up past the Neuadd Reservoirs to walk over Cribyn, Pen y Fan and Corn Du. It happened to be my fifth ascent of Pen y Fan, but I still didn't manage to see the views (something I only finally achieved during a TMS meet in 2018). On the Sunday, after traversing hill country new to us between the Storey Arms and the Black Mountain, I left her and a friend to climb the Carmathan Fan the following day. Over the course of that week, initially by herself and then accompanied by another friend, she worked her way northwards to meet up with me and other family members at the Dyffryn Castell Hotel on the A44.

On the Saturday morning the cloud was down and it was drizzling for our ascent of Plynlimon, the highest hill in this part of mid-Wales. My two previous ascents had both been from the north, starting at Maesnant where the road alongside the Nant-y-moch Reservoir ends, then up over Pumlumon Fach with its views of Llyn y Llygad Rheidol fringed by crags. By contrast, the route up the broad south ridge seemed devoid of features of interest, even allowing for our limited visibility. It confirmed for me that Plynlimon's northern flank is a far more attractive proposition for a way up – which makes me wonder why both the routes Poucher included in his seminal *The Welsh Peaks* were from the south (though in a postscript he does mention a correspondent recommending routes on the north side).

At least the rain had stopped by the time we reached the summit, but progress along the undulating ridge running north-eastwards remained viewless for much of the way. After a small detour to see the sign-posted source of the River Severn and some rough-going along the upper reaches of the Afon Clywedog we eventually ended up at the Dylife Inn. This turned out to be the outright winner of our worst overnight accommodation award – hopefully it's now under new management. On the Sunday, Andy, my long-term climbing partner, accompanied Ruth and me on her next leg to Commins Coch just off the Dovey valley, a day when the view to the north was dominated by the landmark of Cadair Idris, a mountain she would soon be climbing.

Here she was picked up by a friend with whom she was staying in Dinas Mawddwy for three nights. A dreich walk the next day, giving them close-up views of a lot of wind turbines, was followed by a day of incessant heavy rain; that it just happened to have been planned as the solitary rest day in her walk was a stroke of good fortune. By the time she set off the next morning the weather had improved, and it remained fair for the following days when she climbed Cadair Idris and traversed Diffwys, Y Llethr and Rhinog Fach.

With the walk still proceeding according to schedule, family and friends joined her for the Saturday of the final weekend, an ascent of Rhinog Fawr in sunshine. It's one of the rockiest mountains in Wales, particularly on its north side which we descended to the Roman Steps path. Leaving Ruth and the others to follow this down to Cwm Buchan, Andy and I continued traversing northwards over Craig Wion to pick up another path leading back down to Cwm Buchan. Harold Drasdo, in *The Big Walks*, described this section of the range as 'a splendid mile of Celtic Badlands', and I don't think I've ever encountered terrain elsewhere in Wales to rival it in terms of sustained arduous going. We found it very hard work negotiating our way through the jumble of small, broken crags, rough heather and boulders underfoot, let alone the several deep rocky canyons bisecting the terrain that were hard to see until we were actually standing above a steep drop.

On the Sunday Ruth, Andy and I set off up Clip to traverse the ridge to Diffwys in the opposite direction from our earlier effort back in May. It was another sunny day and the terrain entertaining, unlike that previous occasion when navigation sometimes hadn't been straightforward. In fact, it became so hot that when we reached Llyn Corn-ystwc, the (to me) unthinkable happened: Ruth and Andy stripped down to the basics and went for a swim with the dragonflies - I opted instead for a nap. Suitably refreshed we carried on over our old friend, Foel Penalou whose ring of crags now appeared far less forbidding. At Diffwys, leaving Ruth to carry on to our overnight accommodation in Maentwrog, Andy and I took what turned out to be a rather wretched descent route to his car left at the road end at Llyn Llenyrah. After he dropped me off at Maentwrog, it was just Ruth and I tackling the last four mountain days.

Ruth swimming in Llyn Corn-ystwc
(Mike Weedon)

The next morning was very hot. Fortunately, our path alongside the narrow-gauge Ffestiniog railway took us through woodland partially shading us from the sun. But once out in the open the heat became quite oppressive, and the paths up to Llyn Stwian and from there to the col between the two Moelwyns were taken at a very slow pace. I hadn't previously climbed Moelwyn Bach, so leaving Ruth to a well-earned rest, I beetled up and down it. Then came a long plod up over its higher sibling, Moelwyn Mawr, and down to a disused slate mine on the other side. Beyond this we traversed a kind of high plateau, with small tops scattered around randomly and several llyns lying in between them, a fascinating area new to me that's off the beaten track, Cnicht apart. It was still very hot when we reached Llyn yr Adar and, according to Ruth, time for another dip. But she was disappointed to find it too shallow for swimming.

From there we followed a path down past Llyn Llag to a minor road leading to Nantgwynant where we were staying for the night. It had been a long haul in tough conditions and we were understandably pleased with our effort. But at this point we were facing a pressing problem: the grim prospect of a dinnerless end to a hard day. Because Ruth had entertained doubts about getting this far with the walk, she hadn't got round to sorting out where we were going to get our evening meals if B & Bs, like this one, didn't provide them; she simply trusted something would turn up. And maybe we could have got one in Beddgelert, but that was three miles away down the valley and it was already 8.00pm.

Ruth at Llyn Cwm-Corsiog (Mike Weedon)

As it happened, this wasn't our only difficulty. Ruth had booked this particular B & B only after she had started her walk, and although she knew the cottage's name, she hadn't checked its exact whereabouts beforehand. Now, Nantgwynant is only a small habitation but it does straddle both sides of the A498 running down the valley, and we naturally chose the wrong side, following fruitlessly what turned out to be a long cul de sac. The penalty was an unwelcome extra couple of miles of walking and arrival at the B & B even later than it was already going to be. I kept discreetly in the background as she apologised to mine host for our tardiness and then, as winningly as she could, asked if an evening meal could be provided. Fortunately he took the request in his stride and managed to rustle us up something modest but filling.

Next up was Yr Wyddfa (Snowdon). My first-ever ascent had been via the Watkin path, so I was looking forward to reacquainting myself with this way up. But it was obviously going to be a popular choice judging by the number of people getting themselves ready at the car park; and, my gosh, it was already even hotter than the previous day. A change of plan was called for, and at Cwm Llan we headed off up to Yr Wyddfa's col with Yr Aran and climbed its south ridge. I'd actually descended the mountain by this route on that first occasion, but the upper part had been in cloud and I couldn't really remember much about it at all. Well, it turned out to be a highly recommendable way up: we enjoyed fine views and came across hardly any other walkers using it.

After indulging ourselves with ice creams from the summit café - if there has to be one gracing Wales' highest point, I suppose this reincarnation represents something of an improvement over its ugly predecessor - we joined countless others making their way down the aesthetically awful PYG track before veering off down the path to Glaslyn. Ruth fancied another dip here but it felt just a bit too public, so we carried on down to Llyn Llydaw to pick up the Miners' Track. From there it's a couple of miles to the Pen-y-Pass and a further one mile down the main road to the Pen-y-Gwyrd Hotel where we were staying that night. Shortly after the point when the Pen-y-Pass came into view, about half a mile away, we noticed a bus coming up the road and into the carpark.

Ruth perked up: 'Couldn't we get that and save ourselves the drag down to the Pen-y-Gwyrd?'

'Doubt it,' I replied. 'It's probably come from Capel Curig and going on to Llanberis. And in any case it'll probably leave before we get there.'

I was wrong on both counts. The bus was heading back past the Pen-y-Gwyrd and we reached it in time. A long hot bath compensated Ruth for the earlier dip she'd foregone, and a seven (!) course meal sunk us both.

Ruth en route to Glyder Fawr, with Glyder Fach beyond (Mike Weedon)

It wasn't quite so hot on the penultimate day of the walk when we set off up the Miners' Track to traverse the Glyders, but by the time we were descending Glyder Fawr Ruth was beginning to feel quite whacked and wondering whether to abandon continuing over Y Garn and the tops beyond it and instead descend to Ogwen Cottage via the Devil's Kitchen path and Cwm Idwal, then walk down the A5 to Bethesda. However, the prospect of a lengthy bit of road-bashing along a busy highway didn't appeal either, and after a rest by Llyn y Cwn she decided to carry on as planned.

Carnedd y Filiast, the day's final peak, has a steep northern end, and our initial descent took us over some very rough, awkward ground, all humps and boulders. Neither of us had been down this way before, nor from the looks of it had many other people. The huge Penrhyn slate quarry sprawling across the foot of the mountain provided an obvious reason why, barring any direct route to Mynydd Llandegai where we were staying that night. We managed to bypass it by veering to the west and, after climbing over a number of walls and fences, eventually reached a recognised footpath.

It was a great relief to Ruth when we finally arrived at our overnight accommodation. But we were very hungry and by now it was 9.00pm. Unfortunately, this was another B & B that didn't advertise evening meals and Ruth had assumed we would be able to find somewhere to eat in Bethesda. Well, maybe a meal could be found there, but it was a good mile and a half away and last orders had probably already been taken anyway. So mine host was humbly informed of our dire predicament in a last throw of the dice. Salvation came but, unlike the previous evening, it took a very paltry form: four slices of white bread with accompanying lumps of butter. And it was my birthday!

Breakfast couldn't arrive fast enough on our final morning, and it was galling to conclude afterwards that it was probably the best one of all the B & Bs sampled. Of course, Ruth hadn't booked anywhere to eat for our final evening either, so just in case, we made sure to stock up with some extra food when we passed through Bethesda. From there our route took us up the broad ridge of Mynydd Du to Carnedd Dafydd, then along the connecting ridge to Carnedd Llewelyn and, a mile further on to the north, the very last peak of the walk, Foel Grach. Just short of Garnedd Uchaf we turned off the ridge and started contouring downwards on the long haul to our final overnight accommodation just beyond Llanbedr-y-cennin.

Ruth began to feel very tired now and, as we left the hillside behind, was more or less walking on auto-pilot across the heathland, path, track and finally roads leading down to our destination. Thankfully we were spared a repeat of the previous evening's involuntary fasting: the Bull Inn in Llanbedr was still taking orders as we came by, so we dived in straightaway and enjoyed a hasty celebratory meal before booking into our nearby accommodation.

Mike on Carnedd Llewelyn (Ruth Weedon)

The next morning, at a leisurely pace, we walked along roads the few miles to Tal-y-cafn and stood for a while on the middle of the bridge over the tidal Afon Conwy marking the walk's end. After ruminating briefly on some of the experiences of the previous three weeks, I asked Ruth how she was feeling now her walk was finally over. Elated, she said, especially because she was unsure for much of the way whether she would actually have the strength and stamina to complete it. We carried on to the station, caught the train to Blaenau Ffestiniog and then the narrow-gauge railway back to Maentwrog. Our car had been left there. We got in it to drive home, turning the page on a memorable chapter in our lives.

Day	Start point	Destination	Grid ref *	Hills, mountains and other features *en route*
1	Castell Coch	Risca	237905	Caerphilly Common, Caerphilly, Mynydd y Grug, Mynydd Machen
2	Risca	Ystrad Mynach	143941	Sirhowy Valley
3	Ystrad Mynach	Pontsticill	054109	Gelli-gaer Common, Cefn Gelligaer
4	Pontsticill	Llwyn-y-celyn	973225	Cribyn, Pen y Fan, Corn Du
5	Llwyn-y-celyn	Glyntawe	848173	Craig Cerrig-gleisiad, Fan Nedd, Fan Gyhirych
6	Glyntawe	Myddfai	773302	Fan Brycheiniog, Waun Lefrith

Day	Start point	Destination	Grid ref *	Hills, mountains and other features *en route*
7	Myddfai	Nant-y-Bai	775446	Llandovery, Fforest, Afon Tyw
8	Nant-y-Bai	Rhandirmwyn	785438	Afon Tyw
9	Rhandirmwyn	Blaencaron	713608	Afon Doethie, Esgair Hir
10	Blaencaron	Cwmystwyth	789741	Pools of Teifi, Bryn Dafydd
11	Cwmystwyth	Dyffryn Castell	774817	Pen y Garn
12	Dyffryn Castell	Dylife	862941	Pen Pumlumon Fawr, Pen Pumlumon Arwystli
13	Dylife	Commins Coch	845032	Lluest-Ty-mawr, Tal-y-Wern
14	Commins Coch	Dinas Mawddwy	859147	Mynedd y Cemais, Esgair Ddu
15	Rest day			
16	Dinas Mawddwy	Minffordd	732115	Maesglase, Cribin Fawr, Waun-oer, Mynydd y Waun
17	Minffordd	Llechfraith	668196	Cadair Idris
18	Llechfraith	Cwm Nantcol	641270	Diffwys, Y Llethr, Rhinog Fach
19	Cwm Nantcol	Cwm Bychan	646314	Rhinog Fawr, Roman Steps
20	Cwm Bychan	Maentwrog	664405	Clip, Moel Ysgyfarnogod, Foel Penolau, Diffwys
21	Maentwrog	Nantgwynant	642513	Moelwyn Mawr, Llyn yr Adar, Llyn Llagi
22	Nantgwynant	Pen-y-Gwryd	660558	Yr Wyddfa (Snowdon)
23	Pen-y-Gwryd	Mynydd Llandegai	605659	Glyder Fach, Glyder Fawr, Y Garn, Carnedd y Filiast
24	Mynydd Llandegai	Castell	767693	Carnedd Dafydd, Carnedd Llewelyn, Foel Grach
25	Castell	Tal-y-cafn station	787717	Afon Conwy

—TMS—

North West Climbing

A frozen snotter dreeps down
off the Fhidhler's Nose;
you're face to face with *Fear
of the Dark*: rounded holds
of old red sandstone (friends could be useful),
the quartzite capping it all.

Where does this route, this ascent, begin, man?
Below a prominent chimney line...
up the right side of a wide crack... or
somewhere south of the tropic of Capricorn, an island
surfacing off the west coast
of Africa, 1,000 million years ago or more.

Your amphibian ancestors dragged themselves
from their dubby bivouac, then,
man, you hauled yourself upright out of a howff;
steadying yourself on two feet,
wondered what your next move might be.

1988: Prentice, Dinwoodie. Trace their line
back: Whillans, Cunningham, Weir, Collie,
Aonghas Mór of the Eggs... and there's
a hairy hand's pinch-grip fossilised in a flange.

With the *Wall of Flame* behind you, look
over the moor and rising mist, a summer's sun
descends to Tir nan Òg. Beinn Eighe, Torridon;
this is about as far away as you can get
and maybe that, *Fairytale
Groove*, will be as far as you'll ever go.
Fear and wonder
run in that daisy-chain of your DNA.

This is climbing history.

Image: N. McNab

Stuart B. Campbell

The Cape Wrath Trail

Robin Wallace

With great trepidation I finally set off to walk the Cape Wrath Trail. Self-doubt in my own ability, not to mention a pandemic, had put paid to doing the Trail in previous years, but this time it was a goer. I would at least have a hiking buddy too, my good friend Iain. We've been on many wild camping and bothy trips together, but nothing for as long as this and I have heard stories of hiking buddies falling out with each other! Hopefully that wouldn't be the case for us.

I travelled to Ullapool and met up at Iain's bunkhouse; he put me up for the night and we had a few beers whilst making last-minute tweaks to our gear. Luggage scales out, we weighed our packs with five days' worth of food; Iain's pack came in at 18kg and mine was 13kg.

In the morning, we were all set. Iain's Dad gave us a lift to Inverness where we caught the bus to Fort William. I made a pact with myself to have a social media blackout for the duration of the Trail, so it was a bit of a social media binge on the phone, whilst trying to preserve the battery. On arrival we discovered the passenger ferry to Camusnagaul had yet to restart after lockdown. Thinking quickly, we hailed a taxi and headed to the Corran Ferry instead. This stung us twenty quid, but starting at the Ardgour Inn rather than Camusnagaul would shave off a few kilometres of tarmac bashing.

After some final faffing with the packs and polishing off our Morrisons Meal Deals, we were finally ready to set off on our adventure. It was a fine sunny day and it didn't take us too long to walk along the coast to our turn-off point down Cona Glen. It's a nice feeling as you head off the main road and into the lush, wooded area. The further we travelled down the glen, the more remote it felt. Some early signs of blisters had us both worried; Compeed out, and some footwear adjustments allowed us to carry on a bit further until we decided to call it a day. Blisters a couple of hours into a big hike is never a good start!

Our pitch was perfectly placed for our assault on Day 2; we'd head up and over the pass and drop down to Callop with a lunch stop at Glenfinnan. Burger and chips x2 ordered at the National Trust Visitor Centre. We left the tourists behind at the famous viaduct and continued our journey north. We stopped by Corryhully to check the blister situation; thankfully we caught them early!

We paid homage to Sgùrr Thuilm and Streap guarding either side of the pass as we dropped towards Glen Pean. Rather than cutting around the perimeter of the plantation to Strathan, we cut through the trees to experience some of the worst bog ever. It was short-lived as we got ourselves on the track to A' Chùil where we'd retire for the day, and I would have to address a rather nasty heat rash on my derriere!

After a sunny start to our hike, Day 3 was looking rather gloomy and overcast. Still feeling a bit jaded from the effects of a 31-kilometre walk with 922 metres of ascent the day before, we pencilled in Sourlies as a potential stage end. Whilst it took longer to reach than we expected, it was still too soon to call it quits. Instead, we had some lunch at Sourlies and I wished Iain a happy 50th birthday. I could think of a lot worse places to spend a birthday! We were getting too relaxed enjoying the surroundings. We dusted ourselves down and got around the coast. Trying to make a direct beeline for Carnoch was nigh on impossible. The marshland was waiting to soak up any weary walker not paying attention to where they stepped. With fatigue setting in once again, we found a nice riverside pitch under the imposing Beinn an Aodainn.

Sourlies (Robin Wallace)

The beginning of Day 4 took us into the heart of the Rough Bounds of Knoydart. The River Carnach cascaded deep below us in the ravine and with a scattering of native trees, it felt like the most remote, isolated spot in the British Isles. We eventually reached Barrisdale Bay and feeling strong, pushed on for the rough and never-ending walk along the coast to Kinloch Hourn. Hardened Munro and Corbett baggers will be well acquainted with this path. We managed to blag a cottage for the price of a B&B at Kinloch Hourn.

Under Beinn an Aodainn (Robin Wallace)

The cottage was worth every penny as it rained constantly throughout the night. We sat tight for the rain to die off in the morning before setting off, following the pylons for a short distance before the big ascent up to Bealach Coire Mhàlagain. The Forcan Ridge was looking rather inviting in the spring sunshine. Descending towards Shiel Bridge, I managed to dislodge a massive boulder almost crushing my ankle. Somehow my trekking pole got in the way and took the brunt of the rock and I got away with just a bent pole. We eventually settled on a riverside pitch three kilometres short of Shiel Bridge.

Being fixated on reaching stages set out by the guidebooks, I was disheartened that it took us five days to get to Kintail. In reality this isn't a good approach to any long-distance hike. It should take as long as it takes. Stop when you're tired or push on when you're feeling strong. I learned to listen to my body and not worry if we stopped short of an arbitrary stage.

It was Day 6 and our food supplies were depleted. We picked up our resupply parcels at the Kintail Craft shop and as a thank you for agreeing to hold our parcels we bought some items from the shop. It was now time to tackle the stunning but notorious Falls of Glomach. No difficulty in good weather, we struck the correct path. In poor visibility, this can cause confusion with the lower path which leads to a dead-end natural waterfall viewpoint. We got ourselves down to the track that would eventually take us beyond

Iron Lodge to the remote Maol-bhuidhe bothy.

It was another braw sunny day; the river crossing by Loch Cruoshie presented no problems. We skirted around the east flank of Beinn Dronaig. I would be lying if I said I wasn't tempted to nip up to the summit; however I had other worries. My satellite communicator had failed and I had no means of letting my partner Nicola know I was safe; bumping into two Munro baggers, I asked if they would text her at the summit of Lurg Mhòr and thankfully they agreed.

We headed around to Bearnais Bothy, where I took a tumble in the bog and managed to bash my knee on the only visible rock anywhere. After an extended break we pushed on towards Craig; I finally got a phone signal and checked in with my partner. Feeling overwhelmed I got upset and was ready to quit.

A new day and a new me, I was up and packed before Iain, feeling mentally and physically refreshed. Iain's Dad met us in Craig with re-supplies. My trail shoes were wrecked, but I had a fresh pair waiting. After parting company with Iain's Dad our journey continued over the Coulin Pass and eventually to Kinlochewe. We pitched by the track that leads to Heights of Kinlochewe.

Another bright sunny day and we pushed on towards Fisherfield Forest and marked the halfway milestone of the Trail. Our route would skirt under the southern flanks of Mullach Coire Mhic Fhearchair with our rite of passage at Bealach na Croise. From here we decided against going via Shenavall, taking an alternative route to Lochivraon, eventually reaching Iain's house for a well-deserved rest day.

With a rest day, we were refreshed and raring to go, but our lucky weather streak had finally run out. It was wet and windy as we traversed across Inverlael Forest to reach Glen Douchary. The route to Loch an Daimh wasn't obvious and new deer fencing confused matters, but we were soon back on track making our way to Knockdamph and ultimately to the Schoolhouse Bothy.

Schoolhouse Bothy (Robin Wallace)

I wasn't overly enthusiastic about the next stage. Lots of track bashing to Oykel Bridge and beyond made it arguably the least attractive section of the whole Trail but it would allow us to smash some miles without worrying about rough terrain. We stopped at the hotel for some breakfast and once again hit the track that would eventually take us north of Benmore Lodge and into the mountains of Assynt. We pitched our tents by the river we'd followed for most of the day.

Day 12 beckoned and so did Iain's Dad. He was meeting us one last time with more supplies at Inchnadamph. Breabag and Conival stood in our way with a small narrow col offering passage to Gleann Dubh then on to Inchnadamph. We re-supplied with enough food to get us to the Cape. The lift back to Ullapool was tempting so I made a sharp exit with my heavy pack. I waited for Iain to catch up as we headed into what felt like the heart of Assynt, a complex myriad of rock and confusing terrain for the weary walker. We missed our descent route to Glencoul, heading down a steep hillside and eventually passing Eas a Chùal Aluinn, the tallest waterfall in Britain. The stunning views momentarily took our minds off the heavy packs and tired legs. We were more than pleased to finally reach Glencoul; it was a hard-fought destination.

It was now Day 13 and unlucky for some; we needed to negotiate getting around the sea lochs of Loch Glencoul and Loch Glendhu. This gave us a dog-leg of walking west, then shifting east to reach Glendhu bothy, then heading west again before finally heading north. I had to keep reminding myself that this is factored into the distance, and I was still getting closer to that fabled lighthouse.

Loch Glencoul (Robin Wallace)

With plenty food in our packs, a deviation to Kylestrome wasn't needed and we took the path north to Achfary and Loch Stack. We cheated slightly by doing a short section of road walking to Lochstack Lodge to avoid the pathless section under Arkle. Fatigue was setting in from another big day and the lack of places to pitch wasn't helping, walking further than we had intended.

Pitch under Arkle (Robin Wallace)

We eventually stumbled upon a nice pitch by Loch Airigh a' Bhàird under the impressive Arkle.

Day 14 marked our penultimate day on the Cape Wrath Trail, and feeling positive, we set off north to Rhiconich. The path petered out after around two kilometres leaving us with a boggy section and a substantial river crossing (Garbh Allt) before reaching the desolate Rhiconich. Iain stripped down to his scants for the river crossing. I already had wet feet, so I nimbly crossed over at the mouth of the river. Upon reaching Rhiconich, I was left somewhat disappointed to find no hot food was available. Fortunately, we spotted the Old School Inn a few kilometres along the B801. Burger and chips were eagerly ordered to furnish the famished bellies!

Fuelled and ready to roll we continued on towards Blairmore where we turned off towards Sandwood Bay. I met some day trippers coming back and Iain took a detour to look above the famous Am Buachaille sea stack. I reached the dunes and spotted two or three tents dotted around, but I managed to get the beach to myself. I took a moment to reflect on the last two weeks; it had been an amazing and sometimes testing journey. Yet here I was; hard to believe I could now see the lighthouse 10 kilometres away as the crow flies. Sitting on the rocks above taking in the vista, I spotted a solo figure cutting across the bay; the figure got closer and I spied the big pack and trekking poles and realised it was Iain.

During the planning stages, Iain and I came to a mutual agreement that as experienced hill walkers we would not need to be attached at the hip. So, if either of us wanted to push on or bag a hill enroute then we could. This was pivotal to the success of our trip. Whilst we hiked many miles together, we would often have stages where one of us would be well ahead. Despite this, we always naturally lunched and finished the days together. This approach allowed us to have company and support, as well as that much needed time alone.

It was now the final day; it was warm and sunny as we set off one last time. On the previous day I had experienced a pain in my left shin that increasingly got worse. I was worried a shin splint was beginning to set in. I figured it was most likely down to all the road walking on the approach to Sandwood Bay, but a good night's sleep and some Ibuprofen seemed to have done the trick; phew!

Sandwood Bay (Robin Wallace)

We had phoned ahead to check with the MOD that the firing range was not going to be in operation. They gave us the green light and upon reaching the danger zone, we were pleased to see the red flags were down.

The pathless section across Cape Wrath wasn't nearly as bad as I had expected and after a lunch stop, it didn't take us long to reach the vehicle track and ultimately the lighthouse. I felt completely dumbfounded to be standing in front of that lighthouse. Admittedly part of me also felt subdued to have reached the conclusion of such a fantastic experience. Years of Cape Wrath Trail wanderlust and here I was at the end.

I caught up with Iain at the Ozone Café; we congratulated each other and ordered a bacon butty and a brew. Signing the guest book, the lady informed us we were the first hikers to reach the lighthouse in 2021, a nice little memento.

I sauntered behind the lighthouse buildings and pointed the phone towards the Isle of Lewis to get enough signal to phone Nicola and let her know the good news.

We marked the end of the trip with a night at Kearvaig Bay, finishing off the evening by soothing my worn-out feet with a paddle in the water. The last day presented the final walk of the trip to catch the boat across the Kyle of Durness where Iain's parents awaited to give us a lift back to Ullapool. As a thank you, we bought Iain's Dad a bottle of malt whisky. His help made the logistics so much easier. As tempting as it was to celebrate with a few libations, I decided to head home to finally see Nicola.

The End – Cape Wrath (Robin Wallace)

An amazing experience that will live long in the memory.

Robin has produced a series of vlogs on his YouTube channel following Iain and his Cape Wrath Trail adventure. The videos offer the chance to see exactly what the trail involves, including scenery, hints, tips and some added humour along the way.

Episode 1: Backpacks and Blisters
Episode 2: A Rough Bounds Birthday
Episode 3: Wilderness and Waterfalls
Episode 4: Bogs, Tears and Bothies
Episode 5: The Halfway Milestone and Beyond
Episode 6: From River to Mountain
Episode 7: Operation Lighthouse

The vlogs can be found at:

https://youtube.com/playlist?list=PLeBzJ8jmmEWfHkwvOmB6jk8pEeh2txb

—TMs—

Ice-screw

Glinting, shattered javelins spin
air-bound; loosed from the crater,
fall and melt.

Teeth bite and gnaw and the
inverse Archimedes-screw
digs deeper and deeper, setting
up pressure-waves which
could move continents, create
mountains; and the core,
extruded through the scoured sheath:
frozen, brittle, a breaking incidental.

Fixed on metamorphosed vapour,
here life hangs on
both alloy and analogy;
and the teaching today is: 'believe
this can be trusted';
a myth, so strong, from which
the whole world should be
suspended.

Stuart B. Campbell

Image: Heather Morning

282 Munros in a Day – Carnethy Hill Running Club

Mark Hartree et al

Inspiration and planning

Our inspiration for this challenge came when Carnethy member Iain Whiteside spotted that the 214 Wainwrights were summited in one day. Covid had been dismal for everyone, and we wanted a challenge that would bring club members together while recognising the ongoing restrictions. Other groups had tried to climb the Munros in a day, but the outcome of those attempts was unknown at the time; our focus was to plan how our club could achieve this and how to make it fun and open to all members.

The 'Munros in a Day' became a logistical challenge requiring planning, commitment, teamwork, reasonable weather and a dose of luck if we were to succeed. Some impressive spreadsheet wizardry broke the problem down into short, medium, long and extra-long hill days. This approach used the excellent resource provided by Steve Fallon's website (Steve is a Carnethy member with 16 Munro Rounds under his feet). His site groups the hills into day trips with useful information including run-times; it did turn out to be reasonably accurate although Steve is a strong runner making his time estimates quite sporty.

Club members selected their preferred groups of hills until the spreadsheet had names allocated to all 282 Munros and back-up people allocated. The Carnethy Ladies grouped together and were generally much better organised for the day than their male counterparts under the guidance of Nicki Innes who co-ordinated the master plan with efficiency and friendly persuasion. Various members opted to go solo, or to combine hill groups into larger days. There were several overlaps with some hills summited multiple times in different combinations; some members treated the day as a short day out with family and friends; others treated their day as a hill running race training session; while others used them to recce bigger routes or develop new rounds.

An online planning sheet allowed people to form groups and to be aware of who would be on the hills closest to them. This ensured a minimum level of back-up in case of an incident or if a hill was not summited. Our plan had about ten floaters ready to leap into action to fill gaps if needed. The sheet also allowed transport and accommodation to be co-ordinated and WhatsApp groups greatly enhanced communications. Previous attempts were at a clear disadvantage considering the improvements in communications, equipment, food, travel and navigation that are now available.

The safety of participants was important with guidance for a safe day sent to everyone on the basis that if Storm Apocalypse hit Scotland on the day a commonsense approach would prevail and we would go anyway and see what happened. Everyone was to decide if they were happy to proceed in the conditions that they experienced on the day. No heroics; if necessary, adjust the start time or route. Safety instructions instructed members to treat this as a long hill race carrying full body cover, warm top, food, water, map, compass, whistle, phone, head-torch, midge repellent, mini first aid kit and sun cream. As each summit was completed, a photo with Carnethy clothing was taken and sent in a message to Control proving that that the hill had been summited, and at the end of the day, report in that they were safely off the hill. On 14th August 2021, 53 days after the idea was suggested, we started.

The Day

The weather was mixed with heavy rain in the north-west but better further south. Some on the bigger remoter rounds were off at first light in pouring rain; others had a more relaxed start. One of the first Munros completed was Beinn Dearg (Atholl), summited at 07.55hrs by 79 years young previous President Keith Burns. Soon after, An Coileachan fell at 08.39hrs to the current club President and his dog Barra who saw nothing all day but clag and rain on their nine hills in the Fannaichs. The youngest Carnethy member to summit was Rowan Rawlik who, at the tender age of 3.5, ticked her fifth Munro – Carn Liath (Glen Tilt), accompanied by her Mum, Jasmin Paris, Dad Konrad and dog Moss.

Some big days were put in:

- Alex McVey, Iain Whiteside and Eoin Lennon on the 12-Munro Mullardoch Round, 57km, 4,400m in 12 hours
- Michelle Hetherington on the Monar Munros 50km, 4,300m, 14 hours 20 minutes
- Alan Renville on the Beinn Dearg Munros (Inverlael) 44km, 2,700m, 7.5 hours. Described as 'a character-building day out, rain, thick cloud, wind and a swamp underfoot'.
- Rachel and Will Norman, 35km, 2,700m, 8.5 hours
- Sasha Chepelin and Ali Masson managed 65km, 5,100m in 12.5 hours on a new South-of-Glen Shiel Round which was 'longer than I signed-up for, a pretty spectacular day out though'. It was 14km just to get to their first Munro!
- Kudos though may have to go to Declan Valters who committed solo to the remotest of Munros in Knoydart then adding in the Munros south of Loch Cuaich to make a huge round of well over 55km with 5,000m of ascent on the roughest terrain in Britain.

'The jeopardy' that had us on the edge of our seats like the finale of *Line of*

Duty, was the race by Jamie Paterson and his pal on the Skye Ridge to get Sgùrr nan Gillean done before midnight, having not left Cluanie for Skye until after 08.30hrs! This team was one of the youngest in the club and poor Jamie then had to run/walk from Slighachan back to Glen Brittle as the hotel was shut (well it was 2 o'clock in the morning).

Craig Addison on Sgorr Dearg (Carnethy HRC)

'The Jeopardy' – by Controller Ken Fordyce

This day was without doubt the most thrilling hill-related event in my life and I barely left my kitchen table in 17 hours. My phone was pinging non-stop. It was tremendous watching the hills get knocked off, although it was very difficult to keep up with the reports in the early- to mid-afternoon. A few people went off grid for a while but thankfully re-emerged to confirm another set of hills climbed. It was very hard to work out if it was going to be possible or not; I personally couldn't see how the Cuillin ridge guys were going to get that done, but they assured me they would, and they did, comfortably!

I knew Declan had a lot on his plate (and only found out afterwards that he had set off later than planned because of the awful weather overnight). At 19:35hrs he messaged to say he had done Sgùrr na Ciche and wrote 'four more, next couple are closer and along a ridge, but looking like a late finish'.

The real worry, in addition to whether the Skye boys finished was if Declan would have time to do Gairich. I updated the Twitter feed to say Declan had four more to go and at 20:16hrs John Busby tweeted back 'is anyone close enough to get up Gairich? Not that I don't have faith in Mr Valters'. This intervention would prove key to achieving the final hill. There followed some back-and-forth between John, myself, and Nicki Innes. Mick James established what was required to get to Gairich (40 minutes by car, five miles and 700 metres of ascent). At around 21.15hrs the decision was made; it was now or never, and at 21:23hrs, Mick and Jonathan Marks (fresh from seven Munros earlier in the day) were ready to set off. We wouldn't hear from them again until 23:48hrs.

Declan Valters reached Garbh Cioch Mhòr at 20:19hrs and then Sgùrr nan Coireachan at 21:37hrs but the last two were still far away. Between 22.00hrs and 23.00hrs news came through that the incredible Cuillin ridge guys had finished.

All attention now turned to two hills: Sgùrr Mòr and Gairich and then silence descended. The pinging on my phone stopped. Silence, it was a weird, tense silence. I was thinking of Declan out on the hill; was it silent or was there a raging wind? The clock ticked by; my heart was racing (I'm sure I wasn't alone). At 23.35hrs I headed to bed, accepting we wouldn't know the outcome until the early hours when they were back with a signal. Just as I settled down for the night. PING!! Declan 'Sgùrr Mòr. 23.46hrs' and then, just 2 minutes later, PING!! A photo of Jonathan celebrating on Gairich. And then, Jim Hardie, 'so .... we did it?'. Yes, we had!

The Stories

Wyvis Galore: The Munroist, the Virgin, and the Hidden Treasure – Cat Meighan and Dawn Waitt

Cat and Dawn had never met before this Munro Challenge. There is nothing better for women than to have six hours to drive, walk and chat, especially when you have each other's whole lives to discover! Cat, we discovered, was a Munro virgin whilst Dawn was a recent Munro veteran having completed them all in June of this year. We set off two hours after the planned time, to try and minimise the Met Office's morning forecast of thunder and lightning, and we were delighted to discover it wasn't in fact raining. Cat announced that her second cousin's ashes were released near the summit of Ben Wyvis 22 years earlier and in his memory, there was a secret stash of malt whisky somewhere on the mountain. 'OMG!', not only were we part of the Carnethy Munro Challenge, but we had stumbled upon a treasure hunt. By now the waterproofs were on and we were walking in mist. A call was made to Cat's mother for clues on the whereabouts of the hidden treasure. We can't share what we were told; suffice to say we went up plenty of wrong trails looking for the elusive treasure but failed. We summited Ben Wyvis, the 89th Carnethy Munro of the 282 to climb. On our descent, passing An Cabar, we agreed to have another go at finding the treasure; we re-read the text of instructions looking for cryptic meaning to help find the 'needle in the haystack'. We had zero visibility

in the rain and wind and wandered off the path a few times. Just as we were about to give up a few clues seemed to match up and unbelievably we stumbled upon the treasure; it was utterly thrilling, emotional and, wait for it, worth every moment, for there, hidden under rocks, was a crystal glass to pour a 'Cardhu Gold Reserve single malt whisky' into. We had never tasted a dram so delicious, and we toasted my second cousin. The rest of our descent was surprisingly free and easy and even the midges in the lower section could not dampen our 'spirits'.

Kirsty Campbell on her first Munros after joining Carnethy on Carn a' Gheoidh (Carnethy HRC)

Are You Geocaching? The Bizarre Tale of a Run for Glory up Gairich – Mick James

We'd got back to Cluanie from our original Munro runs of 26km, 2,500m of ascent around 5.30pm and had spent the time until 9pm firing up the hot tub, having a nice pasta feed and seeing off a few beers. We'd been musing at the likelihood of the Skye boys completing in the light and wondering when the Sasha would get off the South Shiel ridge. Both teams had been casual that morning when they left Cluanie, the Skye team not leaving until 8.30am for the drive to Glenbrittle; after all, how hard could the Cuillin Ridge really be on a damp and foggy day? Sasha's team left after a porridge fest with youth and enthusiasm gloriously triumphing after what turned out to be a 65km run. But, back to Gairich. Blissfully ignorant, we were having a fine time waiting and watching the Munro map change colour as more and more ascents were reported. In steps Nikki Innes – 'Mick it looks like we have a problem, can you get up Gairich, Declan's running a bit late?' What can you do though? Not much time to think, unfortunately, we actually had a sober driver, so I put on my last remaining dry clothes, re-packed my sack, found a map and a fully working torch so we were set to go. The drive round to the dam was a blur, dodging deer all down the single-track road. We arrived at 10.10pm, leapt out and started up. Fair to say it was a dark boggy stumble for most of the way with the occasional submersion, but the track is good, and we were making progress by using a single headtorch. The rocky top section was a welcome relief as we knew we were in touching distance and then we were on the plateau and there was a tent with a light on! Too tired to process this we headed for the cairn and took a photo at 23.48hrs, the last of the Munros in the bag. No time to celebrate though as we realised it was very cold and we were shivering in our wet t-shirts. We piled on all the clothes we had and started to realise how poorly we'd planned this. We'd genuinely not thought this through; if Declan wasn't there we would have to wait; after all, you can't leave your mates out on the hills. We'd no bothy bag and were not really equipped for sitting around for hours. Unsure of the etiquette for approaching a stranger's tent, at midnight, on the summit of a Munro, when you are soaking wet, I just unzipped it and crawled in. Our two new best friends were actually happy to see us! Buoyed up by the empty Prosecco bottle at the far end of the tent and a genuine sense of incredulity the young lovers asked us 'are you geocaching?' I didn't really know how to reply. Inside the tent, and now about 10 degrees warmer, we set about trying to explain why we were there and what our plans were. We'd had the phones off for the ascent, trying to save battery in case of a forced descent by iPhone torch, but now the messages came flooding in. Declan had made his summit two minutes before us and confirmed that he was going to bivvy, and that meant we could get the hell out of there. Our new tent besties gave us some gels, in return for a story that no one will ever believe, and then it was back outside for an equally stumbly and occasionally submersed return to the dam. 3am and we were back at Cluanie for the remains of the pasta bake and a welcome bed.

Unexpected Items in the Bagging Area: Tales from Knoydart and Beyond – Declan Valters

It's usually a sign that things haven't gone to plan when you're writing 'DAY 2' in your journal of a 24-hour running challenge. I set off from Kinlochourn at 5:30am, intending to cover the Knoydart and Loch Cuaich

Munros, finishing back at my bike at Cuaich Dam.

This was already 'Plan C'. Plan A had been to walk in to Knoydart as far as possible on Friday afternoon, and bivvy at Barrisdale Bothy saving at least 10km, maybe even 15km if the weather was nice enough to bivvy near the summit of Ladhar Bheinn. The weather in the north-west on Friday afternoon and Saturday night had been awful and MWIS had forecast near-gale force winds on the summits. I decided not to risk it and wait until morning to do the walk in instead.

Progress to Barrisdale was slow. The rivers and burns were in spate from the previous night's rain, and the start of the path was chest-high wet bracken, soaking me through within about 10 minutes of starting. At Barrisdale Bay, I was so wet I figured there was nothing to lose by wading across the river (fortunately at low tide), which saved a couple of kilometres trekking upstream to the footbridge at the bothy.

I reached Ladhar Bheinn around 10am; it was clagged in on the summit but it seemed like I was making reasonable progress. Fate duly tempted, the route to Luinne Bheinn quickly became pathless, and navigation was by compass and dead reckoning for a while until finding the path up to the summit, and quite a bit of time was lost here. At Meall Buidhe the clag lifted for a while and there was a fantastic view across the Sound of Sleat, with the Cuillin Ridge visible in the distance.

I started feeling a bit rough heading down Meall Buidhe around 3pm. My knees were really feeling the rocky descent, and the line I picked turned out to be awkward and

Nikki Innes on Ciste Dubh (Carnethy HRC)

required a bit of scrambling to get down to the main path. I dropped back down to sea level, and jogged along to the ruins at Carnoch. I wasn't feeling great there; I'd started feeling a bit nauseous on the descent for some reason. I stopped on the bridge not far from Sourlies Bothy, seriously considering it as a potential bail-out option. I was looking at the climb up Sgùrr na Cìche and the distance left to go. The climb up to Sgùrr na Cìche was boggy and pathless, I'd lost all the height I'd gained from earlier and my final line up to the top, now clagged in again, required yet more unexpected scrambling to reach it. Finally, back in contact with Carnethy HQ on Sgùrr na Cìche, it was early evening. I'd slowed down a lot and was exhausted from the long climb up to the summit.

I was really feeling the day's mileage and ascent, and my feet/legs/knees were knackered and struggling with anything other than flat ground (which there wasn't much of up there). I think I had just done the third to last Munro, Sgùrr nan Coireachan, and was about to switch off my phone to save battery until the next summit when a message came through 'is anyone close enough to get up Gairich? Not that I don't have faith in Mr Valters'. Clearly John had been following the map and the drama and realised I was pushing it to be reaching Gairich anywhere this side of midnight.

Brief panic ensued. Later in the day the messages on the main WhatsApp group had transitioned from summit pictures, to reports of folk being back at base and enjoying beer, pizza, and even hot tubs, and now to a tense scramble to get someone up Gairich. It was clagged in again and starting to get dark and I was still on the hill! I got the map out to reassess. Gairich seemed further away than ever. It might as well have been Mount Keen in Aberdeenshire. I was now not just worried about not reaching Gairich in time and being the only Carnethy not to complete their assigned Munros, but also facing a benightment on the hill.

Back at Carnethy HQ a rescue plan had swung into action. Mick James and Jonathon Marks were heading off to bag Gairich and save the day. I just had to make it to Sgùrr Mòr before midnight and disaster would be averted. Buoyed on, albeit very slowly now, by lots of supportive messages from the WhatsApp group, I headed off in the dark towards Sgùrr Mòr.

Sgùrr Mòr is preceded by the deceptively named Sgùrr Beag (little peak), which somehow seems a bigger hill, despite its name. I was following the vague path under torchlight but really, I'd no idea what the terrain looked like in front for more than a few meters; the hills were shrouded in thick fog.

The last climb seemed to keep going forever; the path twists and winds its way up to the rocky summit of Sgùrr Mòr. There is not much there apart from a small cairn. I double and triple checked I was on the actual summit. I was. I texted Ken 'Sgùrr Mòr, 23:46', 14 minutes to spare. A few minutes later a photo came through of Mick and Jonathon at the summit of Gairich.

We'd done it.

Epilogue: I couldn't face moving on any further past Sgùrr Mòr. My feet were badly blistered from being continuously wet through for the last 17 hours. I told HQ I was bivvying there for the night and would walk out in the morning when it gets light. I put on all my remaining layers and crawled into the bothy shelter/bivvy bag. I think I managed a few hours' sleep, but as soon as it started to get light, I decided not to hang around shivering and hobbled off the hill. I headed out down Glen Kingie and back to Cuaich Dam. Gairich loomed, almost mockingly, high above Loch Cuaich. My bike was there waiting for me. At around 11:30am I got back to my tent at Kinlochourn, 30 hours after I'd set off the previous morning. But all-in-all, a grand day out on the hills.

Ruth Paterson and family on Beinn Eighe
(Carnethy HRC)

Maybe we weren't the first!

In 1988 over 2,000 people tried this in the 'Boots Across Scotland' challenge; they failed to summit two Munros. Water Aid has tried several times and in 2007 came close.

After the news broke on our completion, we were contacted by members of the Edinburgh University Mountaineering Club with a claim that they did the Munros in a day between the 16/17th June 1979. Their approach seemed to be slightly different from ours grouping the hills into smaller groups and completing them from mid-day to mid-day over a 24 hour period. There were 279 Munros then and they completed with 75 people. With no lightweight kit, communications limited to payphones and letters, and hill-walking the hills, this is an outstanding achievement. The passage of time leaves limited diary entries as evidence and an entry in the Edinburgh Evening News. Carnethy congratulates this achievement.

Our time to complete 282 Munros was 16 hours 48 minutes from the first summit to the last.

Mark Hartree is President of Carnethy HRC.

LOCHS and LOCHANS

Above – Rùm from Loch an Fhir-bhallaich. One morning in June 2005 I had been walking in Coire Làgan and captured this view of Rùm and thought one day I will visit. I have yet to go. *Bill Wheeler*

Below – Reflections in Loch Etive. *The David Batty collection*

Coast to Coast

Andrew Fraser

M y first coast to coast walk was in July 1979 when a friend and I walked from Cape Wrath to the Cromarty Firth. A year later TGO magazine came up with their Challenge and I was attracted to their idea for a longer expedition. However, it is normally held in May so my job as a teacher ruled me out of taking part, but it did not prevent me from attempting the journey at some other time. So it was in July 1985 that I planned to walk from Inverie to Inverbervie.

TGO hold their challenge in May partly because it is often a good month weatherwise, plus it is before the midges have multiplied. July's weather can be more problematic and that year was one of the wettest, as Craig Caldwell testified when describing his continuous Munro and Corbett round. On our much more modest two-week trip it rained at some point every day but one, though we did have four nearly dry days to compensate for a slightly larger number of very wet ones.

One of the attractions of the TGO Challenge is that participants can plan their own route within minor constraints. I really enjoy the planning process so many happy hours were spent in preparation. Some people like to take reading material when they go to the loo but I preferred poring over OS maps. Thus a route was worked out, avoiding public roads as much as possible and creating opportunities to bag hills along the way even though we would have heavy packs.

The route selected, the logistics worked out, I had no difficulty in recruiting friend Ranald to accompany me. For the first few days his pal Robin Campbell (no, a different one!) came with us. We all met up at Fort William station to catch the Mallaig train and then Bruce Watt's boat to Inverie, all in teeming rain. Watt's usual boat was out of commission and its smaller replacement was already pretty full, but the ferryman listened to our pleading to be allowed on board. An hour later we reached the Inverie pier, and our great 200-mile adventure could begin.

Mercifully the rain now ceased so it was not too unpleasant plodding up the path to the Màm Meadail even though the cloud base was about 500 feet. At the pass the rain returned and the zigzags beyond were more like a stream. When our destination of Sourlies bothy came into view I was dismayed to see so many tents outside - two school D of E expeditions; the kids were in the tents, their leaders in the bothy, but there was just enough room for us to squeeze in.

136

Sourlies (Andrew Fraser)

Next day began encouragingly; no rain, even a blink of sunshine, but it did not last. The plan was a high-level traverse from Sgùrr na Ciche to An Eag before descending a stalkers' path into Glen Kingie to finish at Kinbreack bothy. It was duly done, though it was disappointing that I had to describe from memory the magnificent views from Sgùrr na Ciche to the other two whose first visit this was.

Kinbreack is a favourite of mine but the same cannot be said of Glen Kingie. It is good greenshank country but that tells you it is often very boggy. The original plan was to traverse Gairich but the other two were still recovering from the previous day's exertions. Once we reached the forestry plantations a track provided better walking and thereafter, we followed a mix of track and paths and left OS Sheet 33 behind. Our finish was near where a bridge crosses the narrow part of Loch Garry. Friends of Robin had a house there which we had permission to use for a night. Home comforts, even a bottle of Bell's left for us, and we could watch highlights of Becker's first Wimbledon title win on TV. Why did it just not feel right?

Day 4 would take us to the Great Glen along forest tracks south of Loch Garry, once more in steady rain. At Invergarry the other two caught the bus to Fort William, Robin to catch his train and Ranald to replace his boots which had fallen apart soon after leaving Kinbreack. Walking beside the busy A82 was not pleasant so I was glad to reach the canal towpath at the south end of Loch Oich for the last lap to the Youth Hostel where Ranald later joined me.

Forest tracks zigzagging up the very steep east flank of the Great Glen gave us an easy start until we had to fight our way through trees and then steep grass to the head of Coire an t-Sìdhein where the first heavy shower of the day caught us up. Then steeply down to Glen Turret and Glen Roy and a good sighting of the Parallel Roads. The fine path heading south-east out of Glen Roy at Annat was in sharp contrast to the very rough going up to the bealach north-east of Beinn Teallach. The Beinn gave us a rare summit view and a final chance to see the Western Ocean in the shape of Loch Eil. That night we camped on a nice haugh between where there are now two plantations.

We woke next morning to the pitter-patter of rain on the flysheet. The forecast said it would rain all day and turned out to be depressingly correct. At Roughburn we were faced with four unavoidable miles along the A86 before we could enjoy relative peace at Luiblea. Morale was low as we sheltered from the rain in a clump of trees. Ranald later admitted he was willing me to call the walk off, but I can honestly say it never occurred to me to give up.

The low moment passed and soon after, Ranald was happy to climb Creag Pitridh, his 200th Munro. Over the next pass a poor path took us down to the Allt Cam which we feared would be much swollen and hard to cross but we found a place to boulder-hop across. We camped near the bridge where the Culra Burn flows into Loch Pattack and were lulled to sleep by the sound of snipe drumming.

Strong winds and rain put paid to our plan to traverse the Fara ridge to Dalwhinnie so it was over to Ben Alder Lodge and out on the estate track. A minibus carrying a group we'd met the day before caught us up and offered us a lift. We explained what we were doing and resisted the temptation but were grateful for them to take our packs to the locked gate. After a pint at the grim Grampian Hotel in Dalwhinnie we walked along the old A9 to Cuaich where my wife picked us up. We 'd arranged to meet our wives and stay a night in Newtonmore where we could restock our food, enjoy some clean clothes and swap over maps.

Reaching the A9 seemed like a big milestone so when we were driven back to Cuaich and shouldered our horribly heavy packs we really felt up for the second half of our journey. The hydro track to Loch Cuaich got us into our stride and there was a good path up the steep headwall of the corrie beyond. The real drama of the day came after crossing the plateau to Sgòr Dearg which gave an eagle's eye view of Gaick Lodge and a wall of screes behind it. The scene with its braided river reminded me of Iceland except with vegetation. So far it had been dry but soon after we fell victim to what forecasters like to describe as 'showers will merge to give longer spells of rain'. It became so heavy we decided in the glen leading to the Minigaig to call it a day early and get our tent up.

The following day was the driest of the trip thus far. I took an early detour to climb the Corbett Carn Dearg Mòr from which I got a last sighting of Ben Tee

Gaick Lodge (Andrew Fraser)

which we had first seen in upper Glen Kingie in what seemed like ages ago. We waded the Feshie and joined the route through the lovely upper glen. The long-considered road through to Deeside would be handy but it would ruin this beautiful glen. Besides, An Sgarsoch would then become just another Munro instead of the challenge it now presents the would-be Completer. At the watershed we left the old Inverness-shire for the first time and when the rain began opposite Geldie Lodge we decided to camp at the next favourable spot. The rain passed overnight to give us our first dry day for the walk to Braemar. It would be a day when we met more walkers than any other, plus tourists at Linn of Dee. We kept to the quieter north side of the river until Victoria Bridge after which there was no real alternative but the public road. The Youth Hostel was surprisingly quiet but gave us a chance to clean up and eat before paying our respects to the Fife Arms.

The three miles east along the A93 to Invercauld Bridge were not pleasant - busy and little verge for avoiding traffic. Across the bridge was a notice announcing, 'Private Estate: No Entry'. The Royals were not yet on holiday so we ignored it. We did meet an army patrol but they paid little heed to us. There is a maze of tracks in Ballochbuie Forest but we eventually found the one to take us up to Gelder Shiel, encountering an adder on the way. The bothy provided shelter from the newly arrived rain and a chance for lunch and a brew. We crossed some rough, boggy ground to reach Inchnabobart and finally waded the Muick before the woods above the Linn. We were still

Upper Glen Feshie (Andrew Fraser)

in bare feet when we met a very large, bad-tempered adder which hissed menacingly at us. A quick detour across the road and so to our intended camp site.

Next day would see us on our last Munro summit, Mount Keen. I'd climbed it from this side before so knew that we were in for some peat hag country first. The summit was clear, and we could see the North Sea, still two days away. In light showers we continued in a broadly south-easterly direction towards the Water of Tarff, passing the ruined houses of an old settlement at Ardsallary. It reminded me of descriptions in Lewis Grassic Gibbon's *Sunset Song* partly because of the bird sounds; peewits, sandpipers, oystercatchers and, best of all, curlews. Eventually we found a discreet camping spot out of sight of houses in Glen Esk.

Our penultimate day should have seen us on Mount Battock but the bad weather was back. So it had to be down Glen Esk until we could ascend to Sturdy Hill where the cloud and rain obliged us to pay close heed to navigating towards Fettercairn. There were dreadful glutinous peat hags on Herd Hill and the ground below was confusing, but we made it, passing the distillery on the way in. Four and a half miles of road bashing brought us to Laurencekirk where we had difficulty finding lodgings for the night. A clean up and a meal restored morale and we rounded things off by sampling Old Fettercairn.

More than once on our trip we were asked what charity we were doing the walk for. None was the answer before explaining that having been pestered too often by folk looking for sponsorship we had decided against risking losing friends. So, sorry good causes, but we will remember you in other ways.

Our final day might have seen us climb the prominent Garvock Hill but a heavy shower at just the wrong moment put us off. Thereafter it was a matter of picking a route along minor roads to reach Inverbervie. Through the village we went and down to the shingle beach to dip our toes in the North Sea. The trip was deemed a great success, despite the weather, and our thoughts had turned to 'what next?' It was to be the Tour du Mont Blanc, but this time our wives insisted on coming too!

Inverbervie (Andrew Fraser)

The One that Got Away: Knight's Peak – Mark Gibson

Two weeks after completing the Munro Tops, Knight's Peak was knocked off the list. A group of us had accessed it via Coire a' Bhàsteir using number 4/5 gully. Number 4/5 gully was 'sporting' in a bloody-minded kind of way. In fact it was a chuffin' nightmare, wet, greasy, steep and packed with every conceivable size of sharp loose rock just waiting to be sent crashing down the defile. We forked right where the gully splits and ascended a few meters before climbing out onto the rib between the two gullies. Crossing the top of Number 4 gully via a series of narrow ledges brought us into the notch below the summit. Well, at least we did it whilst it still was a Munro Top............

A Wee May Stravaig

Jim McKenna

Have you ever wondered how an osprey chick hatched in Strathspey is able fly solo to West Africa? Haldane tells us in *The Drove Roads of Scotland* that it was common practice for Scottish drovers to release their dogs from as far away as London to find their own way home where they were needed for other tasks. Salmon travel thousands of miles to return to the burns where they had spawned. If birds, animals and even fish can easily navigate then why can't humans? Well, humans were once more able, for it is only a few millennia since we were all hunter-gatherers. There are still nomadic peoples wandering through the deserts and jungles who know so much about their environment that it puts us to shame. Consider the rite of passage of young Australian Aborigine males aged between ten and 16 who, after tuition from the Elders, set off solo on a walkabout which may last six months and may cover in excess of a thousand miles. The only thing that they take with them is a loincloth. However, it is not impossible that such people might inherit our planet! My own rite of passage with the outdoors took place over 65 years ago and was a far gentler affair, but it was done in complete ignorance. This article is about a jaunt I took in May 2002, but this time armed with half a century's experience of mountain travel, often solo, in some of the wild parts of the world.

I first started going to the hills in the fifties as a young teenager, and it was three years before I made contact with, and eventually joined, a climbing club at the advanced age of fifteen. Looking back, those three years were filled with the rich mixture of adventure and discovery. It may seem inconceivable now, but during that time I owned only one map and that was a five miles to the inch Esso road map which covered the southern half of Scotland with Crianlarich at its most northerly extreme.

I did not own a compass, but armed with this map, sometimes

The Esso road map

142

alone and sometimes with school friends, I climbed many of Scotland's significant hills, most of which were not even on my map. The usual mode of transport was hitching, which had a delicious uncertainty about it, and as my *modus operandi* was often to go wherever the vehicle was heading, I consequently reached many unusual places where I climbed whatever hills presented themselves. To this day I am not certain which glens I visited and which hills I climbed, but it was not important to me as I have never been much of a record keeper. However, what is certain is that it has left me with an abiding love for uncertainty.

One legacy that you develop from a lifetime of roaming over the Scottish hills is that you create a mental map of most of the country and consequently much of the mystery of what lies over the hill is lost. However, even in 2002 there were still some areas that were unfamiliar to me. One such area was the vast tract of land between the Garve to Ullapool road and Strath Oykel, and when one of my daughters moved to lower Glen Glass, a wee glen running from the eastern slopes of Ben Wyvis to Evanton on the Cromarty Firth, I realised that she backed onto this area. I then avoided looking at any maps of the hinterland as I nursed a desire to save this area as a suitable place for an experiment - I wanted to climb a hill I didn't know the name of, walk through an unknown glen and sit beside a loch that I did not know existed, and by using only minimal equipment, I would attempt to recreate the mystery and adventure of my early hill exploits. The final impetus came in 2002 as a direct result of staying in grossly overcrowded Alpine huts at the height of the ski-touring season, which triggered a desire for the wild and lonely places of my native land.

In late May 2002 I set out from lower Glen Glass to reach the west coast somewhere, and to return by a different route using minimal equipment. I had no map or compass, or watch, or money or credit cards, or mobile phone, or torch, or tent. In fact, it is easier to list the items I did take, namely a sleeping bag, an open-fronted flysheet, a bit of plastic as a groundsheet, a cigarette lighter, a dixie and spoon. The food I carried consisted of four simple components, being porridge oats, dried fruit, salt, and as a luxury to compensate for my advancing years, a dram. Using this variety of food, it is possible to produce sweet or salty meals which can be eaten hot or cold. This food and equipment fitted easily into a large daysack Finally, I took two trekking sticks which doubled up as tent poles for the flysheet.

It was a beautiful spring morning when I handed over my car keys, watch and money to my daughter and waved goodbye to her and three grandchildren. As I did so, a cuckoo called and I thought that it was a suitable herald for such a daft exploit. I had been up the Glen Glass road before, so the first five miles brought no surprises; however the public road finishes at a bridge with impressive gates. Once through these I was ill-prepared for the pack of barking dogs that surrounded me and was less than pleased when a large dog seized my arm. Fortunately, the pack's owner was quickly on the scene and order was restored, apologies proffered and words spoken, and I resolved to always have a trekking pole in my hand when passing through such habitations.

Cadha Dearg (Norman McNab)

I had only walked about another mile when a passing Land Rover stopped and the driver asked if wanted a lift. As my philosophy was 'to go with the flow' and he was going in my direction, I had no hesitation in climbing on board. The driver was not a keeper but a former civil servant who had taken early retirement and had then spent five years repairing paths in Wester Ross before embarking on his latest vocation writing environmental impact reports specialising in the effects of wind farms on birdlife. We bumped along the road beside Loch Glass, then just before Wyvis Lodge we turned on to a rough track and bumped another two or three miles to reach a fine waterfall. Together we walked another three miles to check out with binoculars an eyrie located just below the top of a craggy hill. As there were signs of rebuilding he had to check it out more closely and our ways parted, with me thinking that there were worse ways to earn a crust.

At last, I was alone in wild country and using the sun as a rough compass I pushed west, confirming my direction by frequent backward reference to Ben Wyvis, making a mental note of the conformation of its snow patches for use on my return journey. It was easier to decide on my route ahead if I went high so I strode out over hills which led on to other hills. I had absolutely no idea what the next hill might reveal - this is what I had come for!

On my way down to a glen which had a road running along it I stopped at a burn to light a fire and made some porridge. For a cooking fire there were three basic requirements – dead heather, dry bogwood and a water supply. As May had been a very dry month, I always lit the fire on the dried-out part of the stream bed so that I could not set fire to the ground below and all traces of my passage would be washed away with the first significant rainfall. I followed this road for a couple of miles and spotted a house that I now know to be Deanich Lodge, but a bit before it I took a much rougher track which was heading in the direction I wished to go. About three or four miles along this track I had just started to look for somewhere to camp when I noticed quite a bit of bogwood had been placed on the top of heather banks to dry. This was a sure sign that there would be a bothy nearby and, on turning a corner, I could see a couple of buildings about half a mile away. Loading myself with as much bogwood as I could carry, I staggered to the Glenbeg Bothies. I chose to stay in the older building as it had an open fire which gave me both heat and light as I had neither torch nor candle.

The next morning saw me crossing a shoulder of what I now know to be Seana Bhraigh when a sudden vista revealed a distant Suilven and the Summer Isles. This confirmed that I was heading in too much of a northerly direction. I was then seduced by a fine hill track which overcorrected too much to the south and eventually led me to the sea at Inverlael. In those days

Seana Braigh (Norman McNab)

145

many cars still had analogue clocks and I was able to peer into a parked car window and discovered that it was only 2pm. I therefore decided that it might be possible to visit an old friend in a nursing home in Ullapool. I had only walked a few hundred yards when a van stopped to pick me up - obviously my practiced limp was working! The driver was building his own house on Loch Broom and we had a fascinating conversation about the problems of lifting the massive stones used in the construction of traditional buildings. As I had been a maintenance organiser for the Mountain Bothies Association for many years, I had been involved in the reconstruction and renovation of many remote buildings, so the conversation became quite technical and I learned quite a few tips. I have found over the years that people that work alone like this chap, and the man I had met the day before, are always keen to talk about their work and they all have a tale to tell.

I managed to visit my old friend in the nursing home but I'm sure that some of the staff thought that I was some sort of vagrant. It was good to leave the bustle of Ullapool but I made an error by heading too far north. Fortunately it was possible to correct this after a couple of miles, by taking a rough track then by faint footpaths into wild country. My final adjustment led me through a natural woodland above a loch which I now know was Loch Achall. The wood, carpeted with primroses and violets, was such an enchanting spot that I felt compelled to pitch the flysheet and soon had a wee fire lit. During the night I was suddenly awakened by the repeated loud screeches of a barn owl which must have been only five or six feet above my head for I could hear the intake of breath after each screech. The noise made sleep impossible so I eventually puffed up my lungs and I gave out a mighty screech. There were no more nocturnal disturbances!

Using the distinctive hill opposite Ullapool, Beinn Ghobhlach, as a rear reference point I headed east along a reasonable road, past a couple of lochs and some estate houses. The road deteriorated and to the east I could see the range of hills I would have to cross. I felt that was heading a bit too far north and at Loch an Daimh – identified by a beached boat bearing that name – I took a steep track to the southeast up the edge of a curious defile called Allt nan Caorach, emerging onto a high plateau with some recently built hill roads. Away in the distance to the south-east I spotted a loch with a building beside it. As I headed in that direction, gradually the magnificent north-facing aspect of Seana Bhraigh revealed itself. It turned out that the building was Loch Corriemor Bothy and as it looked that weather was about to change, I decided it might be wise to spend the night there. The bothy was well equipped with a good Jotul woodburning stove and a plentiful supply of dried bogwood. Reading the bothy book revealed that the source of that wood was about half a mile away and I made several trips to more than replace any wood that I might burn. It had started to rain lightly and I could relax in comfort, and with an abundant supply of hot water I was able to wash myself and my socks. On tidying up the bothy I discovered a teabag and a tin of sardines which were fortunately in oil. The fish I thoroughly fried in the oil until brown and crispy, and they tasted wonderful with a flavour of pine from the bogwood, and the tea was equally delightful. As the proverb says – Hunger is a fine sauce!

That evening, two men from Perth arrived, one of whom was hoping to complete his mainland Munros with Seana Bhraigh. They had an enormous amount of gear for just one night out, so I did them a favour by helping them reduce their food and drink supplies in a late-night session made all the more enjoyable by the rain beating on the roof and the fire roaring.

Jim McKenna on Baosbheinn (Norman McNab)

The others were still asleep when I crept out of the bothy next morning. The rain was off but the hills were shrouded in thick mist. I followed the Allt a' Choire Mhòir and made the mistake of heading directly up the corrie headwall into the mist, and found myself on exceedingly steep ground. It was a bit scary when I could hear dislodged stones bouncing a long way to the corrie floor below. I was forced into a former stream bed and made a few moves that I would have had difficulty reversing but kept telling myself that another fifty feet should see the angle easing. That fifty feet was followed by another, then another, before at last it suddenly eased. I was now in really thick mist and my navigation reliant on wind direction and terrain. With my eyes straining to pick up any clues I had a heart-stopping moment when a ptarmigan rose immediately beneath my foot in a flurry of feathers as I narrowly avoided standing on its clutch of eggs.

The one great thing about travelling in mist is that there is always a denouement when suddenly all is revealed, and so after a couple of miles I found myself looking down at a glen which I recognised as the lower part of Gleann Beag which I had passed through a couple of days before. However, instead of retracing my steps home, I took a more northerly route via Crom Loch which was a wonderful place to sit and enjoy the isolation. I then wandered through a wild and remote area that made Rannoch Moor look quite suburban. In the distance I could see Ben Wyvis with its signature snowfields, and eventually I reached the waterfall and Landrover track leading to Wyvis Lodge where I had my final fire and hot meal of the day. I thought about camping but a few midges and the temptation of a nice cup of coffee proved too much. I took my socks off, turned them inside out and put them on opposite feet and walked the remaining dozen or so miles to my daughter's home.

This stravaig was filled with wonderful flora and fauna plus interesting characters and topped off with a good dose of uncertainty. Did I recapture the spirit of my early travels in the hills? Well yes, but it's only a pity that I didn't recapture the body!

Footnote on Seana Bhraigh.

About five years later I was on my way to a Burns Supper weekend in Ullapool and had set off a couple of days early as I had a wee jaunt planned which involved the Glenbeg bothies. I parked my car at Loch Droma, intending to climb Beinn Dearg, but the weather was rather poor, so I took a lower-level route following a series of lochs including the attractive Loch Prille. This time I stayed in the wooden bothy – now burned down – as I had my Primus to cook on. The following morning was wild with high winds and frequent sleet showers. My plan was to get to Glen Achall by way of Seana Braigh and Glen Douchary. As I gained height the sleet turned to snow

Seana Braigh from Càrn Bàn (Norman McNab)

and the wind became really gusty as I struggled upwards with an arm raised to protect my face. Occasionally there was a brief interlude when the wind tore the clouds asunder letting me check my navigation. Once I caught a brief glimpse of Loch Luchd Choire below and was so impressed that I resolved to camp there in summer. From the summit of Seana Bhraigh I was propelled at high speed down into Glen Douchary. In the shelter of the trees at the bottom of the glen I lit the Primus and had a quick meal as it was starting to get dark. I was close to safety as the rough road in Glen Achall was nearby and it was only about ten miles of easy walking to Ullapool.

Once on the road I had only walked a couple of hundred yards when a Landrover stopped, and a keeper asked if I would like a lift for a couple of miles. Climbing aboard I noted a rifle. As usual he enquired where I had come from and was rather taken aback by my reply. The wild weather had brought the deer down off the hill and he had heard that a sika deer had been spotted, and he was looking for it. Three times he stopped and using a powerful rotating lamp mounted on the roof he scanned the woods. On the third occasion he spotted the sika among other deer grazing in a clearing but by this time we discovered the we had mutual friends and he absolutely insisted on driving me all the way to Ullapool…..'Ach', he said 'I'll get the bugger on the way back up the glen.'

—TMS—

The One that Got Away: Buidhe Bheinn – Stewart Logan

Until 1974 Buidhe Bheinn above Kinlochhourn was a Corbett but it was then replaced by Sgùrr a' Bhac Chaolais on the south side of Glen Shiel. I climbed the latter hill in 1983 during my Corbett round which I completed the following year. In 1997, the latest issue of Munro's Tables had both hills listed as Corbetts with a height of 885m although the drop between them is considerably less than 500 feet. In 2012, a survey by John Barnard and Graham Jackson indicated that Buidhe Bheinn topped Sgùrr a' Bhac Chaolais by 30 cm, and Sgùrr a' Bhac Chaolais was removed from the Tables.

By the SMC recommended rule, if I can use such a word, I can still claim to be a Corbetteer because I climbed the official Corbett in my round. I have travelled down Glen Shiel several times in the last nine years and thought that, for the sake of neatness, I should make an effort to climb Buidhe Bheinn. However, I have normally been going for other targets and continued on my way. I just cannot get the motivation to go over the demoted Corbett and out to the confirmed one all for the sake of 30cm.

LOCHS and LOCHANS

Above – Loch Maree with some of its 60+ islands. In the centre is Isle Maree, named after an early resident, St Maelrubha.

Below – Crag and lochan in the gneiss hills behind Gruinard Bay.

Jeremy Fenton

Part 4 – Round the World

The World Ribus Project –
Towards a Comprehensive P1000m Peak List

Rob Woodall

R eaching in behind the bulge, I'm relieved to locate a good handhold, and I move carefully across the ledge – the drop below me is a few hundred metres. This is Ball's Ledge, half a kilometre of thought-provoking narrowness crossing the east face of Monte Pelmo. Only an Irishman could have thought there might be a way up here! John Ball was an Irish politician, botanist, and early alpinist. He made the notable first ascent of Pelmo in 1857 – after, one imagines, a substantial amount of Irish whiskey, and much time spent studying the peak with a telescope. This was eight years before Whymper's landmark first ascent of the Matterhorn.

3,168m Monte Pelmo, in the Italian Dolomites, has a topographical prominence[1] of 1,191 metres. This makes it a Ribu – a peak with at least 1,000 metres drop on all sides. Ribu is the Indonesian word for thousand, a term coined by Dan Quinn and Andy Dean, when they started listing the Indonesian P1000s after a chance meeting in 2009[2]. Their list can be found at the excellent *gunungbagging.com* website.

Monte Pelmo, Dolomites (Rob Woodall)

151

How to extend the P1000m listing worldwide? High-prominence peaks are often quite isolated, and mapping in many parts of the world is rudimentary or unavailable. In practice, identifying a peak's key saddle – defined by the lowest contour line encircling it but containing no higher summit – is not straightforward.

The world's 50 most prominent peaks were first listed by David Metzler and Eberhard Jurgalski in 1999-2000; Jurgalski also listed the 100 most prominent peaks[3]. Identifying high-prominence peaks on a wider scale became simpler and to an extent, more reliable, with the release of SRTM (Shuttle Radar Topography Mission) data by NASA in 2003-2004[4]. This dataset provided a global Digital Elevation Model (DEM) comprising elevation values representing the Earth's surface at points on a grid size of approximately 90 x 90 metres. Computer programs written by Jonathan de Ferranti and Edward Earl were able to use this dataset to identify peaks and cols, and determine their topographical prominence. Jonathan de Ferranti and Aaron Maizlish went on to publish a ground-breaking global list of 1,500m prominence peaks (P1500m Ultras). The term 'Ultras' had been coined by Washington-based Steve Fry in the 1980s[5], but they were now listed worldwide, published at peaklist.org. Revolutionary as it was, the SRTM dataset had significant limitations: it omitted the circumpolar regions (nothing beyond 60° north or south) and its representation of steep terrain was poor – the heights of peaks such as Everest, the Matterhorn or Chile's Torres del Paine were (and still are) considerably under-reported. The Ultras list, updated based on later data, currently runs to 1,541 summits, as listed at peakbagger.com.

The goal of the Ribus project is to extend the analysis from P1500m down to P1000m. On a local level with good mapping, this is straightforward. Scotland has Ben Nevis (1,344m, P1344m) and Carn Eighe (1,182m, P1147m); Wales has Yr Wyddfa (1,085m, P1039m). Ireland has Carrauntoohil (1,038m, P1038m). Skye's 992m Sgùrr Alasdair (992m prominence) narrowly misses the cut, while England's most prominent peak, 978m Scafell Pike (P912m) is well short of Ribu status. Europe has some four hundred Ribus; the USA has a similar number; these were already listed to a good level of accuracy. With 1,541 P1500m summits already listed, the world P1000m list will clearly run to several thousand, and given the lack of reliable topographic maps in many parts of the world, identifying them relies on a combination of digital (DEM) and other data.

The starting point for the World Ribus project is an astonishing piece of work by Andrew Kirmse, whose day job had been managing the Google Earth team. From 2014 he turned his digital elevation data analysis skills to peak listing, and by 2017 his worldwide analysis of Jonathan de Ferranti's cleansed version of the SRTM dataset, running across a network of computers, had resulted in a list of 7.8 million summits[6] of at least 100 feet of prominence! This

Kirmse dataset included 6,637 P1000m peaks.

The World Ribus project came into being in 2020 after the world went into lockdown during the Covid-19 pandemic, with the team consisting of a dozen peakbagging enthusiasts around the world collaborating online. A web application was developed by Oscar Argudo and the work-in-progress data can be viewed at http://worldribus.pythonanywhere.com. The colours represent accuracy, ranging from green (best), through blue and yellow to grey (unchecked).

Together we are working to refine the Kirmse dataset. The accuracy of the underlying data is limited: whilst saddle elevations are usually reasonably accurate, sampling on a 90 x 90m cell size usually misses the highest point of the summit. Tree cover can also affect accuracy – of saddles as well as summits. Worse still, high peaks and areas of high relief are affected by data voids ('no-data areas'). In such areas, summit elevations are often under-represented by up to 30 metres, and errors are sometimes considerably worse than that. Accordingly we need to analyse peaks less prominent than P1000m from the Kirmse dataset, as some of these will also prove to be Ribus. The team uses a variety of sources to refine the data, including the national mapping agencies where available, otherwise OpenTopoMap, Russian and American military mapping, local peakbagging websites, and more recent higher-resolution Digital Elevation datasets (typically 30 x 30m cell size) including ASTER, ArcticDEM, ALOS and ESA (Copernicus). The final list will probably number around 7000 Ribus.

Ribus by country – largest totals

It will be some while before accurate totals are available for all countries, especially for China, where mapping and accurate peak heights are not easy to access.

However, Canada seems to have the largest Ribus total of any country and has reasonable mapping. 1,000 Canadian P1000s would be very neat.

Country	Ribus total (approx.)
Canada	980
China	880
USA	650
Russia	460
Chile	390
Argentina	260
Indonesia	235
Greenland	230
Iran	210
India	190

The R10 group of Ribu-rich nations

Seamounts – underwater Ribus

A March 2021 paper (UCL Open Environment) gives access to a list of 37,889 seamounts, which are all P1000m –

https://ucl.scienceopen.com/document/read?vid=4e96c0b7-4720-4d6d-b3d6-af777866702d

'Seamounts are "undersea mountains", and although many definitions of this term have been used, they are commonly described as conical features that rise more than 1,000m above the surrounding seabed... Present estimates of seamount numbers vary from anywhere between 10,000 to more than 60,000... This study presents an update of seamount predictions based on SRTM30 global bathymetry version 11... 37,889 seamounts [is] an increase of 4,437 from the previous predictions derived from an older global bathymetry grid (SRTM30v.6). This increase is due to greater detail in newer bathymetry grids as acoustic mapping of the seabed expands.'

Unsurprisingly, then, it is more difficult listing underwater mountains than terrestrial ones. Even so, after allowing for the fact that there is more ocean than land surface, it is apparent that the seabed is more mountainous overall than the land surface. The 'mountain chains' in the ocean (mid-oceanic ridges) are much longer and more continuous than on land, and are primarily volcanic, giving rise to steep-sided cones, often close together (some, notably the Aleutian chain, do include many Ribu islands). Additionally, these totals omit islands which are less than 1,000m above sea-level, but rise more than 1,000m off the seabed. A 'dry-earth' analysis could potentially yield 50,000 P1000m peaks.

(With thanks to Ribus team member Keith Bennett)

Turkey – twin peaks and triple saddles

Turkey has 104 P1000m Ribus, including 24 P1500m Ultras. My first peakbagging visit, in 2011, was arranged by Anatolian Adventures and our local guide Recep was based near to one of the Ultras. Demircazik was the name on the list, but nearby Kizilkaya was very similar in height. Turkish topo maps are classified and hence not available to the public. Jonathan de Ferranti had checked his sources – old Russian military maps (now declassified!) showed heights for both peaks, but different scales favoured different summits. A friend of Recep mentioned that a recent precision GPS survey had determined that Kizilkaya was the higher summit (3,767m, P2347). It involved rock climbing – but Recep was also a climber and agreed to take Andrew and me to the summit. I borrowed Bob Packard's hand level, and this also indicated that Kizilkaya was higher than Demircazik. The peak wasn't suitable for a group ascent, so instead we headed south for Medetsiz Tepe (3,524m, P2058m). Bob Packard is probably the world's most prolific peakbagger, and this was his 75th birthday – and his 150th Ultra. It's an attractive multi-summited ridge; an 11-

hour day. Nine years later, checking the peak's data while working on Turkey for the Ribus project, I discovered Medetsiz has three different candidates for the key saddle. Its recognised saddle is to the northwest (its parent peak being Kizilkaya, as it happens). Another saddle to the southwest is just four metres higher. However, a 50m deep road cutting to the northeast has created a new saddle which is some 28 metres lower, according to the most recent (ESA) DEM data. We decided to retain the lowest natural col, in preference to the manmade col; the latter would increase the prominence by 28 metres. Medetsiz and Kizilkaya both have more than 2,000m of prominence – there are only 487 P2000m peaks globally.

Faraway close pairs

Whilst the Turkish near-twins Kizilkaya and Demirkazik are close together and obvious rivals, such pairings can often be far apart and hard to detect. Monte Generoso (1,700m, P1329) is a Ribu on the Italy/Switzerland border - or is it? 15km to the north-east, Monte di Tremezzo is listed on Peakbagger. com as the same height, 1,700m, P962m. Swiss mapping shows Generoso as 1,701.3m with Tremezzo 2m lower, but some maps show them equal. I'd climbed Generoso in 2017, an 8km round trip on a good trail. In 2020, Tremezzo was a near-drive-up, an easy scenic stroll above the Italian Lakes on a July evening.

In places without good mapping, such instances of faraway close pairs may remain undetected for years.

Wrong summit syndrome

Hillwalkers aren't always the most prominence-oriented of folk. In Scotland, the highpoint is sometimes neglected in favour of a lower cairn nearby. In Indonesia, volcano-baggers are happy to simply reach the crater rim and gaze into the crater. In such spectacular surroundings, it can be difficult to explain why it's considered necessary to bushwhack through unfriendly vegetation to get to somewhere less scenic (but higher). Such was our experience on Sumatra's Gunung Marapi, a justifiably popular trek to an active crater. Our 2007 attempt on the highpoint was a heroic failure – especially bad luck for Adam Helman on his birthday. More recently, during a March 2020 trip to Java, Dan Quinn (he of Gunung-bagging fame) and I diverted to Ungaran (2,050m P1320) when our Sulawesi plans were thwarted by local Covid restrictions. Dan had been there before, and had visited both summits, in cloud – not realising that a third (central) peak, bypassed by the trails, is higher. The very popular Merbabu (3,145m P2432) also has two summits of similar elevation. In that case, both are easily reached but few make the easy five-minute diversion to the true highpoint, Triangulasi. After Semeru, I managed to eke out my trip for another six (unambiguous) Ribus before scuttling home just before Britain locked down (Indonesia never did).

Merapi (Rob Woodall)

Marginal Ribus

Numerous Ribus are on the cusp of qualifying for P1000m status. Two Greek peaks climbed in autumn 2020 are listed as exactly P1000m – often an indication that the data are uncertain. Both are in the north-west.

Kanala (1,520m, P1000m) is an imposing rugged peak with a fine rocky ridge. Cliffs to the east fall to a reservoir. A very steep gravel farm road (such roads in Greece usually have *de facto* public vehicular access) reaches 700m on the west side, where a feasible route can be found, involving a short scramble followed by scree and goat tracks.

Skhizokaravo (2,184m P1000m) was more of an adventure. On my first attempt I failed to even reach the trailhead. Seemingly all bridges had been destroyed by medicane (cyclone) Ianos a few days before I arrived in Greece (there had been two fatalities in Karditsa). I tried again on my way back south at the end

Kanala from the north (Rob Woodall)

of my trip, and this time (perhaps thanks to a Google Maps update) managed to locate the one remaining driveable road. Then a landslide-destroyed track led to cattle-grazed summit slopes and a fine rocky summit. It seemed a lot of effort for a peak that might not even be a Ribu, but both are high quality, very prominent peaks – it doesn't do to be too choosy.

Skhizokaravo (Rob Woodall)

Brienzer Rothorn – a multimodal Ribu – the way forward for peak-bagging?

The Swiss are famed for their integrated public transport – trains, buses, and nowadays increasingly e-bike hire at trailheads, which can be combined to access many alpine peaks car-free. Swiss peak-bagger and accomplished mountaineer Andrej Gerber does all his peak bagging by public transport. He leads the Switzerland P600m Peaks league table by a good margin. Myself, being car-based, in summer 2020 I was often overtaken by e-cyclists on the walk-ins. E-bikes are increasingly popular in the UK, too (albeit they may arrive at the trailhead by car currently).

Brienzer Rothorn (2,348m P1340m) is a classic chocolate-box-scenic peak above Interlaken in northern Switzerland with a variety of ascent options. From the south, a cog railway does most of the 1,700m ascent, leaving a short walk to the summit, typically followed by a long ridge traverse and a descent to a different railway station. From the north-east, a cable car climbs even closer to the summit, with a few descent options. I chose the NE side, but on foot, the 15km 1,100m ascent making for a beautiful ascent on good trails. The view south looks across Brienzersee to the glaciated Berner Oberland giants. An hour's diversion on the way down follows a narrow shapely ridge to Arnihaaggen (2,212m P187 – a Swiss Marilyn). I rounded off the day a short drive along the valley, with the Hängst-Hächle twins, both peaks mapped at

Brienzer Rothorn from Arnihaagen (Rob Woodall)

2,091m currently; whichever is higher has 775m prominence. No Ribu – but bagging the pair, in dramatic limestone karst scenery, is certainly no hardship.

The European Alps is a wonderful playground. One wonders how British mountain access will evolve in a low carbon future.

[1] The minimum vertical distance one must descend from a peak in order to climb a higher peak http://www.andrewkirmse.com/prominence
[2] https://www.gunungbagging.com/the-inspiration/
[3] http://www.peaklist.org/WWlists/WorldTop50.html
[4] https://en.wikipedia.org/wiki/Shuttle_Radar_Topography_Mission
[5] https://en.wikipedia.org/wiki/Ultra-prominent_peak
[6] https://en.wikipedia.org/wiki/Ultra-prominent_peak

—TMS—

The One that Got Away: The Bridge of Orchy Hills – John Owen

Have you ever climbed a Munro, convinced you got to the top, and later discovered that you hadn't? Well, I managed to fail twice on the same day, maybe a record. I was climbing from Bridge of Orchy up Beinn Dorain. The cloud was down, but all I had to do was turn right in Coire an Dothaidh and follow a path to the summit clearly shown on the (1976) map. There was a big cairn, so I returned to the col and headed for the western top of Beinn an Dothaidh, my map showing a height of 996m, which was obviously the highest point, wasn't it? Fortunately, only one subsequent visit was needed to correct my errors.

Life on the Ice

Fran Pothecary

The sun gives me no indication of the time of day when I poke my nose out of the sleeping bag. It circles more or less above us – or rather we circle it – for 24 hours at this latitude at this time of year. It is somewhat disorientating to have no darkness at all. What I do know is that it is cold – my breath coils upwards in thick clouds. Maybe -20° or less. My socks are hanging above me from the tent inner and I reach for them, pushing them inside the warmth of the bag and giving myself another five minutes of rest. My salopettes are stiff and crackly as I pull them on over thermals; any damp has frozen overnight though I know it will be only a few minutes before they thaw out and wick away any residual moisture. A fleece and a down jacket go on next, and over that, my 'working' jacket, an oversized synthetic belay jacket. My black and yellow expedition down parka, used as a pillow and neck muffler overnight, waits for my sortie outdoors. Lastly, I step into my 'baffies' – not slippers as the nickname would indicate back home in Scotland – but Baffins, thermally lined double boots, suitable for working in temperatures of well below freezing.

Fran with king penguins, South Georgia (Fran Pothecary)

159

My fingertips nip as I lift a fuel bottle to re-fill the Primus and the Tilley lamp. It is a reminder that you can never take handling anything for granted after a long 'not-night' at 76° South. The mantra is 'gloves always' – but I still end up bare-handed for delicate, quick tasks inside the tent. Smaller gloves for female hands are easier to find these days but often are limited by overstitching and concomitant lack of dexterity. And despite the wealth of full-on mountaineering gloves available, my favourites this season are a pair of fleece-lined leather industrial working gloves – probably a tenth of the price of a technical pair. I empty a flask of water in the pan and bring it up to the boil; the Primus putters along in a friendly fashion and on cue, my companion, the Canadian air mechanic Jason, stirs in his bag. Looking at last at my watch – a $10 Casio special (I have three, they go forever and don't seem to mind the cold) I am shocked to see it is already 10am. At least I didn't have any hourly weather observations to do today. Once he is up, Jason fills the big pan with ice – a little melt water in the base to stop any burning – while I make cowboy coffee, real coffee in a plastic jug, good and strong. I make herbal tea for myself too in the name of keeping hydrated. Bored of a porridge-based breakfast, I opt for a smoko brunch of 'biscuits brown', cheese and jam. The cheese is frozen twice over, once on its journey south by ship and now sitting in blue barrels on the tent valance.

Outside I turn in all directions and survey the sky. Pale yellowy-blue from horizon up, deepening towards the zenith. The sun blazes without emanating any heat. A tiny sliver of cloud to the southeast, on the deck. Bad weather comes from that direction, so that's one to keep an eye on. The view is the same in all directions, flat white ice unbroken by contour or feature. A volcano, Takahe, 60 nautical miles towards the coast, is the exception, and a bump of three peaks to the northwest. It feels lonely out here, a four-and-a-half-hour flight from Sky Blu, the British Antarctic Survey (BAS) deep field base we flew in from, and another couple of hours from the WAIS (West Antarctic Ice Sheet) Divide, which is one of the US Antarctic programme's forward operating bases. I have my passport with me. If we have to be uplifted in the event of an emergency, the chances are we are closer to US operatives and they come and go to Antarctica from New Zealand.

Jason and I are waiting for an aircraft to arrive but we don't know when: two days or a week. There have been some issues with test flights and instrumentation back at Rothera. We are the advance party who have set up a field camp on the Lower Thwaites Glacier for an aero-geophysical survey intending to make 11 flights over the area – around 10,000 kilometres of flying in total. 'Glacier' seems stretching the term given its absolute flatness, apparent lack of crevasses etc. but it is still moving at over 1m a day, one of the fastest moving ice sheets in Antarctica and hence of great scientific interest. It has an austere beauty to it, and a frictionless near-silence, apart from the gentle susurration of wind over the wind-sculptured snow.

The great flat white of Thwaites Glacier (Fran Pothecary)

While we wait, there are jobs to do. First off, and most importantly, we need to make sure our power supplies are functioning. Solar panels charge a bank of batteries and we have a couple of 1kW Honda 'handbag' generators, and two 2kW ones for beefier jobs. At the moment we have just an Iridium phone and a couple of laptops to keep charged – but when the scientists arrive there will be a raft of other requirements. An HF radio is set up and the main choice for regular chats (known as 'scheds') to Rothera, the BAS Research Base on Adelaide Island. HF is available to other field parties to listen in, and therefore social – but this far south, the reception and transmission can be sketchy. It works well in the mornings on a wavelength of 7775Khz but often fades later in the day.

Secondly, we need to attend to the Primus stoves and Tilley lamps, servicing them and changing parts if necessary – they are our only source of heat for cooking and keeping warm. Thirdly, we need to cut blocks from ice as a 'throne' to support our field toilet seat. The seat itself is a length of ply-board with a hole cut in it. As I saw blocks I look closely at the layers of snow and think about snow structure and avalanches – not a risk here obviously. But it brings my thoughts to an upcoming April trip to the Lyngen Alps in north Norway, and I wonder if I will be fit enough to skin up any hills! We walk the length of the ski runway a couple of times a day for exercise and contemplation – it is a thousand metres of snow and ice, delineated by black radar flags and bashed out by a Pisten Bully a few weeks earlier courtesy of a US traverse party going through. I have a pair of cross-country skis as well for a change. My daily yoga routine has been somewhat curtailed – Downward Dog in three layers of down feels bulky and awkward.

People often ask what it is like for women working on the ice. First off, there are many more than you might think working for BAS in a range of jobs from scientist to air mechanic to chef to 'sparky' to field guide – the latter being my role. I would say it is not a role for the 'girly-girl' – though we all brush up nicely on a Saturday night, as do the lads! In the field (what we call being away from Base supporting a science project, or managing a remote fuel depot) you have to go for long periods of time without showering or washing with water. It is not quite as gross as it sounds as you tend to sweat far less and with a bit of care, regular application of wet wipes and damp flannels can take care of your needs. Keeping feet dry and warm is essential. Cleaning teeth never gets ignored. Your clothes very quickly absorb the odours of Avtur (aviation fuel), kerosene and methylated spirits thereby helpfully over-powering any of your own. Every now and again, especially if you are working on a hot water drilling project, hot water might come your way in sufficient quantities to mean you can throw a bucket over yourself. Complete bliss even though you are generally standing in freezing air when you do so! Your skin takes a hammering, although regular applications of Factor 50 and covering up all bits before we step outside protects from the sun. Hands are a different matter. Fuel, dry air, manual labour all take their toll – any break from work finds me massaging thick dollops of hand cream into the cracks and splits that are an inevitable and painful part of life on the ice doing manual labour. These hands will never make it into a photo-shoot for hand lotion! You become very attuned to the more basic functions of your body. Feeling cold? Have a pee. Pee very dark? Drink more water. You get quite happy talking about bodily functions even with people you have only known a few days. Likewise, living so closely to other people, especially when there are only two of you, finds you moving to a range of intimate subjects quite quickly – relationships and the state of them (living apart for extended periods can exert stress on the most robust of relationships); family tensions and fall-outs; dating and sex; food you crave for when you are back in the real world; pets that you long to see and spend time with.

A few weeks later and I find myself flying out on a day excursion to Coal Nunatak on Alexandra Island. We are there to dismantle an old, and erect a new, Automated Weather Station (AWS). It is a relatively quick hop from Rothera – a two-hour direct flight by Twin Otter to the site – piloted by Vicky and accompanied by the Met guy, John; Ali the science lab manager and Pete the incoming over-wintering generator mechanic, brought along for his youth and muscle. It is quite a big job; my role as a field guide is to lead the team roped over a short stretch of crevassed glacier, then hump loads back and forth to the plane. John and Ali take on the job of construction, swapping out batteries and SD cards, and making sure it all works. Vicky helps but also takes the opportunity to rest, the pilots having a pretty punishing schedule at what is now the end of season. The site is stunningly beautiful; at the very southern tip of Alexandra Island it is a great example of a 'cold desert' with dry riverine features in an area that sees literally no precipitation at all in an average year. The day is

Jason refuelling the Twin Otter (Fran Pothecary)

crystal clear, as it needed to be to do a landing on a glacier, Vicky 'trailing skis' to check the landing site before she properly touched down. Despite the busyness of the day – eight hours of non-stop labour – we do take the opportunity to eat a sandwich and appreciate the arid beauty of mountains edging George VI Sound. I'll be leaving in under two weeks and I know already that I want to come back for a fourth season. Something about Antarctica really captures my imagination but without the vibe, the bubble of brilliance that is working with like-minded people, it would count for nothing.

Fran left a secure, well-paid job-for-life to go and work in Antarctica for six months. Eight years later, she still opts to travel thousands of miles every year to experience the highs and lows of life on the ice, or on the South Atlantic islands. She has done every job from waste recycler, fire fighter, plant operator, fuel pump attendant, base commander, co-pilot, bar manager, accountant, weather checker, snow shifter, avalanche forecaster, warehouse operative to field guide. She is most likely to say 'I don't know but I'll find out' and least likely to say 'Yeah, yeah I totally get this'. She skis more than she walks these days; bikes more than she climbs – but has done 80% of the Munros. The rest are waiting for a retirement that looks no closer year by year.

—TMs—

LOCHS and LOCHANS

Above – Reflections of An Teallach's spires in Loch Toll an Lochain after the October cloud lifted for a few minutes to reveal all.

Below – Lochan na h-Achlaise reflects the snow-dusted peaks of the Black Mount summits in brilliant winter sunshine. ***Alan Rowan***

Captain's Log, (Star)Date 1770

Alec Mamwell

Sadly no Starship, nor Enterprise but the H.M.S. *Endeavour*, a bark designed as a collier, out of Whitby, and a long way from home. Starting out from Plymouth in August 1768 the *Endeavour* had sailed for Tahiti in the Pacific to record the transit of Venus. This was a perfect cover for newly promoted Lieutenant James Cook's secret orders from the Lords of the Admiralty, opened only after sailing, to complete the scientific work and then search for Terra Australis, the fabled southern continent. The Admiralty had no desire to alert other nations for commercial and political reasons and hence the 'cover story' of a small scientific expedition with a civilian component. Having observed the transit Cook sailed to 40 degrees south finding no land and as a consequence altered course towards New Zealand, first sighted by Dutch explorer Abel Tasman in 1642, and thought to be the tip of Terra Australis. Six months of intensive survey work proved this speculation to be wrong and, in consultation with his officers, Cook decided to search for the east coast of Australia. Leaving New Zealand Cook bumped into Australia on the 19th April 1770 slightly too far north to establish whether Van Diemen's Land was an island or not. Nevertheless, having found land he proceeded to sail north along the coast and, as he went, he named various natural features that he observed. Although some places have been renamed, many have stood the test of time and are still in use today.

Two hundred and forty years later my youngest daughter, Rebecca, set off with her then boyfriend to start a new life in Australia and it became almost inevitable that part of my retirement would be spent visiting her. This was compounded when her sister Heather joined her a couple of years later, and to date I've spent 30 weeks down under spread over four trips. Whilst bemoaning this disruption to exploring the hills and mountains of our own island group and, at times, those of the rest of the world, it has opened other possibilities which I have subsequently followed up.

As Cook sailed north on 22nd April he spotted: 'At noon … a remarkable peaked hill laying inland, the top of which looked like a Pigeon House, and occasioned me giving it that name.' A few weeks later on the 15th May 'A tolerable highpoint of land' was named Cape Byron and 'It may be known by a remarkable sharp peaked mountain lying inland NW by W from it.' Even today whilst experiencing the flesh-pots of Byron Bay it is usually possible to see this on the horizon. The natives in those days '… were quite naked; even the woman had nothing to cover her nudities' and today matters are only slightly different! The day after 'We saw the breakers again … this situation may always be found by the peaked mountain before mentioned … And on their account I have named it Mount Warning … The point off which these shoals lay I have named Point Danger'. As always, his nomenclature was based on his experience and was, I believe, designed to help any who should come after. Indeed, the very next day he referred directly to this possibility when describing some hills north of where Brisbane would eventually develop. 'These hills lay but a little way inland and not far from each other; they are very remarkable on account of their singular form of elevation, which very much resembles Glass Houses, which occasioned me giving them that name'. As a visiting Yorkshireman, Cook's mountains had a certain attraction.

Mount Warning (Alec Mamwell)

Obviously my first visit in 2011 was preceded by some research aimed at making sure that there were some targets where I could offset the hill deprivation that an urban and beach holiday might create. Along with my wife and hill companion of many years, Angela, a week after our arrival we set off north for a road trip in this new continent. Our first port of call was to be the Glass House Mountains and transport was in a hired 'Wicked' camper chosen because their depot was within walking distance of our daughter's flat. This small and ageing van was not only covered inside with, mainly juvenile, graffiti but was also, on the outside, emblazoned with lurid graphics depicting gun-toting worms. Later in the trip at some traffic lights we heard a rich Aussie voice informing his mate that 'Struth I've never seen anyone that old in one of those before!'

Just over an hour out of Brisbane we arrived at the Glass House Mountains, a set of volcanic plugs that are an important part of the Gubbi Gubbi people's creation stories and beliefs (Beerwah – mother; Tibrogargan – father; Coonowrin – eldest child). We had discovered that the highest hill, Beerwah, was currently out of bounds following a massive rock fall. Given that this was our first choice we felt a bit miffed but decided to give the one nearest the Bruce Highway a try. This hill called Tibrogrogan turned out, despite its lowly height of 364m, to be an impressive lump of rock. That is where you could see the rock for the trees. We were about to start to learn the important difference between fell/mountain walking and bush walking. Navigating our way to the trailhead car park we kitted up and started walking. We knew that some scrambling would be involved but nothing had prepared us for the sign that met us when the flat path suddenly swung left and immediately launched onto steep rock. 'WARNING' it said, in big red letters 'Climbing and walking the steep terrain and slippery rocks on the mountain is dangerous and may lead to serious injury or death'. Fortunately, we both come from a climbing background so I guess we knew this already but to have it thrust in your face was quite disconcerting. In our naïvety we had thought that snakes and spiders would have been the problem.

Tibro with summit path (Alec Mamwell)

Despite our newly found trepidation we set off up the rock to find an open and steepening scoop that was slightly loose. This did not help! However, a quick pull on some huge, and fortunately solid, holds saw us access a ribbon of slabs that lead directly to the summit of the mountain – a clearing in the bush. There was no clear view whatsoever apart from where we had emerged from the slabs. This proved anticlimactic and with nowhere to sit we quickly started to descend, passing a couple of youths equipped with shorts and trainers. We made our way carefully down and eventually arrived at the ledge above the scoop. Just below we met another young couple clearly out of their depth and pointed out that although the bit they were struggling with was the steepest part of the ascent, the slabs above were definitely more technical, and suggested that they may wish to reconsider. As we arrived on terra firma we were glad to see that they had heeded our advice. By this time, although it was mid-morning in winter, we were lathered but quite chuffed with our hill and its challenging nature. Later on this trip, we came back and did a smaller hill in these mountains called Ngungun and enjoyed a short but delightful walk with mild scrambling to a summit with excellent views. This was followed by a dip in the Pacific and a close-up of an osprey taking a fish out of the water just where we had been swimming. This was a much more relaxing and leisurely day that the one on Tibrogrogan.

Ngungun summit view towards Beerwah and Coonowrin (Alec Mamwell)

A few weeks later, after suitable family time we escaped again and headed south. We were intent on Mount Warning, having seen it on a recent trip to Byron Bay. Having found a campsite close to the trailhead in our fresh 'Wicked' van, this time emblazoned with a dishy blonde, we got up early and set off. The main difficulty was finding somewhere to park at the end of the road. Apparently, it is an Australian custom to be on the top for sunrise – it is the first place in the country to see the sun – and hence the difficulty in

Beerwah with the first part of the trail (Alec Mamwell)

parking. Setting off, it was gratifying to see other late-comers experiencing the same problem!

The path was extremely well engineered and solidly built. It zig-zagged uphill at a reasonable angle with occasional views until it ended abruptly about a hundred metres from the summit. From here a chain led up some rocks and this was obviously the way to go. Eschewing the chain, we enjoyed a pleasant and, if somewhat polished, easy scramble to the summit which was, again, a clearing in the bush with no view. Fortunately, the powers that be had seen fit to build a walkway with three viewing platforms around the top of the hill and the view from these was quite spectacular, especially that towards the Gold Coast with the surreal towers of Surfers Paradise figuring prominently. Mount Warning is the spine of an old shield volcano and the other lookouts took in the whole of the eroded rim. On the way down we found an Australian woman sobbing at the base of the chain. Angela asked what was wrong and was informed that she couldn't do it. 'Have you tried?' responded Angela, 'It really is quite easy.' After further womanly encouragement she grasped the chain apprehensively and tried the bottom few feet. 'It's no harder anywhere' she was told and with much further exhortation she proceeded to weep and scrabble her way upwards. Later we met again on the path and she told us that 'I'm 40 and I can't believe I've just done that!'. Whilst Angela patted her on the shoulder and congratulated her, I told her that I was '61 and incredibly handsome'. We left a very confused looking woman.

Pigeon House Mountain on the ladders (Alec Mamwell)

Scroll on a few years to 2014 and we flew down to Melbourne to pick up a camper and spend the next month driving back to Brisbane, knocking off a few hills en route. The trip had been a success so far and we had already been to the top of Australia – an easy stroll on the longest lightning conductor in the world – and were moving north along the Pacific coast towards Sydney and the Blue Mountains when we thought we'd stop and see if we could do Pigeon House Mountain in the Budawangs (some great names in Oz!).

Although the hill seemed easy enough from the description, the access to the trailhead mentioned unsealed roads and we were not supposed to use these with the camper. Needless to say, we decided to give it a go. Sadly, once started we were committed with nowhere to turn. After four or five miles when we were really hoping to reach our destination, we came across a massive grading machine complete with driver working and filling the only turning point we had found on this dirt track. As we ploughed through the six-inch deep sand that the grader had churned up we felt that we might have over-stretched ourselves on this occasion. After a dozen miles or so we eventually came to the car park complete with toilets, shelter, signage and amazingly another car. Restraining our inclination to turn round immediately and escape we decide to don our boots and do it. We followed a sloping path up towards the castle-like summit of the hill and, when reaching the cliffs, met a couple of young women on their way down who informed us they had just had an encounter with a copperhead. Further enquiry ascertained that this was a venomous snake. Fortunately it had scooted off as we followed a ledge to a series of ladders. Whilst we were expecting this we were astonished by the industrial scale and nature of these but pressed on upwards. The ladders followed a steep broad gully and made access to the summit rocks technically easy. We followed the trail to the summit belvedere and trig point.

Pigeon House Mountain summit (Alec Mamwell)

Having enjoyed the fairly extensive views over the bush we set off down and made good time back to the car park and felt mightily relieved when we hit tarmac an hour later, so much so that we treated ourselves to pies when we hit civilisation and stopped at a layby to consume them.

Sitting in the front seat of the camper I noticed that there were some leaves that appeared to be trapped between door and the front wing. Between bites I pulled one out and, in doing so, disturbed the biggest spider I had ever seen, which promptly ran onto the wing mirror. Not usually squeamish about spiders, this one instantly changed my views and I quickly vacated the camper and warned Angela to do the same. For some reason the next thing I did was take a photo before extending a walking pole to full length and flicking it away. Unfortunately, it wasn't going to go away because it ran across the bonnet and disappeared underneath. I'd obviously not learned, because after cautiously lifting the bonnet, it was sitting on the engine block and at my second flick it ran away again. Sadly I had not closed the door on the camper so guess where it went next. All our searching failed to locate it, so we crammed clothing into all the available orifices to try and make the cab spider secure and drove on.

Our fellow traveller (Alec Mamwell)

In the next town we visited the Tourist Information office and showed them the picture. Unlike us they were not impressed. 'It's just a little tarantula. It could give you a little nip that might make you "crook" for a few days but it won't kill you.' Apparently they like the warmth of cars and quite regularly pop out to startle drivers, causing a fair number of road accidents. We carried on not particularly reassured but when we arrived at the next campsite, we emptied out all our gear and started searching all over again. No sign of our friend so, before bed, we used all available clothing to stuff any cracks and crannies which might allow access to our sleeping area.

We spent an apprehensive night but over the next few days in the Blue Mountains we relaxed somewhat. It was another surprise therefore, a few days later, when loading supplies that he popped out of the boot. Wiser now, I closed all the doors of the camper and, armed once again with trekking pole, managed to flick him onto the adjacent car park pillar. We quickly jumped in and drove off very happy to leave him for subsequent Aldi customers. As we headed north towards the Warrembungles (who could resist such a name?) we felt much more relaxed and decided to stop at a café/museum which housed the fossilised remains of the largest marsupial to walk the planet. We were about to leave when a car screeched to a halt and four young ladies jumped out and started unpacking all their kit. We smiled smugly at each other because we knew exactly what their problem was!

In 2014 we finished our trip back to Brisbane at Point Danger right on the New South Wales - Queensland border. On our return we discovered that Beerwah was still closed, so the last link in our pursuit of Cook's mountains was out of reach. However, in 2017 we found that it had re-opened and although we were keen to try it, a trip to New Zealand got in the way. Our one opportunity was thwarted by the threat of thunderstorms and we went a little further and walked up Mount Coolum as compensation.

In 2018 though we did have the time and set aside a number of days whilst watching the daily forecast. Having chosen what we thought was the right day, we drove out of Brisbane early and were on the trail by 8.00 am. Temperatures were forecast to be mid to high 30s C and hence such an early start for the 558m hill, but as we approached the sweep of slabs up which the route goes, we met a couple who had just descended and they commented, in passing, that it was warming up. They were not wrong!

On arrival at the base of the initial slabs the normal start was very obvious from the high degree of polish and, a few feet up with sweaty palms, bendy boots and time pressing, I decided that this was not for me on this occasion. I had heard of an easier start to the left so I scuttled off and found a groove system that seemed promising with very little polish and a few holds. This time I decided to go for it and Angela followed after I arrived at the first ledge. From here we were not only able to re-join the main route but see the real easy start which came in from much further left – a useful bit of knowledge for later. We carried on up the slabs from ledge to ledge with increasing exposure and a certain amount of trepidation, knowing full well that what goes up

Alec on the slabs (Alec Mamwell)

must come down. We were certainly aware that this was a route on which to exercise care and caution as each section of slab threw up another set of problems. Eventually after several hundred feet we came to a large and thankfully shaded belvedere below the overhanging upper cliff. Time to swig some of our only climbing aid, water, and cool down a little before stepping back into what was gradually becoming a furnace.

The route at this point swings hard right and follows the base of the upper cliffs past bizarre, sculpted rocks and fallen blocks to emerge on a stepped ridge that follows the edge of the cliff over a number of small problems. Some of these proved quite tricky but relatively enjoyable given the reduced exposure. Higher still the scrambling ended, and we sweated up a vague path through stunted scrub which led to a short pleasant and easy summit ridge. We were well pleased to have finally managed to get this one under our belts.

Beerwah is the highest of the Glass House Mountains and, as such, afforded us great views over all the other peaklets and out towards a decent stretch of the Sunshine Coast shimmering in the distance. Flies and heat suggested that it might be a good idea to get down before we relaxed too much. Thankfully this proved much easier than anticipated using the arse-brake to compliment the normal four points of contact. Similarly, our earlier discovery of the easier pitch at the base proved a boon because by the time we arrived temperatures were in the very high 30s – so high in fact that Angela sustained burns to her hands on this last section. This did not dampen our pleasure as we rattled back to the car and headed for Brisbane and a nice cold beer.

Although this ascent brought an end to our pursuit of Cook's Australian

Mountains there are still a few loose ends for the future. For example, there are several other small peaks in the Glass House Mountains to do, some hopefully with our grandson. One, Coonowrin, is spectacular and out of bounds, closed to climbers by the National Park on pain of a hefty fine. Similarly, subsequent study of Cook's log has highlighted other possible hills he named such as Mount Dromedary down in New South Wales. Who knows? The end might be further in the future yet!

Left: Beerwah summit ridge
Below: the easy start or finish (Alec Mamwell)

Image: Derek Sime

Six Thousand Feet Beyond Man and Time
(John Tyndall: the 3rd ascent of the Matterhorn, 1868)

'every pain and every joy and every thought
and every sigh... in your life must return to you.'
Nietzchze 1882

After years of wooing and rebuttal, the Matterhorn
was no longer virgin; he was not the first man.
He looked down to Breuil, from where
Carrel had begun his conquest of the mountain
and he looked down also to Zermatt, down
the route Whymper had taken before them both.
He saw chalk-white houses and slate-green pastures
as unremarkable now, as small as rock samples
he had on his desk; indifferent and indiscriminate
as the degrading summit, hacked and hurt by age.

Above him was the deep blue of the morning
sky, so filled with stars and planets; it seemed
as if he was able to look back in time. He saw
aeons of shifting glaciers, mountains being born
in the birth-canals of volcanoes before frosts
cracked them into brittle teeth, decaying
year on year into the stumped remains
of majesty. He saw past all this to plates
folding over nascent fossils; the one great sea
receding and the rise and collision of continents;
and further back, out past the earth, the moon,
the morning star, in the gasses and carbon motes
of space, his own genealogy evolve; as if in that
nebulous haze lay the origins of his feelings;
the progenitor of this present thought; all his
traits and whims and sadness, his disappointments
being conducted back to their ancestral home;
all his endeavour telescoped into this perspective.
He turned to retrace dim footsteps downhill;
ones which might very well have been his own.

Stuart B. Campbell

Karakoram Experience

David Gibson

It's August 2005, I'm lying in my tent, my back wracked with pain and my throat, stomach and rear end sore from repeated vomiting and diarrhoea. Barely conscious, I had achieved something I never thought possible just a year before. Starting that morning from Concordia, I walked and staggered for seven hours along the Godwin Austen glacier, passing Broad Peak, to K2 base camp at 5,100 metres. What caused my physical state was a combination of inexperience, altitude sickness, Diamox and giardia, resulting in a challenge I will never forget. Once at base camp I couldn't raise the energy reserves required to climb the last few extra metres up to the Gilkey Memorial.

Fast forward to June 2021, I'm lying in Ward 12 in Dundee's Ninewells Hospital after an emergency operation, and I realise once again that chance events have the power to change our lives. A completely unpredictable health issue, or a visit to a bookshop, can have serious consequences!

You're probably wondering where I'm going with this, but back in 2004 I purchased Andrew Greig's Summit Fever from Ottakars in Aviemore. I became captivated by Greig's account of his and Mal Duff's 1984 expedition to the Karakoram, which culminated in Duff's ascent of Muztagh, accompanied by Sandy Allan, Tony Brindle and Jon Tinker. Greig is an accomplished author, but described himself with some modesty as an 'armchair climber'. His description about the expedition and experiences on the journey from Islamabad to the Baltoro Glacier in Gilgit-Baltistan portrayed a great adventure ... and inspired me to go!

My only other experience of trekking before K2 was a tame 10 days in the Carpathian Mountains of Romania. Despite being caught in a scary thunderstorm on a summit, and what could have been a serious head over heels fall backwards off a limestone ridge due to a misplaced hand hold, I hadn't been put off. I wanted more and I wanted go somewhere really challenging and different.

I remember being unable to make the final decision; there were just so many things to worry about: lack of experience and fitness, altitude sickness, remoteness, the unpredictable local population and their propensity for violence against trekkers (a bus load had been attacked by gunmen recently in Gilgit). All these mitigated against going. But I found sufficient courage and signed up. Then just a few weeks before departure, four terrorist bombs were set off in London on 7th July 2005, with resultant carnage. The bombs were linked to Islamist extremists who were trained in Pakistan or Afghanistan and the Foreign Office advice was not to go, but my trekking company didn't seem at all stressed by these events, no doubt needing the cash. And so it came to pass, I was on my way.

The detailed itinerary for the journey from Islamabad to Skardu then to Askole and the 80 miles up the Baltoro to Concordia and K2BC is available on the Internet, so I won't repeat it here, but concentrate on my stand-out moments.

Flying to Islamabad on a Pakistan International Airways jumbo is something I wouldn't wish to repeat, especially the toilet experience, and the somewhat pessimistic announcement near arrival: 'Inshallah we shall be landing at Islamabad'. Fortunately, Allah's will was on our side and the landing was uneventful. The journey from Islamabad to Skardu and Askole was simply a fantastic experience, and the trek still hadn't started!

A two-day drive for much of the length of the Karakoram Highway (KKH) in a hire bus from Islamabad, passing Osama bin Laden's compound in Abbottabad, then along the road clinging to the side of somewhat surreal, vertiginous gorges, the KKH found its way through the mountains, following the Indus River to our overnight stop near Gilgit, then on to Skardu.

At Skardu we stayed at the Mashabrum [sic] Hotel, where they had recently had a visit from none other than the first controversial ascensionist of K2, Lino Lacedelli - his recent portrait in traditional Balti dress featuring

On the Karakoram Highway (David Gibson)

prominently in the dining room.

We journeyed from Skardu to Askole in jeeps without suspension on rutted roads, another experience my posterior will never forget. The roads were simply made, mostly by men using picks and shovels cutting a track into the side of a mountain. Narrow, often washed out due to storms, or trashed due to avalanches or rockfall, the journey proved to be better than the destination, the campsite at Askole. We were five days into the journey and the night in the campsite bought my first bout of vomiting. A great start. 'Better out than in' became my motto for the trip as I was never far away from stomach problems. Setting off the next morning took us through some simply delightful country. Hundreds of years of careful management of water from the mountains enabled the desperately poor local people to fashion their own mini-oases, growing crops and apricots, whilst above, the vast and arid wastes of the mountains looked down.

From below, the snout of the Baltoro Glacier rose as a solid wall of scree. We climbed the 150 metres to get on to the glacier in good company, with a small squad of Pakistan Army soldiers armed with rifles, on their way to man the forward positions in the war with India. As if to emphasize the ongoing conflict, we occasionally heard the sound of gunfire in the mountains.

I remember we were accompanied on this early part of the trek by two worried looking goats. When we reached the campsite at Paiju I understood why they were worried! Paiju was the stopping point for some of our porters who were paid off, but only after the goats had been slaughtered and roasted for dinner. I suspected the goats caused my giardia and I've never tasted the stuff since, although I'm now a big fan of goat's butter!

Our trek leader was a guy called Nick from New Zealand. He was an affable, easy-going character and admitted this was his first trek in Pakistan and the Greater Ranges. Nick must have told the crew about his lack of experience, as he turned out to be a complete liability, with the group finishing the

Balti porters (David Gibson)

177

trek near starvation point because the sirdar and his buddies were skimming off the provisions throughout the journey.

After Paiju our trekking group began to morph in character. From being an excited and expectant group, keen to engage with each other, questions started to be asked about the lack of provisions and why we were expected to subsist on a tin of tuna for lunch and not much else for dinner. Serious divisions emerged and different factions created an uneasy atmosphere, especially at mealtimes and overnight stops.

Group members came from the UK, New Zealand, Australia and Ireland, which proved to be an incendiary mix as the trip progressed. As a solo traveller, with ample supplies of munchies, I maintained my neutrality and tried to get on with everyone, especially my tent companion, Vitus Ackermann, a farmer from Hamilton, New Zealand, who was a tower of strength and great company.

After Paiju campsite the mountain scenery is simply incredible and despite the passage of 16 years, the impact of that breathtaking landscape remains with me as a constant and inspiring memory. The Karakoram is massive in scale but young in age compared with other mountain ranges. As a result, the vertiginous peaks are relatively less eroded and rise directly from

Vitus and porter (David Gibson)

the lateral moraines for up to 7,000 metres and more in altitude. Famous peaks now came high and fast, and with eyes constantly looking up, conditions underfoot required care due to walking on moraine and stone-covered ice, with the occasional deep hole caused by water eroding the underside of the glacier. Not all the holes were obvious as the ice was constantly eroding, and the trail could be unpredictable as the glacier moved down from Concordia.

On the day following departure from the campsite, we passed Paiju Peak (6,610m), then walked to one of the most inspiring places I have ever experienced, camping opposite the Trango Towers. Great Trango Tower at 6,286m is the highest point and features the longest nearly vertical drop in the world on its east side. Next is Trango Tower (6,239m) sometimes unimaginatively called Nameless Tower.

I've never been a journal keeper, and for years never even took a camera with me on trips to the mountains. But my little notebook from the K2 trek is worth consulting, despite its limitations. It confirms that from here the trail became more demanding, noting: 'really tough, suffering from altitude headache, felt ok after paracetamol and rest ... others less affected ... maybe rushed too much at start of day'.

As we approached Concordia, altitude induced headaches would become a daily occurrence; we were now at over 4,000m and climbing. Take Thursday 18th August, day 12 ... 'a very tiring day which finished with a splitting headache and retired to bed feeling lousy'. My notes also record 'good photographs of Masherbrum (7,821m), and Gasherbrum IV (7,925m) at different times of day; lovely in the evening sun. A choir of Balti porters sang me to a sleepless night'.

The following day we arrived at Concordia, crossing many crevasses and passing what is still my favourite mountain view - the Mustagh Tower (7,276m) from the Baltoro Glacier. There were great views of Broad Peak and, due to low cloud, only the tip of K2 on that day. My notes confirm the beauty of Concordia, which, at the confluence of the Baltoro and Godwin-Austen Glaciers, enjoys views of many mountain peaks, but also note it's 'rather like an open toilet'.

Gasherbrum IV with Gasherbrum I to the right
(David Gibson)

While there weren't any other trekkers heading in our direction, we saw a number of mule trains providing food and supplies for the Pakistani army soldiers manning their rather primitive rock-built, tarpaulin-covered sentry posts. I also remember a large Italian group we passed returning down

Mustagh Tower (David Gibson)

the glacier, sitting in comparative luxury around tables in director chairs, with typical style.

The weather at Concordia wasn't brilliant that day and my notes recall that the camping place was very cold and hard. Despite assurances to the contrary, in the pre-trek information pack, we had to erect our own tents. Often these didn't arrive until late in the day and my notes confirmed 'getting desperate, tent and kit bag arrived very late'.

And so it came to pass, Sunday 21st August, and the trek to K2 base camp. A note of caution here in that some companies offer the trek to Concordia, with an optional day to go to K2BC and return the same day, a round trip of 10-12 hours. I doubt that anyone with average trek and mountain fitness would want to do this, and at the same time give up a valuable rest day at Concordia. Check the trek notes with care! I won't deny that the big day was a real test. From Concordia at around 4,500m you leave the Baltoro Glacier and cross over to the Godwin Austen Glacier, over some difficult terrain. Then a further six hours and 600m altitude gain to K2BC.

My notes tell the story: 'One of my desperate days. I have diarrhoea and back pain. Felt like death for most of the walk which took seven hours. Unable to take lunch and dinner, and missed the scramble to the Gilkey Memorial. Need rest'.

The following day back to Concordia wasn't much better: 'I wish I was twenty years younger. At least my back is better and settling down. No appetite. Glad to be in camp at Concordia and very pleased to have made it to

K2 from Concordia (David Gibson)

K2BC'. From Concordia, I fared better. I stopped taking Diamox and finished a course of antibiotics I had been taking for my stomach problems. I had also lost a lot of weight in a very short time and lack of nourishment was affecting my fitness. My notebook tells me to 'get a grip!'

The return down the Baltoro Glacier was anything but an anti-climax. As it runs approximately west to east, the sunsets were fabulous, looking down the length of the valley to Paiju Peak in the far distance. Despite the limited relief offered by the loss of altitude, the walk into the Paiju campsite was one of the longest and toughest days with ten miles on the glacier and a further two miles to the camp. At Paiju, Brenda, one of the four ladies in the group, collapsed and it looked serious. Luckily there was a doctor at the campsite in another group who was able to offer assistance and administer drugs. His advice was immediate evacuation to lower altitude and much discussion followed about the options available. Well, there weren't any, other than a ride on a mule back to Askole. Frank, Brenda's partner, parted with $500 to hire two mules and their owner for the journey. At the end of the trek, Brenda had recovered sufficiently to fly home.

I've mentioned the lack of provisions earlier and that had been a feature of the journey. After returning to Askole, we headed back to Skardu in our jeep convoy. We stopped for lunch at a breeze-block cafe and Nick, our guide, put two packets of cracker biscuits on the table. This was to be lunch for 16 people! To say that a lack of constraint followed is an understatement. A scrum across the table ensued as the UK and Antipodean factions scrambled for the TUC crackers. Nick was asked politely to organise Mars Bars and more biscuits but pleaded that his budget had expired. FFS! I bought a few rounds of crackers and others chipped in for the chocolate. After spending more than £3k on the trip you can imagine that everyone was rather annoyed …

Like many mountain locations, flights from Skardu can be unpredictable and depend upon weather conditions, but we were able to fly back to Islamabad, missing out on the return drive down the KKH, but enjoying fantastic views of Nanga Parbat. Following our return, the group united for once to claim compensation for lack of food and other issues. Surprisingly, a 10% refund arrived! Those downsides pale into insignificance over time, and were arguably, part of the experience.

The trip was unforgettable, challenging and sometimes painful, but the vibrant memories are undiminished. Trip of a lifetime? Probably - despite subsequent trips to Nepal, Peru and the Alps, nothing compares with the Karakoram.

Go, if you get the opportunity!

—TMs—

Desert Island Hills: The Seven Summits – Derek Sime

Ben Cleuch is a modest rounded grassy hill in the Ochils and my usual route from The Nebit to King's Seat takes in seven summits and gives a respectable day out with about twelve miles of walking and 1,000m of ascent, all within a 15-minute drive. The views all round are excellent, if not perhaps spectacular, with the whole of the Forth Valley in view right down to North Berwick Law and the Bass Rock, while to the north, the Highlands. On an exceptionally clear day, it's even possible to see The Cheviot, 80 miles away. Then to round off the day, a cappuccino at the Coffee Bothy in Blairlogie. That would keep me happy on my desert island until I was rescued.

The Alps

Stewart Logan

I have walked and climbed in the Alps several times over the years and I describe here some of the more interesting experiences. The one thing which I have never got used to in the Alps is the sheer scale of things. A hill which seems to be only a short distance ahead and not too high can take an age to climb. Also, I never did enjoy the Alpine starts to climb the big hills. This is where you start in the middle of the night to be safely off the hill before the sun softens the snow making progress much harder. More important, it releases rocks from their icy grip and they come tumbling down the mountain sides.

The Chamonix Committee

Our Club had organised a summer trip to Chamonix. Because it would coincide with the sixtieth birthday of one of our number, we decided to do things in style and organised accommodation in four flats in a block of the same. The organisation of the flats was such that, to get from two of the flats to the other two, you had to descend in a lift to the ground floor, cross a large entrance hall and ascend another lift at the far side. Many of the flat occupiers were still in residence and a gentleman, who turned out to be the chairman of their organising committee, had occasion to speak to us. He reminded us that we were in their flats and could we please be a bit quieter and not keep rushing around the place.

One day, after a long overnight trip in the high Alps, we got back to the flats in early afternoon. After a shower, I decided to go over to see our colleagues in the faraway flats to share some refreshment. It was extremely hot, so I descended the lift in bare feet and wearing only shorts and carrying a bottle of wine.

The doors opened on the ground floor and I stepped out to be confronted by a table, round which the chairman and his organising committee were sat. It was too late to turn back so I strode over the hall wishing them 'Bonjour' and shot into the lift on the other side. You could have heard a pin drop, but we never had another visit from the chairman. I think he probably thought that we were beyond redemption.

Wine at the Goûter

We were on our way home from Courmayeur via the Mont Blanc tunnel and decided that there was time in hand to climb the hill if we went to the Goûter Hut that day. After three weeks in the Alps, funds were running low so we knew that we could not afford the food and drink that would be on offer at the hut. We went up from Les Houches by way of the téléphérique and tramway and eventually reached the rocky spur leading up to the Goûter. I was wearing the kilt, intending to leave it at the hut when we made our attempt on the summit the next morning.

Aiguille & Dôme du Goûter (Derek Sime)

We were halfway up the spur when a violent hailstorm suddenly descended on us and the temperature plummeted, and visibility went. The others stopped to pull over-trousers over their shorts but that posed a problem with the kilt. I therefore decided to scramble on up. After about ten minutes, the hail stopped, and visibility improved such that I saw the hut just above me. People were coming back out onto the terrace and saw me in a kilt emerging out of a snowstorm. By the time that I had reached the terrace quite a crowd was watching me, and one chap stepped forward and thrust a half-bottle of wine and a glass into my hands, pointed at the kilt and gave a thumbs up. I shall never forget the looks on my mates' faces when they arrived and saw me sitting on my rucksack sipping a glass of wine.

Early next morning, we failed on the attempt on Mont Blanc because we got surrounded by a violent thunder and lightning storm. We could not even get into the Vallot Hut to shelter because the lightning was constantly striking its roof. Some years later, we got turned back at the same point by gale-force winds. A Scottish climber was blown to his death off the Bosses Ridge that morning.

Zermatt Adventures

We were camped at Täsch, the last place before Zermatt where the general public is allowed to drive to. We wanted to start with a relatively easy acclimatisation day so took the lift to the summit of the Klein Matterhorn, roped up and climbed the Breithorn. We carried on over to climb Pollux, which was not in our original plan and the second rope of three was struggling, so any thought of carrying on to Castor was forgotten about. The last moves to the top of Pollux were on very icy ground and we advised some Italians who were about to descend that they should keep out in the sun where it was not so icy. Whether they did not understand us or chose to ignore us, the pair of them, roped together, proceeded to descend on the icy slopes in the shade. Within moments they were away and went sliding down the fortunately rock-free slopes with cries of 'Gelato, Mamma mia!' We never heard of any disasters so presumed that they survived.

Pollux (Derek Sime)

Castor (Derek Sime)

We started to descend north and soon became separated from our second rope of three who said that they were okay but would take their time. We came to a very steep convex slope of soft snow which looked as though it might avalanche. We therefore roped down it one at a time to a reasonably secure halfway stance and then repeated the manoeuvre to the bottom. Donald knew that an apparently easier route led to an area of séracs and had to be avoided (the second rope got benighted in this area as they found the séracs in the darkness - they realised that they would have to re-ascend to avoid them so had a very uncomfortable night on the slopes). We had an interminable journey down to and across the Gornergletscher and up to the top terminus of the Gornergrat railway. We were now in darkness and the last train had long since left. We walked down the railway track to Zermatt. At one point, there was a hollow sound under our footsteps and Donald explained that we were going over a bridge and to keep away from the side. Next morning, when I saw the bridge from Zermatt, I was horrified. It is an enormous span over a gorge. We got down to Zermatt after all the pubs had closed and Donald and I lay down and fell asleep on the pavement whilst Ian went back to camp for his car. At one in the morning, you don't see police stopping you from driving up to Zermatt.

Next day, we went up to Zermatt to wait for the others to return. We found that a supermarket was having a promotion of a new wine and customers were being offered a sample glass. You then had the back of your hand stamped so that you didn't get another free glass. Every time I passed that corner of the store, I was given another glass although no one else got more than one. Eventually, the girl said that she liked the look of the kilt and was encouraging me to come back for more (if you see what I mean!). I kept Ian and Donald supplied with free wine. When the others eventually appeared off the train, they were rather displeased that our interest in the wine was greater than that of their well-being.

A few days later, we set off to climb the Monte Rosa. We took the Gornergrat railway and then walked over the Gornergletscher to the Monte Rosa hut for the night. When we got there Donald, who had stayed in the hut some years before, shot off to the toilets. When he came back, he said that the state of the toilets was disgraceful, and the smell was terrible. A stranger who overheard this comment pointed out to Donald that these toilets had been closed two years before and the new ones were at the other end of the building. Very early next day, we climbed with head-torches up to the Silbersattel between the Dufourspitze, the main summit, and the outlying Nordend. There was a very strong wind at the saddle and the steep slope to the main summit did not seem to be a sensible proposition in these conditions. Instead, we went out along to Nordend keeping back from the south-facing cornice, and found that we were protected from the wind. The last climb to the summit of Nordend is a short scramble. Now as we traversed along to it, we had never seen over to the Italian side as we were down the slope slightly on the Swiss side. Donald led up to the summit and the route spiralled round towards the Italian side. He quickly reached the summit and called me to follow. He was taking in the rope and I was entering the last short chimney to join him. He asked me to pause a moment and look down. The fields of Italy were thousands of feet below me and I was at the top of what is one of the highest cliffs in Europe.

Monte Rosa (Derek Sime)

'You won't get a view like that in Scotland' was Donald's comment.

Courmayeur Capers

Our annual Alps trip was to be based in Courmayeur in the Aosta Valley in north-west Italy. The day before, Italy had beaten France in a World Cup qualifier. When we crossed into Italy on the Great St. Bernard Pass, the score was emblazoned all over the Customs building, the officials were well into their wine and we were waved through non-stop. This was in the pre-Common Market days when border crossing delays were often extensive for foreigners.

I had never been to Italy and did not appreciate the value of the lira. We stopped to pick up provisions in Courmayeur and I led the way into a public toilet in the square. The concierge asked me for 100 lira and I walked straight out and relieved myself in a garden off the street. Donald came out of the toilet laughing. 'The cost was thrupence-halfpenny', he said. I was soon to find that any loose change due in a shop was given in the form of a handful of sweets.

We set up camp in the official site some distance from the town and went to the local shop to buy wine supplies. We decided that one 1.5 litre bottle per couple every second day should suffice. Over the next few days, after we discovered how cheap the wine was, the consumption progressed through 1.5 litres per couple every day to 1.5 litres per person per day before stabilising at 2 litres per person per day. This, I should hasten to add, was only on rest days.

Relaxing above Courmayeur with Hamish & Donald (Stewart Logan)

One of our major trips was an attempt on the Grandes Jorasses. We started off directly from our camp as opposed to the normal point nearer Courmayeur and so missed a vital notice. When we reached our planned stop for the night at the Boccalatte hut, we found that it was closed for renovations. Luckily, we had bivvy bags and food but were short of a night-cap. The front door of the hut was all boarded up with a gap at the bottom, but we could see about nine feet inside a bottle of wine. I ashamedly have to admit that, using a plank of building material lying outside, we managed to 'rescue' the bottle. We had no water but were right at the snow-line, so set to melting snow for tea and cooking. Donald had brought with him a brand-new lightweight stove which he had tested at home. At this altitude, it just would not melt the snow - the flame stayed stubbornly yellow instead of going blue. Its gas-bottle was separate and joined to it by a flexible tube. In shear frustration, he grabbed it by the gas-bottle, swung it around his head and with an oath, released it over the glacier below. As it arched over in the night-sky, its flame turned blue. 'It's working now', said Gordon.

Next day, we got up to Pointe Whymper and started the traverse to Pointe Walker. By this time, it was getting late in the morning and the snow was getting soft and heavy. We abandoned the traverse when we saw through a hole in the cornice to the fields of France. A pretty horrific descent on mixed ground led to a second night on the hill. We only had one regret about this trip. The Club members who had stayed in camp told us that we had missed the very pleasant sight of a nearby group of German Fräuleins who had spent the day sunbathing in the nude.

One morning back at camp, we wakened up after an especially cold night. Donald wandered down to the toilet-block. The toilets were in cubicles, but each was simply a hole in the ground with a constant run of water coming along a gutter at roof level with an offshoot into each latrine. Donald came running back. 'Quick, go and use the toilets now. The water has frozen in the night and they will soon be unusable'. We quickly used them but he was right. Half an hour later a gas-mask would have been necessary.

On our last evening, we went out for a meal and, with our group of twelve, the eating-house was obviously going to do quite well. As a thank-you, the proprietor provided free home-made grappa which everyone found quite revolting. We were seated in an alcove with a shelf behind us lined with potted plants. I'm afraid that when the proprietor was looking the other way, his plants got a liberal dosing of grappa.

We had been going to the same taverna each night and after our final meal, we returned there for the last time. I wanted to celebrate with a cigar and eventually got through to the barman what I wanted. He disappeared through a bead curtain into the back-shop and returned with an enormous cigar in a metal container. He would not take any money for it. As I was contentedly puffing away in a corner, an old, wizened

Rest-day at Courmayeur campsite
(Stewart Logan)

face peeped through the curtain and then retreated. Immediately, there was the sound of very raised voices from the other side. Donald turned to me. 'They've given you his cigar, you know'.

I acted as the bank for all expenditure and paid the camp bill at the end of the trip. It was actually quite cheap but sounded ridiculous at three quarters of a million lira. When I redistributed the small change from the kitty, Donald chucked his in the bushes with a comment (to the effect) that it was useless.

Fear

Recently, I walked the Grande Randonnée 5 (GR5) from Lake Geneva to Nice. The first few days went well but the weather began to threaten as I left Samoëns. I was planning to pass the Alfred Wills Refuge, go over the Col d'Anterne and stop for the night at the chalet-refuge beyond the top. Halfway to the Alfred Wills, the heavens opened, the wind blew up strongly and a thick mist came down. Ominously, I could hear thunder in the distance but, of course, could see nothing.

The thunder came closer and closer and eventually, the mist was being lit up by the lightning flashes. It got to the point where there was no delay between the flashes and the thunder. I could not see if there was any shelter, so I began running blindly in the direction of the refuge. By now water was streaming off the hillside and the rain was so torrential that I was soaking and starting to shiver. I was never so glad to see the refuge emerge out of the mist. The warden persuaded me not to go any further, but I had no intention of doing so in these conditions.

Two days later I learned that a walker had been killed by lightning less than 10 kilometres away in the same storm.

National Celebrations

It was Bastille Day on the GR5 and we were close to Briançon. By now I

Walked with this couple from Oregon for two days. Refuge below Col de la Golèse.
(Stewart Logan)

had teamed up with my neighbours, Bill and Christine, who had started out on the walk shortly before me. We were climbing to the Col de Dormillouse and they stopped for a rest and a bite to eat. I said that I would wait for them at the col. I got there and the first people up after me were a group of about twenty French. I got out the camcorder and asked them to do something relevant to Bastille Day.

That is why I have a wonderful recording of a group of French people singing the Marseillaise on a col high in the Alps. I, of course, had to reply with Flower of Scotland which they all seemed to be aware of from rugby internationals.

Bill and Christine arrived shortly afterwards and asked if they had been hallucinating!

Taxi for Logan

My wife, Eleanor, and daughter Julie had joined me for the last three days on the GR5. They had done very well on the first nine-hour day which ended with us in a rather poor self-catering gîte because the local hotel had closed. They had only agreed to join me because the accommodation towards the end of the walk was much superior if a trifle more expensive. We were lucky to get any food that evening because everything was shut, but one shop opened for an hour in the evening.

Next day was very, very hot and, by the halfway point at Levens, we were all dead-beat. We still had about three hours walking to do. Julie made the comment that, if there was a bus from there to our stopping point at Aspremont, she would take it. To cut a long story short, Eleanor haggled with a taxi-driver and arranged a lift for the two of them. To make it easier for me, they took most of my luggage and left me with a small rucksack loaded with

On the GR5 with my wife, Eleanor, approaching Nice (Julie Logan)

water. I estimated that I would reach Aspremont by 5pm. I would phone from the mobile if there were problems.

After a three-hour walk in extremely sweltering conditions, I entered Aspremont at 4.55 and went straight into the Tourist Office to ask where our pre-booked hotel was. I was round there a couple of minutes after 5. The chap at the desk said that my wife and daughter had gone out for a walk so I had a quick wash and settled down with a beer. After half an hour, they had still not appeared, so I did a quick tour of the small town without success then went back to the hotel and had another beer. I don't know if it was the effect of the heat, but it never occurred to me to try to phone them.

Sometime after 6 they returned, and I heard their incredulous voices as they were informed by the Manager that I was out in the beer-garden. They came out and their emotions veered between relief and anger. They had left the hotel just before 5 to meet me. We reckon that, at that moment, I must have been in the Tourist Office. They had then walked a considerable distance up the first hill crying out plaintively for me and then returned worried stiff thinking that they would have to report me missing.

At least they had feelings for me.

Tunnels & Falls

We were staying in Grasse with my brother-in-law and his wife. I had a day to myself and decided to go for a walk in the villages and hills behind Grasse. I would be dropped off in Gourdon, a hill-top village, and could walk back down from there. I was duly dropped off and enquired of a local if there was a path down towards Grasse. He directed me to the end of the village and said that a walker's signpost would keep me right. I found the start of the route and then found that there was a choice of descent – one out in the open and the other, which I was told went periodically into tunnels, following the water-supply pipeline to Cannes. I chose the latter route as sounding a bit unusual. It did not have any route markers which should have warned me that it was not a normal route of descent. It was alright where tunnels were dead straight. However, where a tunnel had bends in it, it became pitch black and I had no torch with me. I had to carefully feel my way down these sections but luckily it had no steps in it. The views from occasional windows were truly magnificent. Eventually, I came out of the last tunnel just before a quarry but could not find the open-air path which was obviously meant to be the walkers' descent route. I went into the quarry offices to enquire. My French was awful and I could not get my question understood so they called in a worker who could speak English. He misunderstood me and thought that I was trying to climb from Grasse to Gourdon. 'You go over the road and slightly downhill, you will see the route marker. Do not go into the tunnel where the pipe comes out. It is very dark in there and, even with a torch, people have panicked and turned back'. Some things you do not want to know beforehand.

A few days later we all went out with members of a French walking club into the hills on the Italian border. The day started in glorious weather but steadily deteriorated and it started to rain. The French all put on capes which totally enveloped them and their rucksacks. Kitted out in that gear, they all looked identical. We were traversing a hillside on a path when there was a cry at the front of the crocodile and a figure started to roll down the hillside. The fall was stopped by a tree a short distance down the slope. We found that it was one of the ladies in the party. She had been winded and was shaken but otherwise unhurt. I was a bit surprised that someone phoned the rescue service and said that a call-out might be required if she needed help later to get off the hill. I volunteered to carry her rucksack back to the car and we all got back safely. Returning in the outskirts of Nice, we were somewhat alarmed when a car wheel came flying down the road towards us. We swerved round it and, at the top of the hill, found that a car had shed a wheel without apparently being involved in a crash. We commented that things can happen in threes, but we got back to Grasse with no further excitement.

—TMS—

Desert Island Hills: Tinto Hill – Susan Lunn

It isn't a Munro but my Munro trips can all trace a path back to Tinto in South Lanarkshire. It's my 'local'. Feel like a leg-stretch one morning? Tinto can be summited by lunchtime. Need hill time in preparation for a big trip? Tinto offers a quick blast of training. Its Bronze Age round cairn at the summit links this need to reach the top of hills with countless previous generations – long before Hugh Munro set his challenge – and views to Ben Lomond and beyond give a glimpse of the enticing treats that await just a little further away.

LOCHS and LOCHANS

Above – Sunset lighting the Ghost Slabs above Dubh Loch. On the right is the causeway which separates this loch from Fionn Loch, once a subject of litigation over fishing rights.

Below – Linear lochans in the sandstone below the Green Lochs, in the Coulin hills.

Jeremy Fenton

Kayaking in Patagonia

Will Copestake

T oo hostile to be paradise, too beautiful to be hell, Patagonia was carved into the southern tip of South America by an eternity of ice and wind. On the eastern edge of the Pacific a ragged fringe of fjords is shadowed by vast mountains of the southern Andes. Between the sea and the eastern pampas grasslands these mountains are capped under the third largest continental ice cap on Earth. East of the icecap is the mighty Torres del Paine mountain range in Chile, whose yellow granite spires capped in a black cap of gabbro draw trekkers from around the world. It is here which now feels like a second home to me. This is the story of my journey.

Acrobatics in front of glaciers (Will Copestake)

When I first set foot in Torres Del Paine in 2014, I was fresh off the back of the largest adventure in my life, which I'd coined 'The Machair to Munro Project'. Over 364 days, starting in May 2013, I'd taken four months to kayak solo around the coast of Scotland, then re-packed onto a bicycle and cycled home via a continual, mostly winter, round of the Munros.

As it turned out, a largely winter round of the Munros would prove perfect training for a life as a newly appointed kayak guide in Patagonia. For all those nights spent huddled in my tent, damp sleeping bag frozen over me, toes cold and my face stinging from a day in a whiteout, I'd learnt to deal with life in the elements. Now it was my chance to lead in it.

In the summer since finishing that trip, I'd lived by hitch-hiking across Scotland, guiding freelance hillwalking. I'd bivvied outside carparks before leading three-peak challenges up the Ben, or Duke of Edinburgh trips across the moors. So it was with a twist of irony as I flew south for the winter to the ends of the Earth that I had committed to the most stable life I'd have for almost two years.

I arrived in Puerto Natales, my new home, in the dark after almost three days of bus and plane journeys. Greeted by my new boss Herman and his wife in a snowstorm, they ushered me to my new abode, a rented house on the edge of town. Of the three guides Herman had hired, I was the first to arrive, and upon moving in, set about building my bed, which was a flatpack on the floor. The only other furniture was a large cable drum in the main room, a single heater (which didn't work) and a parasol mushroom growing out of the bath plug. At least the street dogs kept me company until the other guides would arrive. But it didn't matter - as soon as I woke up to first light, I scraped the frost off the window, and looked outside to see a horizon of mountains taller and more remote than I'd ever seen. I'd arrived at an adventure playground!

Unlike my American co-guides, who were fresh from a degree in Expeditionary Studies (I know right! Dream course!), I had no formal

Camped at Bernal Glacier (Will Copestake)

qualifications in kayaking. Herman had hired me solely on credit from my expedition and mountain leader tickets and training would be done 'in house'.

'Mañana' Herman kept saying when it came to our first staff expedition, 'tomorrow'. We waited for almost three weeks before 'tomorrow' became 'today', which, as it turned out, Herman had been waiting for the strongest winds possible. His idea was that if we survived three days down the river at its worst, we could lead safely in lesser conditions.

Camps hidden beneath ice (Will Copestake)

Having once paddled solo from Puerto Montt to Cape Horn in a blacked-out kayak to avoid the Navy (who were looking for him as he had not got permission to go), Herman was a bit of a legend in Patagonian Paddling circles. His expedition pedigree strongly reflected in his leadership style, which took a more 'expedition' approach than formal guiding. Make headway, when possible, with brute strength and tactics, or wait in a tent occasionally a day or so longer than the scheduled tour length. It didn't matter if you were late - 'this is Patagonia'. When the wind got too strong for his guests to paddle, he would take out his towline and go into 'beast mode', literally dragging them through with him, often four tandems at a time lashed together.

I'd idolize him as we got to know each other better, but for now I tried my best to lip-read what I thought said, 'This is a sheltered spot' over a 45-knot headwind.

I'd never paddled in winds this strong before, and it pushed me hard.

Posing in front of a remote glacier on a solo trip (Will Copestake)

At times we waited, at others we battled on; even with the river flow in our favour it was brutal. Clinging to our kayaks whilst hidden in a bush watching a tremendous wall of water roaring over us, no longer in the river but in the air, I remember the look in my American colleagues' eyes which unreassuringly reflected my own, 'how the hell do you even lead in this?'. Herman trained me well, taking me under his wing and teaching me the secrets of the Rio Serrano, the 70km long glacial river which now dictated my life. He taught me how to tow in extreme wind, how to read the weather from the clouds and how to use the eddies and meanders of the river to pull weak guests where you wanted them or more importantly away from the trees. He showed me hidden channels and 'secret walks', reliable campsites and lots of places he promised shelter but in my experience never were.

Most influential of all, Herman introduced to us the concept of tracking and portage. It is for best purposes a thuggish activity performed like a delicate art form and involves the dragging and towing of kayaks upstream and overland. Portage brought you to places hitherto unexplored, unreachable on foot and un-paddleable on water; these places hid glaciers, icebergs and a sense of 'Huckleberry Finn' adventure which I'd only dreamt and read about. Even today on over the 100th time leading guests up-stream, I still get the same sense of this untapped adventure by towing a kayak up a river.

Portage in Patagonia also throws back to the natives, the Kawesqar people. These hardy men and women lived in the western fjords, naked using goose fat for warmth in a climate fringing on a Scottish winter. They used in their canoes a clay floor and a fire to stay warm, proving 'you can have your kayak and heat it too' to misquote a pun. I for one prefer a Gore-Tex dry suit and a fireless boat, but their same principle applies today; when you can't paddle, you can always drag.

My season culminated in the honour of leading the one and only coastal expedition that year. A ten-day expedition to the Canal de las Montañas, a 100km long fjord filled with glaciers west of the mountain ranges.

Dropped in by boat, I was left alone with a single guest and as she and I ventured north into the narrow fjord the heavens opened. For the duration of the trip, it rained torrentially, except when it snowed. Evading spindrifts, we snuck along the coast, which was impossibly steep in places and overgrown in others. Finding camps often involved bashing through the undergrowth or risking a camp at the top of the tidal beaches. Here, every part of my experience gained in Scotland as a sea kayaker was combined with the tent discipline of winter Munro bagging.

Unfortunately, just after our first glacier, my guest became too ill to paddle and after two days awaiting rescue, we were picked up with seven days complete and half the fjord un-paddled. The trip had been equally brutal and exhilarating and instilled in me a deep desire to return as soon as I could. But the year was over, and I was headed home to Scotland.

The next winter I returned to Chile for a second year. The same company,

Glacial calving (Will Copestake)

(Tutravesia) was under new owners, David and Carlos Dittmar. They were two brothers who ran a trekking and biking business in the National Park and had the same knowledge of kayaking as I did of golf – little.

As such, I in part had been hired to teach them how to operate a kayak company, which was novel as I'd never really run one myself, but I saw it as a huge learning opportunity and leapt at the chance to come back with a deal. I'd agreed with the brothers that come the end of the season I'd take two kayaks for a month, and with my friend Seumas from Scotland, we would embark on a big expedition into the fjords, turning our sights far further than the Canal de las Montañas.

With the added knowledge of season one, my second season went smoothly on the whole. I shared my guiding with another American expedition studies alumni, Matt. Between us, we developed a new game of paddling and portaging to the remote glacial lakes that fringe the Rio Serrano. Each one, in their own right, a short but genuine expedition. Matt decided pretty early on that I'd grown unhealthily obsessed with 'type three' fun, where at the time progress is grim and memories are fond; whereas I felt I was training for the bigger trip and an obsession to find ice. These short adventures, including winching a sea kayak up a cliff in one instance, had gained us the ego-boosting nickname 'El Machinas', (the machines), amongst the local guides, many of whom I now knew as friends. It was unusual

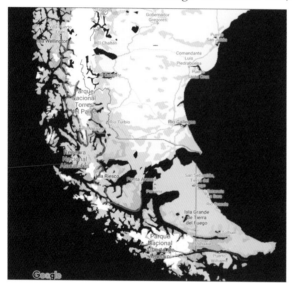

Seumas (Will Copestake)

Landing at PioXI Glacier, the largest in South America (Will Copestake)

for guides to return for more than one season, and I'd noticed a definite positive change to how I was received the second year, much more seriously.

Ultimately as friendships grow that nickname has faded and devolved into what has now stuck circa 2021: 'Willy Wonka', perhaps for my love of snickers bars on trips, or goofy style.

As the season ended, I had a route penned on a chart ready to come to life. An 850km passage from the small township of Puerto Eden back to Puerto Natales. Between the two there would be no roads and no option to escape through a labyrinth of fjords.

Matt & Will at Glacier Geike (Will Copestake)

201

As the ferry took off from Natales I stood by my best friend Seumas, who had arrived from Scotland, and waved farewell to Carlos and David. Below deck two MK1 P&H Scorpio sea kayaks sat overladen with 120kg of food and camp kit, enough to stow away for 45 days alone in the fjords. A Navy inspection was due on arrival, and we hadn't even tested that the kayaks floated yet.

Perfection in Peel Fjord (Will Copestake)

Unlike Herman I didn't fancy a blacked-out kayak, and sought permission from the Navy to navigate, an infamously difficult request, but they are the only rescue option even if they may take a week to reach you. Thankfully, we passed the test, and after three days' stay with a local fisherman, we were given the red stamp to continue. The adventure was on.

The winds in Patagonia blow ferociously with a predictable north to south bearing which we hoped to harness. Our route had only three northern detours, all of which were to reach glaciers whose iceberg-filled fjords had an appealing draw. For Seumas this was his first sea kayak expedition longer than a few days, but he is a strong paddler from a childhood of river kayaking, and through his job as a gamekeeper, reliably tough. To add to our 'firsts' within the first week, we reached Pio XI. As Seumas's first glacier the 11km long wall of shattered blue ice, the largest in South America, was a spectacular start. We spent a whole day wandering beside it, watching it calve huge chunks into the ocean with deafening booms and splashes.

The wettest place on earth, we were unsurprised to have near constant rain or snow throughout, but Seumas brought with him a good omen, which we've since coined 'the Nairn effect' after his surname. Whenever we paddle together, we seem to get horrendous rain until the moment we reach our goal, upon which the wind dies, and the sun comes out. For all three of our glacial detours this happened, and subsequently on our later trips together too.

At our side as we ventured through the fjords, we often saw penguin and albatross, beneath us dolphin and icebergs. Equally they shared the forests with hummingbirds and parrots, flamingos and fuchsia flowers, an unlikely combination.

Between paddling beneath the labyrinth of granite walls and thick, overgrown temperate rainforest, we had planned three portages to bypass the most exposed headlands. Even in the shelter of the fjords the winds, which often blew to 30-40 knots, brought steep waves of several metres; where the sea became more open, we hoped to drag between headlands and into the next narrow passage. In part this was for safety, in another to reach lesser explored fjords and lastly, I felt it was a homage to Herman and the Kawesqar who, for several of our routes we'd chosen to drag, were their own.

Dragging 100kg+ of laden kayaks up to 4km across impossibly dense and inexplicably spiky vegetation was definite 'type 3' fun. To find rhythm to each lift, taking the boats a foot at a time, we recalled Gladiator Ready in a throwback to the '90s TV show. It took an entire day per portage, but we always arrived with a great sense of achievement and a lot of sweat.

Progress went smoothly; despite a few days ashore in bigger gales and the slow pace of portage, we had gained days ahead of our plan. As we ventured north again, this time to the glacial lagoon of Peel Fjord, we arrived at our halfway point and our second light of 'the Nairn effect'. A bottle-neck lagoon with a hefty tide had led us into the most ice-filled fjord of our lives – three tremendous glaciers in a 20km narrows calved ice into the water with regular tent-shuddering booms. To escape we hopped behind the eddies of icebergs, timing our passage to avoid being crushed as they rolled through the tidal fjords.

Scale in Peel Fjord (Will Copestake)

203

On day 25 we reached the Canal de las Montañas. It was very different from how I'd first seen it the year before. This time the rain had gone and I could see the mountains. A weather window of calm conditions and sunshine arrived as we did to the glaciers (the Nairn effect strikes again!). We had less than a week of paddling to return to Natales and were so far ahead of schedule we felt it OK to stop. For four days we explored, camping beneath the ice flows and climbing ridge lines to view the valley from above, lining up a river and weaving into every nook and cranny of the ice-filled lagoons. This was the adventure I'd dreamt of for two years on the Rio Serrano, which lay a little beyond the far side of the mountains from where we now stood.

After our final portage, we arrived east of the mountains chuckling at Herman's description 'a short bog drag', which had turned out to be a 200m high mountain after 4km of bog. Puerto Natales was in sight!

Smiling through rain on my first trip to the Canal de los Montañas (Will Copestake)

33 days since we set off, for the first time we saw other human beings. The sense of isolation turned to a longing for a hot shower and pizzas at the local bar, which we noted hadn't particularly been missed in a month in the tents. We'd been distracted throughout with the sense of adventure, the urge to explore and the logistics of the days ahead. In our wake we'd left the wildest place we'd ever been behind us and a longing to explore more in future.

Over the next few years, I've returned to Patagonia for a further two seasons, now working for a new company: Kayak

Training guides in the wind (Will Copestake)

en Patagonia. Continuing adventures, Seumas has joined me for a second expedition further south, venturing through to Punta Arenas over 14 days in the fjords. We now hope to return a final time to continue to Cape Horn, a plan that was curtailed in 2020 by Covid, just a week before it started.

Looking back, the comparison between Scottish mountains and Patagonian paddling can find many parallels, be it the addictive challenges of venturing to wild places in cold conditions, or, when sheltering in the towns, the hospitality of the locals. One thing I can say for sure is that the finest adventures take a little dose of cold, a lot of rain and perhaps an element of suffering before the reward. In the meantime, I'm based in Scotland until I can return south again. I'll be finding home back in the Munros and hope to see you up there.

—TMS—

Desert Island Hills: Ben Wyvis – Julian Foot

As any DID fan will tell you, it's not always the best but the one holding the most sentimental value. Every day we are home we look out onto Ben Wyvis, a mighty mountain but not the most dramatic or shapely. It's there every time we pull back the curtains, even if the clouds are down, we know it hides behind. When we've been away on our travels, it heralds our approach to home. We have climbed it numerous times – in thick snow and in shorts and tee-shirts and usually in high wind! One of my crowning achievements was digging down and unearthing the top of the trig point from the deep snow.

LOCHS and LOCHANS

Above – Fionn Loch and its neighbours from Beinn Airigh Charr. According to the reflections it is a fine day.

Below – Loch Ghiuragarstidh on the Inverewe estate, with a fine example of 'patterned bog'; this is caused by the slippage of the surface of the peat.

Jeremy Fenton

The Luck of the Irish

James Forrest

I lift my head to the heavens and laugh maniacally, like an evil villain. Am I losing my mind? 11 consecutive days of relentless rain has left me on the brink of madness. 'Arrrggghhhh, is that all you've got?' I scream, a deranged war cry taunting the weather gods. Being out in the worst Storm Ali can throw at me is horrific, demoralising, joyless; but also, strangely thrilling and soul-stirring. Horizontal rain pummels into my exposed face, dripping off my scraggly, ginger-tinged beard; and gale force winds throw me around, buffeting my sodden Gore-Tex layers. I am wet and wretched – and I don't know whether to laugh or cry. I choose the former and begin cackling hysterically, disinhibited in the knowledge I am alone in these rugged mountains. This really is putting the wild into the Wild Atlantic coast.

Fifty-three mountains is my tally for the past 11 days – and I've barely seen a view from a single summit. I feel like giving up. I'm exhausted and crestfallen. All I want to do is get the ferry home, curl up on the sofa with my duvet, binge-watch Netflix while eating pizza, and forget all about this horrible nightmare. But I can't, I mustn't, I won't – no matter how badly I want to. Why? Because I'm here on the Emerald Isle with a very specific peak-bagging mission: to climb all 273 mountains in Ireland and Northern Ireland. The so-called Vandeleur-Lynams – Irish mountains over 600m with a minimum prominence of 15m – are my *raison d'être*. And I want to be the fastest person ever to complete them and the first person ever to do so in a single-round. But will I make it?

The finish line seems a long way off, as I arrive back to the sanctuary of my hostel. I shower, put on warm, dry clothes, and make pasta with chorizo for dinner. Outside the merciless rain continues to batter Connemara National Park. County Galway is in the grip of a brutal storm and I've never felt happier to not be in a tent. Flashbacks of a foul, sleepless, damp night in my storm-tossed Terra Nova, just days ago in the Bluestack Mountains, make me shudder, as if experiencing an episode of PTSD. I shake off the feeling and sit down in the lounge with my heaped plate of pasta. 'You look tired', says Serena, a pretty French girl with long dark hair and a nose piercing. 'I'm absolutely shattered – I've climbed 178 mountains in the past 41 days', I reply, glancing at my journal to check the stats. 'In this weather? You're mad', she replies, chuckling.

I proceed to tell her in great detail the story of my adventure so far: of how I'm climbing all of the mountains of Ireland and Northern Ireland, solo and unsupported, walking up to 40km a day, sleeping wild under the stars in a one-man tent, hitchhiking when I need to, and driving between ranges in my VW Golf, which is packed to the rafters with hiking gear and expedition food. The look on her face is somewhere between impressed and bemused. 'So where have you been so far?', asks Serena, seemingly intrigued by this mad Englishman's eccentric travels. I draw a crude map on the back of a napkin, with arrows highlighting my journey: ferry from Liverpool to Dublin; three weeks travelling clockwise around the coast, ticking off the mountains of eastern and southern Ireland; leap-frogging to the north-east – due to a spot of illogical adventure planning – for a mini-break with my girlfriend Nic; and then a further three weeks of looping north and west, in an anti-clockwise arch through the Mournes, Sperrins, Donegal, Mayo and Galway, again mostly sticking to the mountain-rich coastal regions.

'Has anything funny happened?', asks my French friend, who seems to be enjoying the conversation. But I don't really need any prompting. My monologue – perhaps geed by a dire lack of human contact over the past month – is in free flow. I reel off a long-list of anecdotes and tall tales: in the Wicklow Mountains I forgot my lighter, couldn't boil water and had to resort to eating freeze-dried meals mixed with cold water – they tasted like dog food; in the Comeraghs I got stranded in the middle of nowhere, tried and failed to hitchhike a ride, and came very close to sleeping in a squalid roadside ditch, until a lovely couple rescued me in the eleventh hour; and in the Galtees I fell violently ill, my upset stomach perhaps victim to my laissez-faire approach to water filtering.

Waking up above the clouds on Knockowen (James Forrest)

'But it hasn't all been calamitous and miserable', I add, reaching for my phone. 'Check this out', I say, playing a video of me opening my tent on Knockowen, a 658m mountain in the Caha Mountains of the Beara Peninsula, an area of wild and rocky uplands in south-west Ireland. Serena is mesmerised, watching as I unzip the door to unveil a perfect cloud inversion. Craggy mountain tops pierce majestically through a sea of fluffy white clouds, like the fins of dolphins breaking the waves; while the sun paints a Brocken spectre masterpiece on the white cloud canvas, a double-rainbow halo forming around my shadow. 'Wow, that is so beautiful', says Serena, smiling as she hits play for a second time. 'It was my 100th mountain, so it felt doubly special', I reply. 'It was one of those moments that make enduring all the rain and wind worth it.'

The following morning, dreary-eyed and clutching a mug of hot filter coffee, I check the forecast on my phone. Grinning, I read it twice to make sure I'm not imagining things. Storm Ali is no more – and maybe, just maybe, the sun will shine during my final 95 Vandeleur-Lynams. I'm excited and elated. Thick mists have spoilt so many of my recent walks: I never saw the volcano-like pyramid of Errigal in Glenveagh National Park, one of Ireland's most dramatic peaks; my hike up Croagh Patrick, a sacred and holy mountain with the power to cleanse the souls of pilgrims, was completed in hellish rather than divine weather; and the only thing memorable of my climbs in the cloud-cloaked Ben Gorm and Partry mountains was fearing for my life atop Devilsmother, as I desperately hung to a fence in an attempt to stop 60mph gusts blowing me off a ridge and into the abyss. But now, perhaps, all of that hardship is over – and, I hope, I pray, the good times lie ahead in the high peaks of County Kerry.

I drive into Killarney, the gateway town to the mountains of Kerry. The sun beams brightly in a cloudless azure sky and my smile beams even brighter. It feels as if my penance has been served in the sodden west coast of Ireland. And now the mountain gods are looking down on me favourably, in recognition of the hardship I've endured. The south-west of Ireland is exactly where I want to be during these sunnier climes too. County Kerry is the promised land of Irish hill-walking; a must-visit region on the bucket-list of every outdoor enthusiast in Ireland. MacGillycuddy's Reeks are the star attraction: a chaotic, gnarly mountain range of inter-connecting knife-edge ridges, soaring rocky summits, and domineering cliff-faces – and home to Carrauntoohil, Ireland's highest peak at 1,039m. But Kerry is so much more than just the Reeks. To the north, the Dingle Peninsula serves up endless skies, sparkling ocean views and pristine beaches; while the Dunkerrons to the south are wild, remote and rugged, a place of tough, pathless walking for tough, fearless walkers. I have so much to look forward to – and I can't wait to get started.

View of Carrauntoohil while exploring the MacGillycyddy's Reeks (James Forrest)

Scrambling on The Big Gun ridge (James Forrest)

The next two weeks are a sun-drenched dream. In the Reeks, I enter a scrambler's paradise, a rocky world that is simultaneously breathtaking and terrifying. From Cruach Mhór I clamber nervously over The Big Gun ridge, a jumbled, mangled puzzle of boulders with precipitous drops on each side, before edging along the crest of the Knocknapeasta arête, a narrow spine of rock I imagine to be the scaly backbone of a sleeping dragon. Forget Crib Goch and Striding Edge, this is some of the finest scrambling I've ever experienced. I top out on Carrauntoohil, a moment that feels like a significant milestone in my peak-bagging mission, and then descend via Beenkeragh, Ireland's second highest mountain at 1,008m, and the Hag's Tooth ridge. The latter is an alpine-esque arête; an adrenaline-inducing, nerve-jangling grade two scramble crescendo-ing at the jagged, fang-like excrescence of Hag's Tooth, a Vandeleur-Lynam in its own right. The scramble to the top looks impassable and perilous without ropes. But this is no time for wimping out. I gulp, wipe sweat from my brow, and go for it. Mercifully it's nowhere near as bad as it looks. I traverse a ledge, scramble up a narrow gully, heave myself over a few rocky steps – and, triumphantly, stand atop the exposed summit, whooping with a mixture of joy and relief.

With the 20 summits of the Reeks in the bag, I head north to the Dingle Peninsula – and it's not just the weather that is being kind to me. The hitchhiking gods are on my side too. Near Cloghane, I only have to wag my thumb for a matter of minutes before getting picked up by Kathy and Paul, friendly and chatty tourists from New Jersey in America, celebrating their

Climbing the Knocknapeasta ridge in the MacGillycuddy's Reeks (James Forrest)

wedding anniversary in Ireland. They give me a ride all the way to the Conor Pass, 15km to the south, and even insist on donating an apple and a cereal bar to my cause. Their kindness and generosity fill me with happiness – and set the tone for a glorious day in the mountains. I climb a sweeping ridgeline to the summit of Mt Brandon, before a magical night under the stars, watching the sky swirl pink and orange over the rippling inlets and bays, and headlands and spits, of the Dingle coastline.

Next, I travel south to the energy-sapping badlands of the Dunkerrons. Like much of Ireland, the mountains are pathless, untainted by stone-pitched bridleways and untouched by human interference. This is a double-edged sword: I love the genuine escapism, emptiness and wildness of the range, but

Hiking in the Mount Brandon range on the Dingle Peninsula (James Forrest)

slogging through knee-deep heather and clambering over boulder-strewn, ankle-jarring terrain for hours on end is physically exhausting. I feel close to the brink; deeply fatigued and mentally broken. But I know the end is in sight – and that keeps me going.

Two days later and I'm almost there. Just 50ft in front of me stands the trig pillar of Knocknadobar on the Iveragh Peninsula, my final Vandeleur-Lynam. I can't quite believe it. I've travelled a long, long way to get here: walking 1,129km, ascending the height of Everest every week for eight weeks in a row, and climbing 273 mountains in 56 days. Slowly, I plod the last 50ft of my journey. I place my hand atop the plinth and spontaneously start to laugh aloud. But this time there is no mania or hysteria in my voice. I'm simply overjoyed to have truly experienced the grandeur of Ireland's wild mountains, no matter how much it rained.

Top 6 must-do mountains in Ireland

1. Carrauntoohil, 1,039m, County Kerry

Centrepiece of the awe-inspiring MacGillycuddy's Reeks mountain range, Carrauntoohil is Ireland's highest mountain – and therefore a must-do for any hillwalker's visit to the Emerald Isle. The safest route is the Devil's Ladder and Brother O'Shea's Gully loop from Cronin's Yard. But to really get your heart racing, take the stunning arête from Carrauntoohil to Beenkeragh, before descending the jelly-leg inducing Hag's Tooth ridge, an alpine-esque grade two rocky scramble. Epic.

2. Cuilcagh, 665m, County Fermanagh

With its famous – and very long – boardwalk known as the 'Stairway to

Heaven', Cuilcagh has become a social media sensation. It is the perfect place to grab some awe-inspiring Instagram shots; the boardwalk means you aren't plodding through swamps or navigationally challenged, which is a novelty in the often rugged, pathless uplands of Ireland; and the views are stunning despite the mountain's small stature. It's the perfect choice for a quick and simple outing.

3. Croagh Patrick, 764m, County Mayo

Croagh Patrick is Ireland's holy mountain: a hallowed place attracting thousands of pilgrims every year, who perform penance at stations along the route before making it to the chapel adorning the summit. It is a busy mountain, plagued by hordes of tourists, and the path is heavily eroded. But it doesn't really matter. Croagh Patrick's huge cultural and religious significance make it a rite of passage for any hillwalker in Ireland.

4. Slieve Donard, 850m, County Down

Set within the rugged Mourne Mountains, Slieve Donard is Northern Ireland's highest peak. The ascent along the Glen River from Newcastle is thoroughly delightful, while the towering summit serves up glorious coastal views and panoramas across virtually the entire country. But why stop at just Donard? Walk alongside the famous Mourne Wall to visit the surrounding dramatic peaks, many of which are topped by granite tors, for an unforgettable day in the mountains.

5. Errigal, 751m, County Donegal

With its dramatic, volcanic profile, Errigal looks like a child's drawing of mountain – a perfect, symmetrical triangle that draws the eye and sets the heart racing. It is the most popular peak in Glenveagh National Park – and it's easy to see why. The climb, once an initial trudge over boggy grassland is negotiated, serves up rugged, exciting terrain and scenic grandeur. Just pray that the weather gods of Donegal are in a good mood when you visit.

6. Mt Brandon, 952m, County Kerry

It might only be Ireland's ninth highest mountain, but Mt Brandon is up there competing for the number one spot in the hearts of Irish hillwalkers. It is a charming mountain, with eye-watering views across the verdant Dingle Peninsula and its island-dotted coastline. And if you're feeling brave, the optional rocky scramble to the Faha Ridge, which looks both terrifying and impassable but is in fact manageable for competent scramblers, will leave you feeling like a real adventurer.

James Forrest is the author of 'Mountain Man: 446 Mountains. Six months. One record-breaking adventure'. This article first appeared in The Great Outdoors, June 2019. James Forrest's website is here: jamesmforrest.co.uk

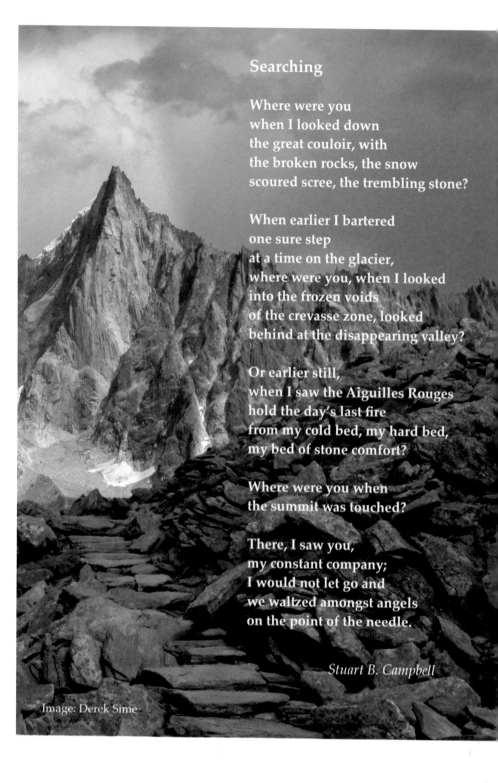

Searching

Where were you
when I looked down
the great couloir, with
the broken rocks, the snow
scoured scree, the trembling stone?

When earlier I bartered
one sure step
at a time on the glacier,
where were you, when I looked
into the frozen voids
of the crevasse zone, looked
behind at the disappearing valley?

Or earlier still,
when I saw the Aiguilles Rouges
hold the day's last fire
from my cold bed, my hard bed,
my bed of stone comfort?

Where were you when
the summit was touched?

There, I saw you,
my constant company;
I would not let go and
we waltzed amongst angels
on the point of the needle.

Stuart B. Campbell

Image: Derek Sime

The Red Tartan Shirt

Elizabeth (Betty) Mellows

Whilst clearing my Mother's house (she passed away aged 100 last year) I came across this article written by an old colleague, Betty Mellows, about 37-38 years ago. Sadly, Betty died of cancer a couple of years later. Betty was no mountaineer but took a great interest in everything, and I remember she had been so intrigued by my tale of the lost/found shirt that she decided to write it up as a short story for the Reader's Digest. I don't believe it was published but being an English teacher, I think she regularly submitted items to magazines.

In essence the story is true, although I think she had to 'invent' some details because she only heard it from me once, and I was surprised when she showed me that the account was surprisingly accurate. We weren't a group; I just went with my friend Neil Heaton (Munroist 956). Paths, gosh I don't remember paths. Slow, not really but would be very slow now. The warden at Glen Brittle had climbed the wall and was descending through the gullies when he found the shirt, and the photo was of myself sitting on a rock in the middle of a snowfield. Still, I warmed to the article when I read it again for the first time in nearly 40 years. The trip took place in 1969 and memorably, as we arrived in Norway, the Americans made their first moon landing.

Peter Barlass

This story is the most incredible one I have ever heard. It is neither sensational nor exciting, but fantastic and unbelievable. It is also true, and in its truth lies its incredulity.

We were sitting in the staff room at work enjoying one of those welcome half hours called, for want of simple description, our 'free period'. Usually everyone worked during this time, caved up in some cubbyhole or isolated table to mark books or prepare a lesson, but on this particular occasion we were circled in a friendly group just talking.

The conversation, as is wont, became somewhat philosophical, but only at a general level, for none of us was qualified to sink into Descartian depths or any other profound analysis. As it was, no names, as such, were even mentioned. Rather we explored a forest of ideas, and the tendency was to quickly become introvertial. Clearings appeared through ideas, ample space for anecdotes and personal reflections to verify the points we made.

We talked, for want of a starting point, about nuclear war and the future, and someone said, 'The world won't be wiped out because God would not let it happen'. We talked about God and wondered about the mystery of the beginning of things, a common enough topic for drifting minds. We discussed the idea of 'Chance'. Peter reminded us of the well-known story of the monkey

215

which you must have heard – 'You give a group of monkeys typewriters to play with and an infinite length of time. Then eventually one will type out the works of Shakespeare.'

I said, in support of this, that my husband John once related a theory about a man who was washed up on a desert island where no human being had set foot before, and there, lying on the beach, was a watch.

I could only remember this vaguely and had even vaguer recollection as to the context in which I had heard it, but it had stuck in my mind and it did seem to support the trend of our conversation which was, that given time, and there being so many billions of permutations and combinations, anything could evolve. This is the theory of 'Chance' explored and expounded by many who believe in it. We tend to accept the expected, but what about the unexpected?

'It's strange,' said Marlene, 'how many people can look like someone else who is no relation and may be miles away.' She then related a story of how, when on her travels in Australia, she went to a dinner-dance and one of her partners looked exactly like Michael Bentine. We were sceptical: 'Are you sure it wasn't him?' 'Oh no. He had a different name, and he was a farmer from Tasmania!'

Gordon remarked, then, how he had seen photographs in a magazine which showed how Princess Anne looked exactly like an ancestor of hers – Queen Charlotte. A painting of the Queen existed. We all reflected on the strong possibility (Gordon said it was a fact) that had we had photographs and paintings of our own long past generations, we too might find our exact doubles.

When the Chance is small, then, we have coincidence. But how small is Chance? It may be vast. It may be the answer for everything that exists, only we haven't discovered enough. There may be, for instance, millions of 'coincidences' that lay hidden; that we never will know about. So the few that exist are so rare that they are worthy of mention. Such was Peter's experience, which I will relate now.

Peter was in his early thirties and his great love was the outdoors. He was a walker and a climber. This had been a source of pleasure to him for many years and his interest overflowed into his working life, where many a young person had benefited from his expertise and instruction and shared his enthusiasm in the practical application of this enjoyable endeavour. He had that marvellous ability to impart enjoyment of the thing he himself enjoyed to others, which is a rare and beautiful quality. He loved talking about the places he had been to and he seemed to have been everywhere.

One summer, and a very hot one, about ten years ago, he was with a group on a walking holiday in the west of Norway. They housed themselves in the pretty village of Åndalsnes, remote with regard to tourists but popular with climbers. Åndalsnes nestles in the Romsdal valley, which itself had access to the famous Trolltind. This was the main attraction. Trolltind, or 'Troll Wall' is one of the most famous of all rock faces in Europe, being the highest. The 'Wall' rises 5,000 feet. It is a haven for the experienced, a challenge to the newcomer and a rare and beautiful sight to the onlooker.

Peter and his friends from the group decided to make the ascent up Trolltind by the easy walking route. They would follow the walkers', not the

Romsdal, 1969 (Neil Heaton)

climbers' path and the day, though hot and unexpectedly dry, promised to be an enjoyable one.

Taking in the magnificent views and experiencing the joy of wending their way up the mountain nearer the sky, which is the unique form of ecstasy experienced only by the long-distance walker, it proved to be a long pull and a slow one as a result of the heat wave.

They sweated up the peaks and one by one shed their top gear, walking naked to the waist, their backs protected only by their packs. They stopped for lunch and once more on their way back, this time in the welcome shade of two overhanging rocks. On reaching the valley Peter discovered he had lost his shirt. It must have fallen out of his pack when he opened the same to get out the drinks. This must have been when they stopped by the outcrop of boulders on their way down. He regretted losing it because it was a new one of good quality, but there was nothing he could do about it except forget about it and enjoy the rest of the holiday. The group split up (they had not travelled together) and Peter came home.

The story moves on now eight years in fact. Peter and three friends, also keen walkers, arranged a holiday on the Isle of Skye. They had not seen each

Trolltind, 1969 (Neil Heaton)

other for some time. Each had gone their separate ways; in fact, Peter only knew two of them through the third member with whom he had been on walks in the past. In view of this they decided to make an evening of it at the hostel in Glen Brittle where they had booked in, by bringing slides of their individual holidays and showing them to each other. The warden of the Youth Hostel, himself a mountaineer, was very helpful and, on request, allocated them a dark room in which to set up their projector.

The idea proved to be an excellent one as each member of the group had carefully selected slides of a place hitherto unfamiliar to the rest. Peter brought slides of his Norwegian holiday eight years before.

The warden, who came in and out of the room during the various showings, happened to be watching when Peter was showing his slides and talking about each one in turn. The warden himself showed particular interest in Peter's selection, expressing the fact that he too had been to the same area. It turned out, in fact to be the same summer Peter had visited the Romsdal valley.

When Peter reached a slide of the two rocks, he related the story of the lost shirt. He was about to go on when the warden interrupted him.

'Was it a red tartan shirt?'

'Why … yes!' Peter said in complete surprise.

Everyone gasped. The warden himself could hardly believe his own explanation.

'I found it' he said. 'I must have walked up the Trolltind a couple of days after you. It was there, new, completely unspoiled, lying on the path. I brought it home, thinking it was such a good one, and wore it until it wore out!'

They could hardly believe it. They pondered over the possibilities – of not going to that hostel, of the warden not being in the moment the slides were shown, the chance of it having rained eight years before that summer in Norway, of Peter bringing a different set of slides, of arranging the trip at all and thinking up such an evening's entertainment … The probabilities of them never finding out were endless.

Trollryggen (Derek Sime)

Having read this, my complete story, you will no doubt search your own minds for similar experiences. Chance? Coincidence? What do you think?

(Written circa 1983)

Trolltind, 1969
(Peter Barlass)

LOCHS and LOCHANS

Above – Autumnal colours reflected in Loch Tuill Bhearnach under Sgùrr na Lapaich in the Mullardoch hills.

Below – Loch Monar twisting through snow-laden hills as seen from the top of Beinn na Muice at the head of Strathfarrar.　　　　*Alan Rowan*

Part 5 – Life in the Mountains

Citizen Science – The Secret Life of a Chionophile

Iain Cameron

For the love of it – a (qualified) eulogy to citizen science.

A common response from many people to my elaboration on what it is that I do for a living is, it's fair to say, incredulity. For example, during a recent outing to the hills with a BBC TV crew when filming for an outdoors programme, the presenter asked who employed me to do this work. When I replied that, in fact, I worked for a house-building firm, and monitored long-lying patches of snow on Britain's hills merely as a hobby, his look was unbelieving. 'I just assumed you did this for a living,' he said.

He is not alone to have thought this. Many – most – people I talk to about the subject also assume I am employed in a snow-seeking capacity. Given I have now authored and co-authored over 20 papers on the esoteric subject of how long patches of snow persist in Wales, England and Scotland, coupled with reasonably regular appearances in the media, it is perhaps understandable that folk would think this. I often wonder, though, who they imagine would pay me to indulge in this very niche interest. A university? Some government-funded body? Alas, no. Even if such funding were available, I doubt it would stretch anything like as far as it needed to. No, the innumerable journeys that I and others like me undertake over the course of a summer and autumn are carried out entirely at our own discretion and expense. We are 'citizen scientists' in the very purest sense of the phrase.

What is citizen science?

The British Geological Society rather helpfully defines citizen science as 'a term used for projects in which individual volunteers (or networks of volunteers), many of whom may have no specific scientific training, perform or manage research-related tasks such as observation, measurement or computation.' [1]

This noble pursuit has a long and distinguished pedigree, especially in Britain. Whether it's flora or fauna, meteorology or astronomy, people for hundreds of years have been filling in the blanks that are left when 'real' scientists pack up their equipment and head home. Throughout the ages, folk like Mary Anning and Seton Gordon, both supreme autodidacts, have

Braeriach, August 2018 (Iain Cameron)

contributed hugely to the fields of study they engaged in. Their legacies endure to this day.

The thing that drives us citizen scientists can be distilled down to one basic ingredient: passion. When you strip everything else away this is always what is left. The excitement of seeing or experiencing that thing is what makes the driving, the walking, the climbing, all worthwhile. It is what fuels everything else. The genesis of such passions is trickier to establish. I can trace mine back to when I was nine years old. Why it should be that patches of snow fascinate me is a question I have been grappling with for almost 40 years. I still don't have the answer.

Aonach Beag,
September 2018
(Iain Cameron)

Childhood fascinations are often fragile things, being both whimsical and ephemeral. Here-today-gone-tomorrow interests picked up by infants are legion, but, just occasionally, something sticks. An idea or experience attaches itself to a child, where – allowed to blossom – it can remain for the rest of his or her life. There is an *ad nauseum* number of accounts of respected scientists or naturalists having read something inspirational or memorable as children. In their memoirs many of these people seem to be able to recall the event with almost perfect clarity, despite it sometimes being many decades since seeing it, and which has gone on to inform their life's study. So it was the case for me.

Despite this passion, which can light a spark on even the dreariest autumn day, it is not always sunshine and glistening landscapes that are experienced when conducting research. Being a citizen scientist engaged in snow-patch observation carries down-sides. Firstly, it can be a thankless task. How well I remember spending ten hours in the pouring rain and driving hail one day, only to find no snow at a location where I was expecting it. 'Are you sure you were looking in the right place?' came the unhelpful reply from an acquaintance when I messaged him later to break the bad news. Then there is the business of scattering one's sopping-wet clothes across various radiators in the house, much to the delight of one's partner. No university facility or drying area is available to us, nor – for that matter – are there cameras or IT equipment for recording and cataloguing our results. When something breaks or is needed, we must put our hands into our own pockets.

But honestly, we wouldn't have it any other way. Well, I wouldn't.

Aonach Mòr aerial survey, August 2020 (Iain Cameron)

223

The benefits

What I describe below is very personal, and refers to the niche area that I am interested in. However, it is hard not to assume that these feelings are experienced by all citizen scientists, to a lesser or greater degree.

Before discussing the pros and cons of gathering data, I should perhaps describe what data we collect as part of our research. First and foremost, we are concerned with counting the patches of snow which generally persist on Scotland's hills from one year to the next. Or, to put it another way, patches of snow that almost never melt. Fortunately, the locations where these are found tend to be the same every year, which makes planning and multi-year comparisons easier.

Typically, when we go to one of these far-flung sites where snow reposes, we record the maximum length, breadth and depth of the snow, and the date on which the trip was made. These data are then noted and compared with measurements from previous years. By so doing we can form an estimate of how long a particular patch is likely to persist, assuming the weather patterns are normal. This – it must be said – is in no way an exact science, as there are too many British weather variables to consider. But it is fair to say that if, for example, we measure a certain patch of snow high in the Cairngorms in late September and it exceeds 50 metres in length, it is a reasonable and relatively safe assumption that it will endure until the lasting snows of the new winter arrive.

Ben Nevis snow tunnel, August 2020 (Iain Cameron)

But we are also interested in what I call 'bellwether' patches. These relics of winter will typically be ones that are prone to melting at various points throughout the summer and autumn. By monitoring them and when they disappear, we are able to formulate a good estimate as to the likelihood of survivals elsewhere, even from a relatively early point in the year (in Scottish snow-patch circles, July 1st is considered 'early').

It is to be hoped that by recording the sizes and dates of various patches over a period of many years and publishing it, researchers in the future will be able to compare their findings with our own.

The main advantage of publishing work as an amateur, so far as I am concerned, is the freedom to issue the data without any pressure to spin the results a certain way. No institute or body has, for example, leaned on us to 'talk up' the effect of climate change on the increasing disappearance of Scottish snow patches in the last 25 years. In a world where funding for research can be influenced by political agendas, there are no such worries for us. We simply report the data and let others interpret it as they see fit.

Another benefit of being unrestrained by timescales or supervisors is that we can pick which mountain range to go to, and when. If the weather forecast for a certain day is miserable then we may simply decide not to go, without worrying about the consequences. In my day-job, like many other people, I am controlled by deadlines and a line manager. And although working to targets can often bring out the best in people, it can also be enormously stressful.

As far as enthusiasm goes, the keen amateur is likely to go above and beyond what is, scientifically speaking, considered statistically good sampling. Someone with emotional investment might want to count and measure every patch of snow. It is not difficult to become somewhat jaded in a job if it's conducted routinely and at someone else's behest. The citizen scientist, however, fresh from his or her day job and unencumbered by expectations, leaps into the same task with enthusiasm bordering on obsession. Added to this is the immensely satisfying feeling of having contributed to the collective understanding of the subject matter in which we are engaged. This feeling can do nothing except enhance the love we have for our chosen subject.

Last, but by no means least, is the camaraderie and sense of community that seeking out patches of snow has engendered over the years. Since being engaged in this study properly (approaching 20 years) a hard-core of people has built up - people who meet and accompany each other to locations where the snow lies latest. There is little doubt that the internet and social media have helped hugely in this respect, drawing people to special web forums as moths do to a flame. It is no exaggeration to say that a community has formed around this subject, and although it may justifiably still be called niche, it is becoming increasingly less so as people see the value in the work we do.

Creag Meagaidh, September 2014 (Iain Cameron)

The challenges

It is often the case that the simple logistics of snow-patch recording are its biggest challenge. For example, each August bank holiday since 2008 I have organised an all-Scotland survey of every patch of snow still extant on the hills. Though in some years this endeavour is reasonably straightforward, with – say – only about a dozen-or-so to record, other years are not so easy. In 2015 there was a minimum of 678 patches across a bewilderingly large section of the Highlands. I had to put out pleas on social media for volunteers, and a total of about 30 people stepped up to the plate that year and went out into the hills to count snow. An educational establishment would, perhaps, have enough resources to deal with such a Herculean task, but we as amateurs had to rely on the good will of enthusiasts and hillwalkers. This task is exacerbated by the fact that patches of snow often linger in places that are very difficult to get to.

And then there is the not-insubstantial cost that needs to be met each year. Boots, coats, trousers, petrol, stuff. All these things are paid for out of our own pockets. We are not subsidised or sponsored. No outdoors apparel brands come knocking on our doors to offer any freebies, and nor do we have budgets for such things. A rough calculation suggests that the dedicated enthusiast can spend in excess of £1,000 per annum pursuing his or her hobby. Because the rough terrain I often visit plays havoc with my footwear, new boots are an annual expense for me, whereas some walkers need only buy new ones every few years.

Creagan na Beinne – the last sub-3,000ft snow patch, July 2014 (Iain Cameron)

The question that often arises from people curious to know more about what we do is, 'How do you know where to look for snow?' This is a very reasonable enquiry. Often when we go to places to look for old patches, we don't know what we are going to find. Yes, experience of spotting long-lasting snow tells us that they appear in the same places (and even take the same shapes) year-in, year-out, but it is not always a given that we find what we are looking for. Trudging eight miles on a cold October day across rough ground, only to find a puddle where a patch of snow used to lie, can be a trifle dispiriting. But the more prosaic of us understand that proving a negative is often as important as a positive. Plus, no walk in the grand terrain of the Highlands can reasonably be considered 'wasted'. This seemingly haphazard approach to scientific enquiry is another by-product of a lack of resources and manpower. Had we the financial wherewithal we might engage the services of a mountain expert to visit somewhere on our behalf, or even in rare occasions hire a helicopter to cover large parts of the Highlands.

Limitations

Is a little knowledge a dangerous thing? Is going somewhere to take readings or measurements as an amateur likely to throw up spurious or inconsistent results? I have often given thought in the past to whether the lack of academic grounding (I left school aged 16 with hardly any qualifications) disadvantages the citizen scientist. The short answer, I suppose, must be yes. Attaining a science-based degree confers legitimacy and teaches rigour. How can someone gather and interpret data, yet expect to be taken seriously? The secret to this, as it has always seemed to me, is to avoid hypotheses or to indulge in interpretation. Luckily for us, and as mentioned earlier, we do not venture into this territory. We merely record the patches of snow on the date we find them. Using a tape-measure or camera requires no special competencies or skillsets. The statistical analysis of our results, so far as it is done at all, is completed by others. Whenever I am asked by anyone in the media what the state of the increasingly small patches of snow tell us about climate change I always refuse to be drawn. It is a subject for climatologists to answer as far as I am concerned.

I am fortunate in that I have never encountered any snobbery among the scientific community in the U.K. On the contrary, I have often been approached by academics from institutions who have asked me to contribute to some journal or paper they're writing. I have read from credible sources, however, that some journals don't publish data that have been gathered by others. Though this is unfortunate, it is I suppose understandable. Academics spend weeks or months in the field gathering data for inclusion in research papers. In a somewhat crowded field, a journal editor cannot be blamed for eschewing an amateur's paper for one done by someone with university pedigree.

Garbh Choire Mòr, September 2019 (Iain Cameron)

In conclusion

There can be little doubt that citizen science is of immense worth to the broader understanding of a subject. It logically follows that – within defined parameters – the more pairs of eyes that are looking at something, the more useful the observations made will be. Take, for example, the RSPB's Birdwatch survey. Eight million birds were counted by half-a-million people over the course of a year. Allowing for mistakes and mis-recording, this is still of incalculable value. [2]

Though I sometimes think it would be nice to have the financial and intellectual weight of an academic institution or research facility behind the work that I do, these feelings last only fleetingly. If I were to be employed to do this full-time then I suspect some of the love I have for it would disappear. I would never want it to become anything other than something that I want to do as opposed to something that I must. I suspect that most citizen scientists share this sentiment. We are destined to work in the shadows, generally outside the gaze of the public. Our work is done quietly, not because it is of no value, but rather that it is unglamorous and unasked for. But, in a hundred years from now, long after we've gone, people will hopefully look back on our work and say 'hurrah' for citizen scientists once again.

And there is no question in my mind that, just as before, so it will be in the future. Citizen scientists will be around for as long as data need to be gathered, and passion runs through the veins of the data collectors. For sure technology will change, and is changing, the way in which we collect data. During the Covid-enforced lockdown that affected everyone during spring 2020, for example, no field visits could be undertaken. Luckily, we were able to utilise the daily photographs taken by the Sentinel satellite which, on the rare days when there was little or no cloud-cover, showed patches of snow up superbly against the brown and green terrain of the hills. Such technological advances will be used by us as readily as it will be by the professionals.

Nevis range, August 2016 (Iain Cameron)

Footnote (November 2021):

In recent years, Scottish snow-patches have attracted a level of national and international interest that was hitherto unknown. It is not difficult to understand why. In 2018, all snow disappeared at Scotland's snowiest place, Garbh Choire Mòr of Braeriach, for the second consecutive year. This was unprecedented. Prior to the 2017 and 2018 disappearances, all snow at Garbh Choire Mòr had disappeared only in 1933, 1959, 1996, 2003 and 2006. The rate of complete melting is accelerating. In late October 2021, the Sphinx snow-patch in Garbh Choire Mòr melted completely for the third time in five years (2017, 2018 & 2021). Prior to 2017 it had melted five times since the 1700s. It is clear that the frequency of total disappearance is increasing, and quickly.

With the COP26 conference in Glasgow still making headlines, the Sphinx's departure attracted international interest. The passing of this small, lonely lump of winter induced radio stations and papers from all over the world to enquire on its history, and to publish and broadcast it. Let us hope that the trend reverses and the Sphinx remains un-melted for many years to come. However, the portents are not good.

Iain Cameron is a citizen scientist whose work is published each year in the Royal Meteorological Society's Weather journal. He has authored and co-authored over 20 papers and one book (The Vanishing Ice – Diaries of a Scottish Snow Hunter, published by Vertebrate Publishing, 2021, ISBN 978-1-83981-108-1) about long-lying snow on the hills of Britain.

[1] https://www.bgs.ac.uk/geology-projects/citizen-science/
[2] https://www.rspb.org.uk/get-involved/activities/birdwatch/results/

—TMS—

The One that Got Away: Pen-y-Fan – Anne Butler

Certain hills seem to lure you in and invite you to climb them, and Pen-y-Fan caught my eye. Its graceful grassy curves, the layers of rock and the endless views made a city-bound London girl want to head west and climb it. Our planned trip to Talybont-on-Usk was cancelled due to the 2001 foot and mouth outbreak. Since then we have moved to Scotland and Pen-y-Fan remains unclimbed to this day. I still look lovingly at its long sweeping ridges and wonder if I will ever get there. Maybe one day, but the 10-hour drive from Aviemore is rather off-putting.

The North Face
(in memory of WH Murray)

After the heat of battle,
the cold night of the desert
creeps through his bones
with a dislocated familiarity;
this is when he surrenders, admits
'It's as cold as a mountain top'
He is the captive his captor
salutes 'To the mountains!' then
drinks. He replies 'The mountains
have taught me three things...' then
drinks deep and smashes the bottle
off the armour-plated panzer.

This is the moment he sees
how Nevis snow sparkled red
at sunset, the frozen towers
of Bidean burning
in the moonlight can sustain;
how even the abstract: Rubicon
Wall, Agag's Groove, Crowberry
Tower are greater than his being
there, a captive on a cold desert
night; in Italy; Bavaria; Marisch
Tubia, Czechoslovakia: all
the concentration camps
contained was a soldier,
the man escaped; giving himself
up, surrendering to what
the mountains had revealed,
'The beauty is life'.

Stuart B. Campbell

Image: N. McNab

The John Muir Trust, Wild Places and Climate Change

David Balharry

Edinburgh's city centre is the last place I expected to contemplate the idea of 'wildness'. But as I passed a restaurant that proudly advertised its 'wild food', I was reminded of just how heavy the 'wild' bandwagon has become. Whether it's attached to coffee or swimming, the word has been increasingly adopted to appeal to, and appease, a primal part of ourselves.

As a wild places charity, the John Muir Trust is constantly trying to establish what we mean by the word 'wild' in a conservation and land management context. And unfortunately, the UK has little left in the way of authentic landscapes to offer as a definition.

I recently had the pleasure of walking a short way up Ben Nevis with a hiking group focused on connecting minority ethnic groups to the outdoors. Most of the group had travelled from London, Coventry and Manchester, and were in awe at the beauty of the environment they found themselves in. None read the landscape as a monoculture of overgrazing, devoid of trees and impoverished biodiversity. They showed a genuine interest in an ecologist's view of what lay before them, and we had a fantastic discussion.

Giving nature the freedom to restore itself is critical for our future. If the UK is to meet our targets for mitigating the climate crisis, we must use the natural solutions we've got on our doorstep: most obviously native woodland, which captures carbon, helps prevent soil erosion and contributes to flood defence. We must also ensure people continue to have the freedom to enjoy these special landscapes and recognise, understand and appreciate wild places when they see them. And, we must ensure this will be to the benefit of local economies and thriving communities.

This is what the John Muir Trust has been working on for the past 40 years. The organisation came into being with the purchase of Li and Coire Dhorrcail in Knoydart in 1983, which was bought for two reasons. The first – to prevent the Ministry of Defence from using it as a bombing range. The second – to make sure the public could continue to access the Ladhar Bheinn Munro and its wild surrounds. Now, the Trust looks after some of the finest wild places in the UK, including other notable Munros: Carn Mòr Dearg, Ben Nevis, Bla Bheinn, and Schiehallion (as well as several equally impressive Corbetts in Assynt and on Skye). We campaign and lobby for the protection of wild places, collaborate with local partners to expand native woodlands and restore damaged peatland, and maintain around 120 kilometres of footpath each year. Through the John Muir Award, we also inspire and encourage people from all walks of life to get involved in direct, practical action to connect with

Coire Dhorrcail, showing the regeneration which has occurred in 40 years of Trust ownership (Stephen Ballard)

and care for nature. Over 387,000 people from across the UK have completed a John Muir Award to date.

We believe in landscape-scale restoration. That's because large areas with less fragmentation provide nature with the space to move, adapt and become ecologically balanced and resilient. In 2010 alongside 13 other organisations, we helped create Europe's largest environmental restoration project – the Coigach and Assynt Living Landscape Partnership (CALL). The total project area is 635 square kilometres and includes Trust land at the triple buttress Corbett Quinag in Sutherland. At the conical mountain Schiehallion in Perthshire – for many people their first Munro summit – we're proud to be a part of the Heart of Scotland Forest Partnership. This aims to restore 3,000 hectares of mountain woodland from the Keltneyburn Special Area of Conservation all the way to Loch Tummel. And on Nevis we work with neighbouring landowners as part of The Nevis Landscape Partnership to manage visitor impacts and help grow the native pine forest.

One of the greatest barriers to achieving healthy living landscapes – capable of removing carbon and supporting a diversity of wildlife species – is the destructive impact of intensive deer grazing pressure, which prevents the natural regeneration and expansion of native woodlands. Currently, 12 million tonnes of carbon dioxide are absorbed by Scotland's forests and woodlands each year. This number could and should be a lot, lot higher. Deer have no natural predators in the UK, and large areas of land have historically been managed to encourage high red deer numbers. Scotland's woodlands simply cannot sustain the current million-strong population.

Looking at the impact of deer on native woodland, it is clear that effective deer management is essential to Scotland's role in tackling the climate emergency, and a critical part of giving wild places in Scotland the freedom to recover.

The Trust will now be increasing its deer culls going forward, and exploring options for developing long term community hunting models, to ensure deer management will benefit wider society long term and not just a small number of wealthy individuals.

We welcome the Scottish Government's commitment to modernising deer management regulation too. In 2021, they accepted either in detail or in principle 91 of the 99 recommendations made in an independent Deer Working Group report – agreeing in a statement that it will be necessary to introduce extensive legislative and regulatory change over the course of this Parliamentary session.

Large scale reform and big picture thinking needs incentives and regulation. So, beyond deer, we're looking at ideas that encourage Scotland's landowners to work together more broadly to help accelerate the drive towards the target

Glen Nevis, showing the impact of conservation work, supporting the regeneration of this forest through tree planting and monitoring, and deer management
(Alex Gillespie)

of net-zero carbon emissions.

If all land managers in Scotland maximised carbon capture of their peatlands and woodlands, we could reduce our national carbon emissions by up to 13 Mt CO_2e a year – that's equivalent to removing every single vehicle from Scottish roads.

That's why we're advocating for a banded tax on landholdings, based on actual and potential carbon emissions. Those maximising natural carbon capture on their land (through woodlands or intact peatlands for example) would be exempt from the charges, and landowners eligible for the tax would be able to move to lower tax bands by changing land use to maximise carbon capture.

Levies raised would help fund natural carbon capture work across the country – the carbon equivalent of using the sugar tax to help tackle the obesity crisis.

When we published this proposal in early 2021, there was constructive and supportive feedback from scientists, political parties and climate change experts around the UK, as well as the Chartered Institute for Taxation. We took this feedback on board in developing a revised version which was published in time for COP26 – when the world's eyes were on the UK.

What could this mean for wild places? That land management for nature and the planet would be the default position (rather than management for one species – deer or grouse), and that there would be incentives to expand the footprint of wild places. There is currently no map or register of these areas in the UK, so we have no baseline from which to build. The John Muir Trust recently put out a tender for mapping priority wild places across England, Scotland and Wales, to better understand the extent and condition of the UK's wild places, and enable us to engage with a wider range of people to help us prioritise limited resources.

It is our firm belief that wild places are for everyone, and if we're to change the narrative of what a wild place should truly look like in the UK, then we must make sure that the freedom we extend to the plants and animals here also extends inclusively to everyone.

David Balharry is Chief Executive Officer of the John Muir Trust.

—TMS—

LOCHS and LOCHANS

Above – Arkle from Loch Stack on a summer's day when the cloud persisted on Foinaven all day, but Arkle remained clear.

Below – Loch a' Mhadaidh Ruadh, and Beinn Damh, taken in late March on a walk from Coulags to Torridon, taking in An Ruadh-Stac.

Derek Sime

Mountains for All

Lucy Wallace

The golden eagle appeared on the horizon as my husband Wally and I were eating lunch on the highest point of Sgùrr Sgumain on the Isle of Skye. From our lofty perch, we could see the broad wings barrelling along the ridge of the Cuillin, coming from the north and heading our way. The vast shape grew until it seemed that wingtip-to-wingtip, the eagle spanned the full width of the ridge. Over Sgùrr Mhic Choinnich and Sgùrr Thearlaich it flew, until at Sgùrr Alasdair, it banked slightly, and headed in our direction. The eagle entered the rocky gap between us and the summit of Sgùrr Alasdair. It looked close enough to touch. Sunlight was radiating from its golden back, and the wind barely ruffled primary feathers the size of feather dusters. Once in the gap, it picked up an air current that swept it away from us and over the deep expanse of Coir' a' Ghrunnda before soaring away down the peninsula. We watched silently as it disappeared from view, and then looked at each other in barely contained excitement. This was an encounter on a scale as epic as the surroundings.

Why do we climb mountains? That famous response from Mallory, 'because it's there' doesn't begin to cover the thousands of reasons why people choose to reach a summit. Some will climb high for the view, others for the sense of achievement, to push themselves with a physical challenge. Many work their way through lists and tables, meticulously ticking the summits as they are gained, while others are raising money for charity. People walk in the hills to be alone, or to spend time with like-minded companions. Some do it for kudos, or even social media likes. For most of us, there will be more than one reason.

I admit I am not a Munro bagger in the strictest sense. Too many favourite peaks call me back repeatedly, and many smaller mountains capture my attention. Sometimes I choose not to go to the summit at all, preferring to traverse the hills instead. I do have a little list, but I add to it so slowly that I will be lucky to complete in my lifetime. However, I share many of the motivations and passions of readers of this Journal. As John Muir said, 'I climb the mountains and get their glad tidings'. It makes me feel good, and alive, and purposeful in a way that other aspects of my life, however essential, do not.

Muir's famous quote (from his book *The Mountains of California*), continues: 'Nature's peace will flow into you as sunshine flows into trees. The winds will blow their own freshness into you, and the storms their energy, while cares will drop away from you like the leaves of autumn.'

Caught in the moment – perfect winter walking on Gulvain (Lucy Wallace)

The feeling of rejuvenation we get from being in the mountains fills us up, as conversely our limbs become more tired from the journey. Passing time in the here and now, attending to one's immediate needs of refreshment and comfort, while experiencing the elements, seems to put into perspective the cares of everyday life. Sometimes, moments arise that will stay with us long after we have left the mountains. A ptarmigan sheltering in a blizzard, a soaring eagle overhead, a thunderous waterfall that seems to grow in stature as it is approached.

Psychologists have tried to measure and understand what happens to us when nature stirs us in this way. They call it 'nature connectedness'. In the strictest sense, nature connectedness is a measure of how people see themselves and their relationship to nature. Higher levels of nature connectedness are associated with a greater sense of wellbeing.

For those of us who experience a connection with nature in our daily lives, this understanding is intuitive, but during the last ten years or so a huge body of research has been accumulated that attempts to get to the bottom of why feeling a part of nature helps us to feel better – both happier and more fulfilled. What's more, it's been shown that people who feel more nature connected are more likely to care about the planet, the environment, and engage in pro-environmental behaviour.

In summary: nature connectedness makes us healthier, happier, and more environmentally responsible. Much of this work has been done by Professor

Miles Richardson and the Nature Connectedness Research Group at the University of Derby, who have helped create initiatives such as The Wildlife Trust's '30 Days Wild' campaign, and the National Trust's '50 things to do before you are 11¾'.

Some clients scanning the landscape for wildlife (Lucy Wallace)

One of the key findings of this research is that it is moments, not time, spent in nature that increase the feelings of nature connectedness. For example, during my eagle encounter, I felt my connection to nature most deeply – as opposed to during all those hours trudging up the mountain beforehand, when I was trying to think about something else. You don't have to climb mountains to get these moments; they arise with something as simple as taking the time to watch bees visiting flowers, or paying attention to the sound of water tumbling over rocks in a burn.

However, I believe there is something about the experience of climbing mountains that strips away the defences created by the hustle and bustle of life and makes us more open to receiving the full benefit of connecting with nature. These 'moments' arise more readily with the unpredictability and elemental nature of the mountain environment.

As a Mountain Leader and wildlife guide, I work with a wide range of people, albeit generally quite affluent, from teenagers on Duke of Edinburgh expeditions to older holidaymakers. I get to be a part of the experience that leads folk to have these 'wow moments' in nature that deepen their connectedness.

I often say it is the best job in the world. Not only do I have the best office, but also, my clients are endlessly fascinating and insightful people. I never know whom I'm going to meet next. It's a big honour to have a job where I facilitate people achieving goals, pushing themselves, and having an incredible time. I've had clients burst into tears at seeing a golden eagle for the first time, and many that have simply laughed for joy at the sheer beauty of it all.

Enjoying a wow moment high on Beinn Alligin (Lucy Wallace)

Most are not experienced outdoor people – one rather memorably expected there to be 'bin-men' on Ben Nevis. Almost all think it is okay to cast aside apple cores or to cut off corners on paths. My role isn't just to guide and enthuse; I also try to foster a sense of awareness of the mountain environment and encourage people to get out and explore for themselves, teaching them about equipment and mountain safety as we go. Not everyone gets to learn these skills growing up, and although they seem innate to those of us who have been walking the hills for decades, this is in fact, hard-earned knowledge.

I've been lucky in my life to have been brought up with access to the mountains, and an understanding of my place in nature that has been nurtured by committed parents who took me walking and bird watching as a kid.

Some people need a lifetime to find out just how good climbing mountains really is, and some never will. When I think about this, it gives rise to thorny questions for me. Is access to nature a right? Should mountains be for everyone? If I reflect on the huge benefits both to the individual (and as touched upon above, society) of mountain walking and time spent in nature, I have to answer with a resounding yes.

In reality, mountain climbing will never be everyone's cup of tea, no matter what I think. However, access to the hills and nature in general is definitely something that is distributed unequally within our society. It isn't just about whether you have green spaces on your doorstep, (although that helps), but also who brought you up, what activities your school provided, and how easily you can travel away from home to get to the wilder places in our country.

The recent restrictions due to coronavirus exacerbated this inequality. Even as restrictions were lifted, public transport, not always the easiest way to get around once you leave the city limits, is not something we are being encouraged to use for leisure during the pandemic. For some people, this is a genuine logistical barrier to getting to the hills. Other barriers can include not having the skills, the kit, the health or the companions with which to do so. Ramblers Scotland and other walking groups are a fantastic way to break down some of these barriers, but while car sharing was a no-no, those without a vehicle could struggle to get to the start of walks.

As I write this in spring 2021, we find ourselves on the brink of a summer season in Scotland like no other. We were over a year into a global pandemic that has seen our freedoms curtailed and our lives changed, perhaps forever. The mountains that had been off limits for most people for months were at last within reach of the nation. Alongside this, is the knowledge that coronavirus has not gone away. The overwhelming message that we have received over the last 12 months is that the outdoors is the place where we are safest from infection.

Despite the many barriers, people have discovered walking in record numbers, and Highland communities were bracing themselves for visitor footfall that would exceed anything they have experienced before. The more accessible and well-known mountain ranges would see thousands of brand-new hill walkers tackling the hills for the first time.

Fortunately, unlike 2020, National Park authorities, local councils and destination management organisations had some time to prepare, and we were seeing much needed investment in ranger services and infrastructure. I suspect it will not always be enough, and that pinch points will inevitably pop up with associated problems of parking and litter. It tends to be the bad news stories of anti-social behaviour that make the headlines, while most people are of course behaving themselves, and having an amazing time in the mountains while they do so.

Looking further ahead, we need to do so much more. This is why Ramblers Scotland, alongside 11 leading outdoor groups, published a joint Manifesto for the Outdoors. It called for strategic investment to ensure that everyone across Scotland shares the benefits – and pleasure – of being active in the natural environment. It seems to have been well received by the main political parties, with many adopting some of its key asks, such as the creation of a new Outdoor Recreation Champion within government, and a commitment to at least one week at an outdoor residential centre for all schoolchildren.

Meanwhile, what can we, the experienced mountain hardened hill-goers, do to help? First and foremost, we can help to spread the practice of leave no trace, and promote Scotland's world-class access rights. As we know, these come with responsibilities, which are not always so well understood.

We may, a lot of the time, be preaching to the converted within our networks, but the more we share the message, neatly covered by the hashtag #RespectProtectEnjoy, the more chance we have of reaching less experienced people who are heading for the hills. We can also help minimise our own impact, by choosing the less travelled routes, and visiting more out of the way places. Esteemed members of The Munro Society don't need me to tell them that Scotland is a huge country,

Lucy on wildlife watch
(Lucy Wallace)

full of mountains, and blessed with vast wild spaces! Even during the height of the season, much of the Highlands are empty.

There were times when the impacts of increased footfall were writ large in the scars of litter and wear on the most popular hills. It will be easy to fall back on the position of blame, and quite rightly we will feel anger towards those who desecrate our natural heritage. During these times, I will be trying to remember that this is a small but visible minority committing these crimes, and that behind these images, there are thousands more people enjoying the great outdoors as never before.

Every day spent in the hills is special – we are all transformed by these experiences, no matter how battle-worn or experienced we are. This is a unique time of opportunity for social change, and as people discover the benefits of walking in the hills, we can nurture their sense of connection to Scotland's landscape in a way that can benefit us all. I dream of a future Scotland where outdoor skills are a part of our cultural tradition, and everyone feels at home in the hills, understanding the importance of our natural heritage.

I could leave it there, but I want to end with another anecdote, a pivotal moment for me in the hills, not with nature this time, but one that has stayed with me ever since.

I was at work – supervising a Gold DofE expedition in the Rannoch Moor area. Within my care was a privileged and well-trained group of 17-year-olds. It had been raining for days, with rivers in spate and strong winds forcing us to adapt our route. We'd barely slept. It was day four, and we were all soaked to the skin, heading towards Corrour Station and a welcome exit.

My colleague Jan and I stood on a bridge, waiting for our weary band

Home territory – scrambling on Arran (Lucy Wallace)

of teenagers to appear, having left a soggy camp some hours before. They were late, and beaten to the bridge by another group of young people on a similar journey, who had also camped in the area the previous night.

Unlike our wealthy kids in fancy jackets (funded by mum and dad), this group was dressed in the identikit waterproofs and rucksacks that gave them away as an Outward Bound group. They were equipped for a multi-day journey through the mountains. Jan and I nodded at them through a curtain of rain as they traipsed across the bridge, heads bowed. We shared glances from beneath hoods as they passed, acknowledging that we were all tired and wet. I felt a little sorry for them.

The last boy in the group stopped suddenly and fixed us with a piercing gaze. 'Scuse me?!' he said, in a perfect Liverpool accent that took me by surprise. 'Do yous do this for a living?' Jan and I laughed grimly, 'Yes … for our sins'. 'This is f***ing brilliant' he retorted brazenly, his face creasing into a wide toothy smile. 'I wanna do your job. Yous are so lucky. This place is amazing!'

I was astonished. I looked at him, soaked to the skin, knowing the unpleasant night and journey he had endured was no different from ours and saw my experience reflected back at me. He stopped a while to chat to us and told us of his life back home. Without over-egging it, his backstory was standard issue grim. A stark contrast to the space, the freedom and the wildness of the landscape we were now stood in. Despite the rain, the basic kit, the wet feet and the sleep deprivation, this young lad was having the absolute time of his life, fizzing with excitement.

I'll never know if he achieved his ambition, but I like to think that this was a life-changing experience for him. What I do know is that meeting him was pretty life-changing for me.

Lucy Wallace is a wildlife guide and Mountain Leader based on the Isle of Arran. She is president of Ramblers Scotland and a passionate advocate for outdoor education.

—TMs—

Desert Island Hills: Kuwait 1976 – Charles Murray

We had been exploring and when I saw the hill, I wanted to climb it. We drove across the desert to reach it, raising a huge dust cloud. A short scramble and I was at the top. Below, I could see Janina and our Volkswagen. To the north were the Getty Oil burn-off flares at Mena Saud and two miles south was the Saudi Arabian border. To the west lay hundreds of miles of inhospitable desert, while half a mile east lay the azure waters of the Arabian Gulf. It was only about 150 feet high, but what memories.

The One that Got Away: Aletschhorn (4,195m) – Derek Sime

August 1999. We drove from Grindelwald to Blatten, via Lötschberg, followed by the Luftseilbahn to Belalp for the walk to the Oberaletschhütte (2,640m). The original plan was a Jungfraujoch – Fiesch traverse, taking in the Aletschhorn but the weather had changed all that. Next morning, reveille was at 03.00, but as we finished our Frühstück, an almighty flash outside the window. The all-clear was sounded at 06.00 and off we went, but after about 3km, another bright flash up on the ridge. We did what you're not supposed to do in a thunderstorm, and sheltered under a large boulder – then back to the hut for the lunchtime weather report, which was no better. Trip abandoned.

Fast forward one year, based at Blatten. I joined a local guide and his companion, shunned the mechanical lift and slogged up 1,100m in 'dehydrating heat'. Setting off from the hut at 02.30 next morning, this time we made it, in glorious Alpine weather.

Photographing Mountain Flora

Bert Barnett

A mongst my hill friends, I am often surprised how little they appreciate the added enjoyment that plants can give during a short pause to get your breath back (in my case!). I admit that I was equally ignorant until middle age. I know the exact year and place, as it was in 1992 taking in some hills during a break from the Killin Folk Festival. I was descending the south slopes of Ben Lawers following a burn which was lined with a variety of eye-catching colours. I may have taken some 'snaps' with my wee film Rollei 35, but the results were amateurish and of little value.

Over the years I started to put names to plants, collecting ID books and cameras which were more suited to take close up photos. The introduction of digital cameras offered a huge improvement for macro shots as special lenses were not required, which was the case with film cameras. Quite soon I also appreciated the benefits of swivel screens, which reduced the need to grovel in the grass as the camera could be at low level with the screen set horizontally and viewed from above. Importantly, digital cameras gave the ability to view the results immediately, but as screens are no competition against daylight, I simply waited to view the pictures at home on the PC monitor. Needless to say, there was a great deal of deleting, mostly from exposure and focussing problems.

My first folding screen cameras were mostly Canon, as these had optical viewfinders which are better for shooting scenery, so these cameras served for both plants and mountain shots. Optical viewfinder cameras have largely disappeared from the market, but can still be found on eBay. I have tried cameras with electronic viewfinders, but even good cameras like Panasonics are not as readable as an optical viewfinder. My current camera is a Panasonic TZ90 with folding screen for shooting plants. The TZ90 has an electronic viewfinder which is better to use than the rear screen outdoors, but I still use my Canon A1200 in summer and winter for landscapes.

Grass of Parnassus
(pictures by Bert Barnett)

The most significant benefits of the TZ90 are the reliable functions of spot focussing and spot exposure values. I expect that most of the Panasonics in this range will offer these functions. The spot readings are especially useful when taking white or yellow flowers which are commonly over-exposed. This is because average light readings will dwell on the large areas of foliage behind the flower, resulting in good exposure and focussing of the background, but will largely ignore the subject plant. Even using the spot feature, you cannot guarantee good results with tiny flowers, and I have recently adopted a new trick, where I place a written white card directly over the plant, take focus and light readings with a half click, remove the card and then press fully to take the shot. This requires steady hands, but a tripod could resolve any shaky hand issues. The card trick will result in a good exposure for the whites, but the darker parts will be under-exposed, so in Photoshop I use the Image/Adjustments/Levels feature to lighten the mid-tones without affecting the whites. When I am reviewing a batch of pictures, I choose the best and open those in Photoshop for cropping and general enhancement before sharing or storing. Other photo software is of course available and I have seen recommendations for the free version GIMP although I have not used this myself.

When taking close-up photos, I also use the half-click to take light and focus readings on the plant, then keeping the camera at the same distance, I move the scene sideways to obtain a better composition, usually to place the plant to one side rather than the centre.

When taking landscapes, I regularly tilt the camera slightly skyward with the half-click, then lower again to compose the scene, then full click. This

Moss Campion

reduces the risk of over-exposure and can produce blue skies rather than white. It is always best to look at the review screen to check the result – and, if necessary, adjust the level of tilt when taking another shot.

I also carry a loupe, which is a tube that goes over the screen to cut out daylight. This is useful for reviewing shots you have just taken but is very hard to control if you are shooting. Some loupes come with a magnetic attachment to ease this problem, but in general this can be an unwelcome fouter when you are on the hill and on the move. I only use the loupe for rare plants in remote locations where failure to get a good image would be most unfortunate.

Regarding the digital SLR option, I did use one when out on easy plant hunting walks. I bought a cheap Chinese

Yellow Saxifrage

right-angle viewer which attached to the viewfinder letting you use the camera at low level whilst looking down on the angle viewer. I found this was very successful. Historically, the major asset of the film SLR was for taking slides as opposed to film for printing. Slides by nature have to be correct in all respects at the time of shooting, whereas printing and digital images have scope for adjustment at home, so perfection on site is not really necessary. The real benefit of the SLR is that it gives an optical view, exact in terms of focussing and composition, which will always be better than the digital viewfinder version.

Ultimately the size and weight of the DSLR was an added burden and inconvenience so I do not take one in the hills anymore. I should add that if quality of image is your priority, then it is likely that the DSLR will generally have a superior lens to that of a compact. You may be aware that photo journalists all use DSLR cameras, but that is because their work is generally only acceptable to the press if the images have not been 'doctored'.

Without doubt, the digital compact with the folding screen will remain my preferred camera. One slight disadvantage of the TZ90 is that the screen only folds in one direction, which limits the number of shooting options. I have had other cameras where the swivel action is universal and the camera can be held in many contorted positions, but these have been put aside in favour of the TZ90's capabilities. I am afraid that I cannot offer advice on other cameras which can perform as well as the TZ90, but there will be other Panasonics which will be built to a very similar specification.

Starry Saxifrage

As my knowledge developed, partly through books on rare plants and partly through the help of the Botanical section of Perth Natural Science Society, I made efforts to visit sites known to be rich in plant variety. This proved fruitful at times, but occasionally the effort was wasted if the timing was too early, or the plants had passed. Nowadays, I am happy to have a good day of hill bagging whilst looking for good plants in photogenic locations. As an aside, I am vexed by photos taken by friends from the top of a hill rather than part of the way up, a better bet for composition and detail.

In recent times the Botanical Society of Britain and Ireland has posted an appeal to hill walkers to help with the ongoing search for data for the 2020 Atlas which is attempting to include a comprehensive listing of the variety of plants in every part of the country. Botanists have been concentrating their efforts towards filling in the missing areas, but the more remote locations are time and effort consuming. Since hill walkers are regularly on ground which is difficult to access and rarely visited, it would be a real advantage to collect input from those walkers who have a basic knowledge of plant species. I myself have contributed in recent years, but only plants which are both positively identifiable and less common, such as Dwarf Cornel, Purple Saxifrage or Trailing Azalea.

Sightings can be sent to the NBN Atlas Scotland where details and advice can be found. The website is fairly simple and registration is optional, but this requires very little detailed input. I did however register as I now intend using this facility as my preferred method of reporting plants. The information requested at best includes details such as date, grid reference, a named location and a photo, but the accuracy of your named plant can be qualified by 'certain, likely, not certain.' It would be useful in the first instance to record a single plant, to become familiar with the boxes to fill.

Dwarf Cornel

https://nbn.org.uk/record-share-explore-data/start-recording-wildlife/

I hope this piece may awaken members to the rich plant life on offer in the hills, and would firstly recommend the books *Scottish Wild Flowers* by Michael Scott and his more detailed book *Mountain Flowers*. These are very readable with good pictures and descriptions of the locations most suitable for exploration. *Hostile Habitats* published by The Scottish Mountaineering Trust deals with all aspects of mountains, but has a good section on plants, giving brief descriptions with photos of common plants and their environment. I have also been using a free app called 'Seek' on my phone which can help with ID and give encouragement to the beginner. Eyes down and start looking!

Purple Saxifrage

Thrift on Beinn a' Chlaidheimh

Sonnets for Eurydice

(i)

...Oh aye, but see me:
I widnae tak my ein aff ye.
I'd hae your haun in mine (climber's grip)
and wid be tellin ye,
(oh aye, ye'd be near petrified,
me an aw, but I widnae be lettin oan);
I wid turn tae ye, sayin,
    'Dinnae look ahint;
    look at me, dinnae look doon...
    pit your haun there, your right fit there;
    if I can get ye up the Buachaille,
    I can get ye up this, easy peasy...
I wid be watchin ye a the wie,
I'd be watchin, so I wid.

(ii)

If thon nyaff, Pluto, pitched up sayin,
    'We had a deal... give
    her back'
I'd tell him,
    'Did we? Well, we've no noo!
    Whit the hell did ye expect? Awa
    an whistle, ya mug, ye; I've banjo'd
    better than you, noo bog off!'
and up we'd go;
me watching you watching me. I suppose
it'd be like Crypt Route (51m V Diff ***)
and sure enough, we'd exit
into the sunlicht, staunin
like gods on Bidean nam Bian.

Stuart B. Campbell

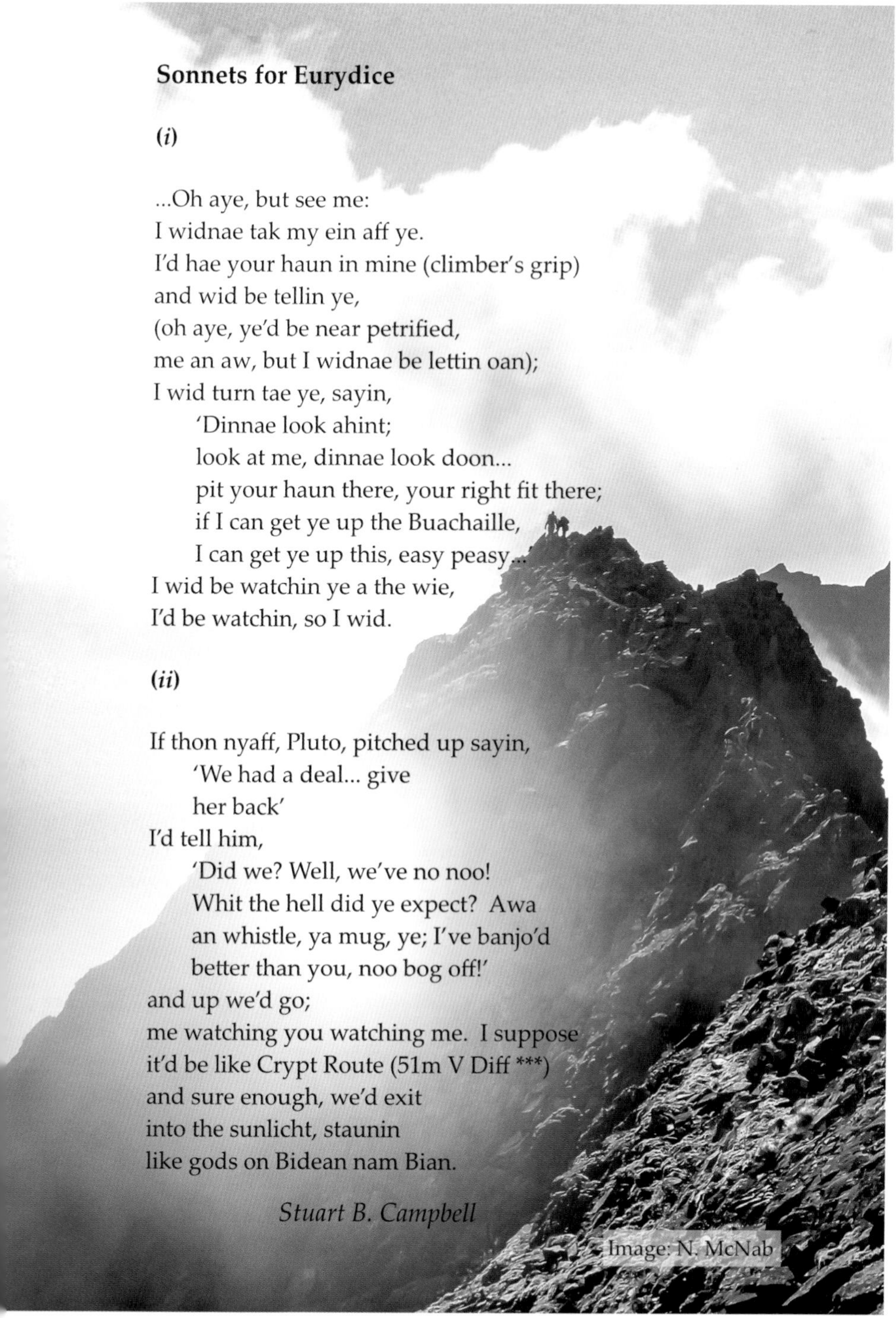

Image: N. McNab

Siren* or Sanctuary?

Heather Morning

Mountain Bothies and Mountain Rescue

Are mountain bothies a haven of safety for those who 'love the wild and lonely places,' or a dangerous Utopia luring the unwary into trouble?

There is no doubt that bothies have featured many times historically in mountain misadventures and this remains so today, as many of us choose to search out remote and challenging environments. Those of us who have had the privilege of spending a wind-torn, rain-lashed winter's night in the haven of a bothy or seen the bothy roof appear on the horizon through the growing darkness after a long walk in, will endorse and empathise with the concept of a bothy as a 'sanctuary'. But have we stopped to ask the question 'Would we be in this location at all, if the bothy did not exist?' Could this question alone suggest bothies, by their mere presence, result in folk getting themselves into difficulty in an environment that they are unable and unequipped to survive in?

Once the whisky-fuelled tales around the bothy fire are discounted, there are strong, well-documented cases of bothies playing both positive and negative roles in some of the most notorious mountain misadventures in Scotland. But first, let's focus on the positives......

The Fords of Avon

The Fords of Avon rebuild and adoption by the MBA in the summer of 2011 ensured the survival of an essential mountain refuge in a remote part of the Cairngorms. The small wooden hut, buried with granite boulders to hold it down in the winter storms, is placed strategically at a crossroad of glens and next to a major river crossing. Originally built by the military in the sixties, the hut has provided a lifesaving refuge to several parties over the years. Winter 2012 proved to be no exception. On 9th December 2012, Cairngorm Mountain Rescue Team (CMRT) was called out to the assistance of two overdue hill walkers, Malcolm Russell and Gerry Weir.

Malcolm and Gerry are both MBA members and experienced winter hill walkers, who set off for a two-day journey in the Cairngorms. Their plan was to head over Beinn MacDuibh from the Coire Cas car park at Cairngorm, spend the night in the Hutchinson Hut and return by a similar high-level route. The first day went according to plan and the boys spent a warm and comfortable night at the newly refurbished 'Hutchy Hut' adding their names to the bothy logbook. With fresh snow overnight adding to the already deep soft snow underfoot, Malcolm and Gerry made the decision not to return via the high tops, but to take a lower route which would take them via the Fords of Avon and out to Glenmore via the Lairig an Laoigh to their car at Glenmore Lodge.

The snow was deep, progress slow and the boys were carrying heavy rucksacks. It was late afternoon and the light was already fading when they finally reached the Avon crossing, well behind schedule. The river was a mixture of frozen ice and icy water. Gerry slipped whilst crossing and was soaked to the skin. They sensibly made the decision to stop, get out of their wet clothes, get into sleeping bags and get a brew and warm food. The Fords of Avon provided the vital shelter they needed.

They were both aware that their families would have started to be concerned, but with no phone reception they were unable to get a message out that they were fine and would continue their journey the following day. They left Fords of Avon refuge early after again noting in the bothy book their details, knowing by now that a rescue attempt may be underway. And indeed it was; their relatives had reported them overdue and Braemar MRT, CMRT, SARDA dogs and the Sea King helicopter from RAF Lossiemouth had all been deployed and were out searching for them.

Fords of Avon rebuild, 2011 (Heather Morning)

The Braemar team found the first clue as to their whereabouts – the note they had sensibly left in the 'Hutchy Hut' logbook. Shortly after, another team from Braemar entered the Fords of Avon and noted their entry from earlier that morning referencing their 'emergency' overnight at the refuge and their intention to continue their journey out via the Lairig an Laoigh. The boys were met by members of CMRT on their way out.

Faindouran

Fords of Avon has a very close neighbour – Faindouran; a remote stalking bothy maintained by the MBA since 1966. On the 2nd March 1992 Faindouran was a key factor in the survival of one very lucky lady. Kathleen Caird was ascending Beinn a' Bhuird with her husband Robert from the Glen Derry side. The pair split and Kathleen waited at the top of the Landrover track near the south top as Robert headed over to the north top. When Robert returned, he was unable to locate Kathleen and asked another party to call the police while he searched for her. Sometime later Grampian Police found Robert on the track.

Six mountain rescue teams, two helicopters and 1,222 person hours later, Kathleen was found in the sanctuary of Faindouran bothy. She had

Craic in Faindouran Bothy (Heather Morning)

crossed the plateau in a wild blizzard, with no map, compass, torch, whistle or extra gear. By sheer luck she stumbled across Faindouran bothy where fortuitously a party of three from Manchester was staying. The party was able to provide essential warmth and food until help arrived. The rescue team log noted: 'Teams were out all night; every team had an epic in wild weather! Temperature dropped to -20 during the night'.

Both of these incidents illustrate the immense importance bothies have played in remote locations and how they have literally saved lives. But sadly, there's a darker side to bothies too and there are certainly cases where the presence of a bothy has directly contributed to multiple fatalities. Both of the incidents described below are a long time ago, but lessons can still be learnt from them today. The 20 fatalities between January and April 2013 in the mountains of Scotland highlight how history has a tendency to repeat itself even with modern day kit and easily accessible training and information.

Ben Alder Cottage

Ben Alder Cottage was one of the earliest MBA projects, renovated in 1969. Most folk will associate the bothy with the infamous poltergeist ghost stories, but that is not my focus here. In December 1951, prior to the MBA's involvement, Ben Alder Cottage was the siren which lured four experienced, well-known and strong mountaineers to their deaths. Only one of the party survived – the lady in the group, Anne Tewnion.

The party from Glasgow planned to spend Hogmanay at Ben Alder Cottage; they travelled by train to Corrour Station then managed to get a lift along the side of Loch Ossian from an estate lorry to Corrour Lodge. Here the party cooked a meal in the shelter of the woods prior to heading up the Uisge Labhair over Bealach Cumhann and down to Ben Alder Cottage, a distance of 11km. The party was carrying heavy rucksacks with three to four days' food, and progress up the glen was slow. After about 4km, the party was exhausted and decided to bivouac. (It is unclear whether all five bivouacked together or whether the party split at this stage). The following morning, they continued their fateful journey in increasingly strong westerly winds. Metrological records show that storm-force westerly winds were experienced across Scotland on this, the second day of their journey, the 30th December 1951. The party realised that to try to continue to the bothy was impossible, so they turned back into the teeth of the storm hoping to return to Corrour Lodge for shelter and safety. Only Anne Tewnion made it back to initiate the rescue.

All four men died of hypothermia below 550m. Notably, the term 'hypothermia' was unknown to mountaineers in the 1950s, even though early research into 'exposure' and the effects of the cold on human victims had been trialled during the Second World War in concentration camps. The wet, cold and windy conditions combined with the equipment and clothing available at the time resulted in their tragic deaths. But it does raise the question as to whether these folk would ever have been in the position they were in, were it not for Ben Alder Cottage. (The full account of this tragic incident is available in *The Black Cloud* by IDS Thomson, ISBN 0-948153-20-2).

The McCooks at Ben Alder Cottage (AE Robertson, SMC Image Archive)

Curran Refuge

Perhaps the most well-documented tragedy surrounding bothies, is the Cairngorm Disaster in November 1971.

The Curran Refuge was built by the military and was one of several high-level shelters built in the Cairngorms during the 1960s. It was named after the person in charge of the build project, Jim Curran. A few years ago, I was introduced to Jim Curran, a very elderly gentleman. His first words to me were 'It wasn't my fault'; sadly he must still have harboured some guilt about the tragedy. A few months later he died. The Curran's construction was very similar to The Fords of Avon, with wooden/metal structures buried beneath granite boulders to hold them down in severe winds, and was located close to the south shore of the Lochan Buidhe on the Cairngorm plateau. (If you investigate closely in summer conditions you can still see evidence of the site of the refuge.) It is worth noting that the MBA never had any involvement with the Curran, nor the St. Valery, El Alamein or Garbh Choire refuges.

On Saturday 20th November 1971, a party of fourteen children aged between fourteen and eighteen from Ainslie Park School in Edinburgh with

The Curran Refuge, Feith Bhuidhe (Heather Morning)

two staff (Ben Beattie and Cath Davidson) set off for a weekend course in the Cairngorms. Their plan was to operate in two groups, both crossing the plateau from the top of the chairlift and descending the Tailors' Burn (Allt Clach nan Taillear) via Beinn MacDuibh to overnight in Corrour bothy. Here they would spend the night; the stronger group would return via Cairn Toul and Braeriach and the other (weaker) group via the Lairig Ghru. Both groups had arranged a pickup at the Rothiemurchus Bailey Bridge. An ambitious route even in the best of weather and underfoot conditions.

The party left their accommodation at Lagganlia in Glen Feshie just before eleven o'clock and Cath Davidson's group was seen on the summit of Cairngorm at a quarter past one. The forecast was for snow and an increasing westerly wind. The stronger party led by Ben Beattie made it across the plateau and into the Curran Refuge for the night, continuing on the following day, down the March Burn and out to the rendezvous location at Rothiemurchus. It was only when Cath Davidson's party did not turn up for this rendezvous that the alarm was raised; the party had now been out on the hill since mid-day the previous day.

Cath Davidson's party were less able and less experienced than Ben Beattie's; unable to locate the refuge they decided to bivouac. The bivouac was approximately 400 meters downstream from the Lochan Bhuidhe and in a low-lying area where the fresh windblown snow steadily accumulated. Over a period of 36 hours, one by one the group succumbed to hypothermia and died. Only Cath Davidson and one boy survived. Five children and the assistant leader perished; the worst tragedy in British mountaineering history. (A full and detailed account of this terrible incident is available in *A Bobby on Ben Macdhui* by John Duff, ISBN: 0-9534534-1-3).

A fatal accident enquiry was carried out and a formal verdict was returned. No blame was allocated and the jury made seven recommendations, one of which was, 'In the matter of the high level bothies, advice as to their removal or otherwise should be left to the experts'. Extensive consultation followed in 1972 amongst the outdoor community, the result of which was the removal of the Curran and St. Valery refuges. El Alamein and Garbh Corrie both remain today.

Both the tragedies highlighted have been instrumental in the development of mountain safety awareness, and Mountain Training Scotland (the organisation that administers training and assessment of mountain skills for leaders in the hills). Anyone heading into the remote mountains of Scotland would benefit from reading about these incidents and take learning messages from them. Ultimately in the mountains, safety and responsibility lies with ourselves. Bothies aren't mythical sirens luring folk to danger; bothies are a fantastic resource which we should treasure and use with respect as a valued part of our mountaineering culture.

*Siren – '(In Greek mythology) women or winged creatures whose singing lured unwary sailors onto the rocks' (Oxford English Dictionary).

Heather Morning has been a member of the MBA for many years and The Munro Society for only two (it took Heather a mere 19 years after completion before she joined!). Her father, Donald Rich, was the Maintenance Organiser for Pinkneys and Kershopehead bothies in Northern England and the Area Officer for Northern England. Heather works as the Mountain Safety Advisor with Mountaineering Scotland and was a member of the Cairngorm Mountain Rescue Team for 17 years. Heather was instrumental in the re-build of the Fords of Avon Refuge.

'To Dad for sharing his love of the wild & lonely places'.

—TMs—

Part 6 – Reflections

The First Munro Compleater:
Rev Archibald Aeneas Robertson 1870-1958

John Home Robertson

F amilies are full of surprises – I had no idea that my father's uncle Archie was Munro Compleater number one until a friend in Berwick-upon-Tweed drew my attention to James Robertson's piece in The Munro Society's Newsletter No. 40 in August 2017. I only had vague memories of visiting a venerable old man in Morningside with my Dad. Archie died when I was only ten, and neither I nor my sisters nor any of our cousins had ever heard mention that the worthy old Kirk Minister had been a pioneering mountaineer.

Although I have enjoyed lots of walks, including a handful of Munros, I'm afraid that this retired parliamentarian is never going to be a proper Munro bagger, but it has been a joy to research the story of the Rev Archibald Aeneas Robertson and our family.

Archie is generally known as A.E. Robertson, based on the phonetic pronunciation of 'Aeneas'. He was born in Helensburgh in 1870 and spent his childhood in the Hillhead area, close to his school, Glasgow Academy. He climbed Goatfell aged just 12 and became a kirk minister after studying at Glasgow and Edinburgh Universities. He climbed his first Munro, Ben Cruachan, in 1889 at the age of 19 – two years before the publication of Munro's Tables. 12 years later, in 1901, he bagged his 283rd and last Munro, Meall Dearg, with his newly-wed wife.

The incentive for thousands of people who follow in the footsteps of the first Munroist will be obvious to members of The Munro Society. It made sense for Sir Hugh Munro to climb the mountains and to check their altitudes while he was

The MacDonnell family, Ardchuilk,
Strathfarrar
(AER, from the SMC Image Archive)

compiling his Tables, and it is a sad quirk of history that the great man died without climbing three of his namesakes. But goodness knows what drove AER, a late-Victorian Glaswegian kirk minister, to be the first Munro pilgrim.

I can trace this part of the Robertson family tree to Archie Robertson's great-great-great grandfather, George Robertson, who was born in Rothesay on the Isle of Bute in 1692. George became Lord Bute's factor. The next generation moved to Greenock, and Archie's father, John Robertson, was born in Glasgow in 1825. John Robertson was an insurance broker, and his wife, Catherine Thomson, was associated with the Caird Shipbuilding company in Greenock. So the family came from highland ancestry but was now part of west-central Scotland's upwardly-mobile urban middle class. The family home was at 19 Hillhead Street, a compact terraced house between Glasgow University and Great Western Road – maybe there should be a plaque there to mark the childhood home of the first Munroist?

John and Catherine had four children; their first son and their only daughter died very young, and John died of tuberculosis at the age of 56 in 1881. Their two surviving sons were my grandfather, Henry (Harry) and Archibald Aeneas. Both boys were educated at the nearby Glasgow Academy. Harry had commercial ambitions – he left school at 16, got a job in a trading company and ended up as the Swire company's 'Taipan' in Hong Kong.

As you know, Archie scaled different heights – starting with Goatfell when he was only 12, soon after the death of his father. He studied physics (then called natural philosophy) under Lord Kelvin at Glasgow University, and then divinity at Edinburgh. All that education must have been costly, and I can only guess that a cherished younger son may have been benefiting from the inheritance of his widowed mother. He became a Church of Scotland minister, initially as an assistant minister in Musselburgh then in Edinburgh's prosperous Morningside. In 1906, at the age of 36, he got the call to be the parish minister for the Braes of Rannoch in highland Perthshire – an extremely convenient patch for a walking and climbing enthusiast.

The Robertson brothers went their separate ways as teenagers. Harry was the classic Scotsman-on-the-make, pursuing business interests in Britain's global empire, while Archie was saving souls and bagging Munros back home in Scotland. But they kept in touch with each other, and they both married MacFarlan girls – daughters of a family with strong highland heritage and a very honourable record of promoting access to our hills and glens.

Harry's wife, my grandmother Hannah MacFarlan, was descended from John MacFarlan, the so-called 'Radical Laird' of Ballencleroch. He had enraged neighbouring estate owners by supporting Thomas Muir and the 'Radical Martyrs' in 1820, and worse, by opening the gates to the Campsie Glen for public access in 1785. Hannah's cousin Kate, AER's first wife, was descended from that Laird's brother, so no surprise that she shared Archie's enthusiasm for walks and climbs.

My grandmother's diary for 17th August 1900 in Hong Kong reads 'Mail in – news that Archie is going to marry Kate MacF. Harry thinks he is mad; she is 20 years older than him'. He could also have mentioned that the couple's mothers were sisters, so in view of such dangerously close consanguinity, it was just as well that Kate was fifty years old. But regardless of the age difference, they evidently had a happy marriage. Kate was a 'daughter of the manse' who knew how to support Archie's parish work and she obviously enjoyed sharing his walks and climbs in the highlands.

Archie climbed his final Munro, Meall Dearg, with Kate in 1901 and he wrote that he kissed the summit cairn before embracing his new wife. His 12-year Munro campaign, as well as a climbing trip in the Alps and a break in America, coincided with his years as an assistant minister in Musselburgh and Morningside. Those excursions required time and money from a junior cleric in his twenties, perhaps depending on tolerant Session Clerks as well as a generous and doting mother, who died in 1898.

McFail (McPhail) family at Strathmore Cottage, West Monar, 1905 (AER, from the SMC Image Archive)

AER was 14 years younger than Sir Hugh Munro, but they were both very active members of the Scottish Mountaineering Club and they must have known each other. I'm not aware of any evidence of a race to be the first to climb all the mountains in Sir Hugh's Tables. But while Munro was assiduously climbing and measuring all the associated Tops as well as the main mountains, Robertson was firmly focused on the 283 main

Kate Robertson, Loch Arkaig, May 1906 (AER, from the SMC Image Archive)

259

summits, which conveniently at that time, did not include the Inaccessible Pinnacle.

There is some controversy about whether Robertson actually reached the summit of Ben Wyvis. Then, as now, compleation relies on honesty, and my reading of Archie's words and his character suggest that he practised what he preached about truth. So, if he did stop short of the summit in bad weather, it seems fair to assume that he will have returned later. Likewise, I don't think he would have shirked the Inaccessible Pinnacle if it had been on the list at the time as he had plenty experience of serious rock climbing.

Sadly, Sir Hugh's death in 1919 at the age of 63 prevented him from climbing the last three of the 283 summits on his list[1]. AER's status as the only Munro compleator stood for 22 years until another kirk minister joined the procession in 1923 – beginning a list that is now over 7,000.

These pioneers did not have the benefit of roads, cars, bridges, or even signposts, let alone mobile phones, GPS or Gore-Tex. The short-lived highland railway network was still being developed; the Mallaig line was opened in 1901. Archie and Kate did a lot of walking, and they also used a tandem bicycle for transit between railway platforms and the foot of mountains. Then they had to find routes to previously unclimbed summits.

They must have depended very heavily on the local knowledge of crofters and shepherds about routes. AER's diaries and photos describe highland hospitality in remote glens, where weary walkers could expect shelter in isolated dwellings. Descriptions of nights in very remote cottages reveal primitive conditions and serious poverty – slightly relieved by the produce of illicit stills. Robertson's presbyterian principles evidently did not exclude the enjoyment of whisky. He made an effort to learn Gaelic not only for travels in the north, but also for his work as a parish minister in highland Perthshire.

AER was an important early photographer, and he has left a truly magnificent record of the landscapes and people of the highlands at the end of the Victorian

Buachaille Etive Mòr and the Kingshouse Hotel, Glen Coe, 1926 (AER, from the SMC Image Archive)

era. His glass slides now belong to the Scottish Mountaineering Club, and they are a wonderful archive of images from that time. It must have been difficult enough to tramp and scramble up rain-soaked Munros wearing sodden woollen tweed clothes and leather tackety boots, but Archie was also often carrying a bulky heavy wooden camera and tripod with fragile glass photographic plates, not to mention an aneroid barometer provided by his old Professor, Lord Kelvin, to check the altitude of summits.

Between 1907 and 1918, Archie and Kate lived in the Braes of Rannoch Manse at Bridge of Gaur. It is a beautiful and very remote location, halfway between the West Highland railway station at Rannoch and the Struan halt on the main line to Inverness – convenient for rail travel to destinations throughout the highlands. Struan happens to be the ancestral heartland of Clan Robertson.

I have inherited documents relating to AER's election by the parish of Braes of Rannoch – the 'call' is signed by 97 kirk members from cottages as well as shooting lodges. It's fair to assume that he was an inspiring preacher, and he and Kate must have provided pastoral support to grieving families through the First World War as well as the 1918 'Spanish 'flu' pandemic. He seems to have been an effective fundraiser too – he set himself the task of building a new church to replace a sadly dilapidated old structure and he succeeded in raising £800 to build the little stone kirk that is still in use today. But his weekday duties to such a small flock can't have been too demanding, leaving plenty time for walking and mountaineering.

The Reverend Archie made himself available for transfer to bigger and more prominent parishes. He compiled a dossier of testimonials citing his learned and 'earnest' preaching as well as his 'lectures with lantern slides from his own photographs about mountaineering, his favourite recreation'. But it seems that that promotion never happened. He retired from his parish ministry after only 12 years at Rannoch in 1918, aged 49, and returned to Morningside in Edinburgh where he just had part-time duties as chaplain at the Astley Ainslie Hospital.

He spent his long 40-year retirement on more walking and climbing excursions and became a very active member of the Scottish Mountaineering Club, the Scottish Rights of Way

The Old Manse (John Home Robertson)

261

SMC's Charles Inglis Clark (CIC) Hut, Ben Nevis
(AER, from the SMC Image Archive)

Society and the Royal Scottish Geographical Society. He seems to have been the unofficial chaplain of the Scottish Mountaineering Club and in 1929 he performed a service of dedication for the new Charles Inglis Clark Memorial Hut on Ben Nevis. He was an enthusiastic amateur woodworker, making a table that is still in service in the CIC hut.

I think it's relevant to mention AER's part in the campaign by the Scottish Rights of Way Society to protect and promote rights of access in the Scottish countryside. Bear in mind at the time, lairds were taking aggressive steps to obstruct access to their sporting estates, to the extent that even the upper-class members of the Scottish Mountaineering Club often did their climbs at night – partly to avoid causing disturbance to landowners, but also to minimise the risk of confrontations with their staff.

As an old red myself, I must acknowledge the fact that great uncle Archie was a true-blue Tory and a natural proponent of the rights and privileges of landowners. But he had a radical streak on the subject of access to hills and glens. He built up an extensive knowledge of historic drove roads, coffin paths and rights of way, and he opposed initiatives by estate factors to obstruct those rights.

The Trespass (Scotland) Act 1865 only applied to camping and lighting fires, so 'trespassers will be prosecuted' signs in Scotland were always a meaningless bluff, but estates went to great lengths to obstruct walkers; locking gates, erecting aggressive signs and deploying staff to frighten people. After years spent tramping so many paths, Archie Robertson knew his facts about routes and rights, and he became Chairman of the Scottish Rights of Way Society in 1931. His encyclopaedic knowledge is demonstrated in the Society's 1941 booklet 'Old tracks, cross-country routes and coffin roads in the north-west Highlands'.

Armed with all that information, AER seems to have had the personality to face down bullying lairds and factors. And he may have been the right man to do it – as a kirk minister and a paid-up Tory who had volunteered as a special constable during the General Strike in 1926, he probably had more influence with landlords than a socialist would have had. But they still found him very irritating; in his foreword to the booklet, he explained that he had acquired a lot of information about access rights, and he quoted an Inverness-shire estate factor's words 'I would like to stick a knife in

Cluanie Inn, Easter 1931
(AER, from the SMC Image Archive)

your ribs… and then all that information would perish with you'. That's why he wrote it all down and published it. I'm rather proud of that important family heritage, and I was particularly happy to use my vote in the Scottish Parliament to help to entrench the statutory 'right to roam' in the Land Reform (Scotland) Act 2003.

Archie's first wife died in 1935. Kate had been twenty years older than him, and was evidently a wonderful companion as well as fellow-traveller in the hills and glens. Within a year of her death, our 65-year-old widower was married to another keen hill walker, Winifred Hutchison. And this time his wife was twenty years younger than him, but he never had any children.

Archie and Winifred spent a long and happy retirement in their house in Cluny Gardens, Edinburgh. I remain puzzled by the fact that a man from an apparently modest middle-class background managed to live such a leisurely and comfortable life, including trips to the USA and Italy in the 1890s as well as countless recreational excursions around Scotland, with presumably very limited income from just 12 years' service as minister in a tiny highland parish and temporary duties elsewhere. I can only guess that there may have been shipbuilding wealth inherited from his mother.

Archie died in 1958 at the age of 88, leaving his mountaineering archive and a wonderful collection of early photographic plates to the Scottish Mountaineering Club, as well as a valuable body of information and rights protected for the benefit of people who enjoy access in the Highlands. And he will always be remembered as Munroist Number One.

[1] Although Munro had not climbed The Inaccessible Pinnacle, at the time it was not regarded as a 'summit'.

—TMS—

John Dow, 1881–1972

Robin N. Campbell

John Dow was Munroist No. 5, completing in 1933 in the footsteps of Archie Robertson, Ronald Burn, James Parker and Rooke Corbett. He went on to complete the Tops in 1947, following Burn, Corbett and Alastair Cram, and coinciding with John and Paddy Hirst née Wells. In 1956 he added the Furths. He is sometimes said to be the first to complete all three of Munros, Tops and Furths, but he was comfortably preceded in this by William M. Docharty in 1949.

Dow was born on 19th November 1881 in Kinning Park, a former burgh of Glasgow lying south of the Clyde between Kingston and Govan. His father Donald worked in the carpet trade. His SMC application form showed early ascents of Ben Lomond and the Arran peaks. Dow trained as a Tax Surveyor with the Inland Revenue. A few years after the death of his father in 1898, Dow's family relocated to Findhorn Place in Edinburgh.[1]

Dow married Violet Euphemia Shaw in 1916.[2] His SMC application form shows that he did not resume his interest in climbing until 1927, when he began to gather Munros, winter and summer, at a steady rate, often alone. His climbing notebooks identify companions only by initials.[3] Even these scanty indications are ambiguous, since he had a curious way with hand-written capitals, but it looks like he had an outing in 1928 with his SMC sponsors Murray Lawson and Malcolm Matheson – possibly suggested by Secretary George Sang to check Dow's roadworthiness.[4] At any rate he joined SMC at the end of 1928, and thereafter took a full part in SMC activities.

Dow made rapid progress towards completion during the next years and completed in 1933. Although he climbed with SMC members at Club Meets, his usual companions in this period were non-members, so far as I can tell. One companion who features prominently in the Notebooks is 'C.G.A.' From other evidence, such as Dow's photographs, it is clear that this is Christopher Gibson Andrews, another Tax Inspector who eventually settled in Perth. Andrews did not join the SMC until 1934. He shared many expeditions with Dow, before and after Dow's completion, and was himself an unrecorded early Munroist[5] Andrews and Dow explored the ridge of Creag a' Choire Aird (now named Mullach na Dheiragain) in clear weather in July 1930, and were able to provide better data on heights and distances of the various points along that troublesome ridge (see D4 in the list of Dow's writings below). One highlight of Dow's round was his blitzing of Aonachs, Grey Corries and Easains with Andrews on 3rd to 5th May 1930 (see D3), and another may have been a week of fine weather in May 1932 when Dow climbed the Cuillin Munros with SMC member Donald Mackay.

Chris Andrews and John Dow, Sgùrr nan Ceathramhnan, July 1930
(John Dow Collection, SMC Image Archive)

By 1933 Dow was on the brink of completion, and he achieved it in attendance at the special SMC Meet at Corrour Lodge in June of that year. Sir John Stirling Maxwell had been an Honorary Member since 1921, and had offered the use of his Lodge at Corrour to the Club. On 4th June Dow climbed his final Munro – Beinn na Lap, accompanied by Percy Donald. When he wrote about his achievement (see D5), he remarked that when stood on each summit 'there was always in my mind the thought that on this peak four grave and reverend men have at one time stood, and that over this cairn, on four great days of the past, four dignified and (more or less) flowing beards have wagged.' After generally abusing beards, and the climbers who used them, and discounting them as artificial aids, he remarked that 'Bearded men cannot, in a civilised society, be reckoned, and that therefore to me belongs the glory and honour of being the first to count as a conqueror of the Munros.' With tongue firmly in cheek, of course. Paddy Hirst might of course have made the same sort of claim in 1947, with a different sort of appendage in mind. After this knockabout beginning, Dow continued with a survey of the weather he had encountered in his round, and some conclusions about Munros – principally that the ranges An Teallach, the Buachailles, Liathach

Group at Corrour Lodge, June 1933. From left, standing: James Anton, Malcolm Matheson, John Dow, Robert Elton, Percy Donald, George Glover. Seated: Stuart Jack (MacRobert Collection, SMC Image Archive)

and Beinn Eighe should each have more than one Munro, a suggestion eventually adopted by SMC after the passage of many years.

In 1931, the new Guidebooks Editor Archie Robertson announced that there would be a 'Lowlands' Guide, covering ground south of the Forth & Clyde Canal and the two Firths, and that Dow would be its Editor – a suitable appointment since Dow had just moved from Edinburgh to Dumfries.[6] Dow published an interesting lengthy article about the Galloway Hills (see D6), and persuaded others to write about the Lowthers and Cheviots (see D7).[7] However, there was a background of Committee and AGM swithering, with the alternate suggestion of incorporating Lowland Hills in the planned Southern Highlands Guide enjoying support.[8] Eventually both new Guide projects were shelved due to the War. According to Dow's obituarist Edward C. Thomson, Dow gave up on the project owing to 'lack of sufficient interest' from other members.[9] Whatever the truth of the matter, it is interesting to note that when Andrew and Thrippleton produced the long-delayed SMC Southern Uplands Guide in 1972, none of the articles prepared or commissioned by Dow is listed in their bibliography, and Dow is nowhere mentioned. Such is the common fate of all scholars: to have their work ignored, misunderstood, or plagiarized.

John Dow completing his Munros on Beinn na Lap, 4th June 1933
(John Dow Collection, SMC Image Archive)

Dow accumulated Munro Tops slowly and it was not until 1949 that he stood on his last, Beinn Garbh of Beinn Dearg in Atholl (see D8).[10] He acknowledged there that whereas those who visit all the Munros are generally considered only eccentric, those who visit all the Tops 'can hardly be [thought to be] quite sane'. Nevertheless, he went on to propose that the criterion for a Top should be relaxed to include 'any obvious knob' over 3.000 feet, in the interest of ensuring that the mountains are better known. As indicated above, Dow's attitude towards the Munros was similarly liberal, and (see D9) he suggested – following a triple criterion of Dip, Distance and Difficulty – that a further 31 Tops should become Munros. The most audacious additional Munro he proposed is the Bhàsteir Tooth, which could only be on grounds of Difficulty. Docharty also endorsed this triple criterion, and in his Supplementary volume he made the equally audacious proposal that Sgùrr Coire an Lochain (Cuillin) should be a 2,000-foot Independent mountain (or 'Graham', as we mistakenly call these), and went to the considerable trouble of climbing it with the help of George 'Syd' Prentice and Jim Walmsley on 25th May 1961.[11]

Dow's final contribution to the SMC Journal (D10) was to present Corbett's posthumous list of 2,500-foot Scottish mountains. In his Foreword, he misunderstood Corbett's method and seemed bewildered by the omission of so many 'heights of equal merit to those listed' but looked forward to a revised edition 'comprehensive of every 2,500-foot summit', as well as to a further list embracing heights 'below that arbitrary limit'. In his Afterword, he reports advice from Edmund W. Hodge and Docharty that Corbett was using a Dip criterion only, of 500 feet, and assents to this.[12] My own belief is that they were all wrong, and that Corbett's criterion was 10 fifty-foot contours (OS Popular Map) between relevant col and summit, which of course enclose only 450 feet.[13]

Dow remained in Dumfries, apart from the War years in which he relocated to Edinburgh, perhaps for War-related work, until his death at 'The Chesters' on 22nd April 1972 in his 91st year. He is buried in Section I of Cathcart Old Cemetery in East Renfrewshire along with his father and mother. I have sought his grave in what has become a jungle, thanks to the Covid pandemic, but failed to locate it. He lived and climbed through the years when the collection of Munros, Tops, etc. was still a rare activity, carried on by devotees commonly regarded as eccentric or borderline sane. Now, of course we regard those men and women as Enlightened Pioneers of what has become an entirely normal recreation. Maybe. But the cutting edge is always eccentric, and they are still among us today.

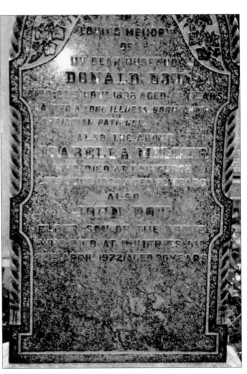

Dow Family headstone, Cathcart Cemetery
(Courtesy of William Dow)

Writings by John Dow in the SMC Journal

D1. 'Day Trips by Rail', Volume 19, 33-40
D2. 'Road Reconnaissances from Braemar', Volume 19, 96-100
D3. 'The Eastern Nevis Group', Volume 19, 132-134
D4. 'The Strath Glass Glens', Volume 19, 284-285
D5. 'Munros, Beards and Weather', Volume 20, 113-118
D6: 'The Galloway Hills', Volume 21, 327-336 & 356

D7. 'Notes on the Cheviot Hills' (with A.W. Peacock), Volume 22, 170-176
D8. 'Munros and "Tops"', Volume 24, 75
D9. 'Munro's Tables', Volume 24, 118-120
D10. Foreword/Afterword to Corbett's List of 2,500ft Mountains, Volume 25, 45-46 & 136

[1] John's younger brother Thomas Miller Dow (b. 1890) attended Edinburgh University and joined the Indian Civil Service. He trained as a pilot around 1930, and flew Lancaster bombers in WW2. His medals, etc. were sold in June 2021 at Thomas Roddick Auctions.

[2] Family background and marriage information all obtained from ScotlandsPeople data.

[3] These are kept in the SMC Archive at the National Library: Acc.11538 items 93 to 96.

[4] Matheson was a Principal Secretary in the Department of Health. He married in his mid-40s, but had the great misfortune to succumb to severe illness while on honeymoon, and died in hospital at Garmisch.

[5] Andrews' completion is noted in a very brief obituary in SMCJ 25 (1954), p.262. His completion date is the subject of research by Dave Hewitt and Andrews' son Chris (Munroist No. 280).

[6] The Position of the "Guide Book" Scheme', SMCJ 19, 266-267

[7] Corbett provided 'The Lowther Hills', SMCJ 22, 287-290

[8] See 1934 AGM Report, SMCJ 20, 352

[9] SMCJ 30 (1973), 200-201

[10] His last Top is not mentioned in D8. I have inferred it from the ticks and dates in his copy of *Munro's Tables*, Munro Society Archives item 254/2/10, Bell Library, Perth.

[11] *The Supplement to a Selection...* , Volume I, Foreword p. 16-17

[12] For further comment on Hodge's role here, see Jim Barton's 'Hodge's Journals & Corbett's Criterion', SMCJ 41, 36-37

[13] See my 'Corbett's Criterion', *Munro Society Journal No. 2* (2010), 31-35

Desert Island Hills: Meall a' Bhuachaille – Anne Butler

Meall a' Bhuachaille is overshadowed by the Munros of the Northern Cairngorms. Whenever I drive up the A9 it is there, a welcoming sentinel, its pyramidal shape reminding me that I am almost home.

The walk in is pretty special; sometimes the weather has closed in and I have just turned round at Ryvoan and headed back, knowing that Meall a' Bhuachaille will be waiting for another day. I can see Meall a' Bhuachaille from my bedroom window; it's a hill that feels like home and I know it'll be there whenever I need it, full of memories.

Star 1:1.618

That star contained all my childhood
wishes. I first sighted it when
the street-lights went out in my home-town
and all the heavens were revealed;
and years later I recalled seeing it then,
in Coire Etchachan when the curtain
of the Aurora Borealis rose above
Beinn Mheadhoin. Everything was starlit;
the snow sparkled like yet another universe
and I looked again amongst the Great Bear
and Pleiades of my inner space for it; to see
if I could see in that five-pointed star,
we describe as children: the architecture of our souls;
the symmetrical perfection of a man fully formed
and naked; the golden ratio of the human
and divine. Yet, looking back now, far
beyond the light of its birth spiralling ever outwards,
into the curled foetal beginnings of its nucleosynthesis,
there was nothing more, perhaps, than the last
will of a god already passed away and
an encroaching time when this anonymous
luminescent here and now would be extinguished.

Stuart B. Campbell

Image: N. McNab

Reflections of an Ancient Hill Walker

Norman McNab

I have been walking among and over Scotland's hills and mountains for 60 plus years in an entirely uncompetitive way, either on my own or with others. 'Completions' were not something that drove me, and forty years passed before I had climbed every Munro; an inevitable conclusion rather than an objective. Indeed, I shrivelled a little inside and still do when the epithet 'Munro Bagger' was applied. I do not feel superior about this. The opposite in fact. I contemplate with awe the multiple rounds and record times that are achieved by others. The passage of time inevitably brings change, and this is a challenge for me. The older you become the less you like environmental changes. I mean environmental in its widest sense, rather than the consequences of climate change which correctly concern us all.

A consequence of these changes is a sense of loss. A feeling that something has been taken away from me. Now this emotion has its origins in selfishness and, although I feel it, I am not proud of it. As an example, many people have happy memories of family holidays in some quiet and peaceful place, pristine and known to few. These places hardly exist now; they have been 'discovered'. A return later in life can be disturbing. The peaceful idyll has become popular. It is cluttered with cars and motor caravans, litter and what was pristine turf for a family picnic, is now a sea of mud. What has this got to do with hill walking? Well, it is an exaggerated analogue for the change in Scotland's hill and mountain environment.

I am well aware that even in the early 1960s things had changed compared with pre-war times when the mountains were only accessible for the privileged or indominable, and remote highland glens still housed shepherds and estate employees before afforestation, the profound landscape modifications associated with hydroelectricity and lifestyle changes emptied the glens. In many ways these glens were less of a wilderness than they are now. A time when Bill Murray's poetic and sometimes metaphysical prose in *Mountaineering in Scotland* became a source of inspiration for many of my generation.

My hill walking pleasure comes, albeit not exclusively, from camping in remote locations including Munro summits, high plateaux and corries, during the short days of winter and early spring. This provides time to appreciate the changing light and weather and to absorb the essence of 'wilderness'. It is living on the mountain rather than a transitory pole tap of a summit cairn. 24 hours compared with 24 minutes. In its own way it is a blend of the strenuous and the idle – a heavy, laden climb with four-season gear,

4th January 1968 close to the summit of Am Bodach at the east end of the Aonach Eagach. Two climbers passed in the early morning of the 3rd, while we were inside the tent and passed critical comments about our Black's mountain tent – I assume they thought the tent was unoccupied! Nobody else was seen over the three days and two nights we spent on the ridge. To camp there now would be like camping in Glasgow's George Square. Note that even 53 years ago there were some thin snow cover times too. (Norman McNab)

snow shovels, saws, the necessary ice axe and crampons plus food, cooking equipment, appropriate clothing and the hard work of digging and clearing a safe haven to pitch the tent. The idle part follows with the sublime pleasure of languishing in dramatic surroundings and watching day change through dusk to moonlight and night change through dawn into a new day, matched by a kaleidoscope of changing colours. Lying in the tent it is possible to imagine a living mountain. Lying halfway between wakefulness and sleep the gentle breathing of the wind and the swish of spindrift is as soothing as a childhood lullaby. Not always though; the mood can change and become profoundly aggressive. The sound of the wind roaring against the cliffs, the whip crack of the tent as the violent changes in air pressure squeeze and inflate the fabric reminds you that the mountain is the master, and you are a vulnerable mortal.

From the early 1960s to the late 1970s, I spent many winter nights camping on the Glen Coe summits and high corries with friends, the Buachailles, Bidean, Sgreamhach, Coire nan Lochain, Sgorr nam Fiannaidh, and Am Bodach. At that time, it was unusual but a pleasant interlude to be visited by a passing climber. By the 1980s, Glen Coe was becoming increasingly popular and it was no longer desirable to camp close to the increasingly busy summits.

A campsite on Buachaille Etive Beag in February 1975. Again, poor snow cover.
(Norman McNab)

The contrast is startling between then and now. In superb snow conditions in January 1965, we camped in Coire nan Lochain for three days and saw nobody, apart from a chat with Hamish MacInnes outside his house before we set off. On a recent return to the same location on a good winter day, parking spaces were at a premium, the corrie was a busy place, full of climbers, hill walkers, mountain guided parties and the happy sounds of the multitude.

So we fled to the hills on the north and south Cluanie ridges and had many winter camping years of adventure. Years where, seeing passing fellow climbers was still rare and our sense of wilderness peace undisturbed. Sometimes we would meet a few others while ridge walking and on rare occasions a return to our camp would reveal, in footsteps in the snow, evidence of a passing visitor. Winter camps in Torridon, the Fannichs and Mamores were equally quiet. The sense of being alone can still be experienced because most sensible people have left the high tops before sunset and have not returned in the hours before and after sunrise. These are the 'magic hours', and a compelling reason for dwelling in high silent places with only the moon and stars for illumination.

This quiet vastness of a mountain top at night can deliver a sense that we are the intrusion, which indeed we are. Humbled by our surroundings, conversation is muted, as is our illumination. We took great care to ensure our feeble torches were always aimed downwards lest a flash of unintentional light was interpreted as a distress signal. By contrast a high camp on Beinn a' Chrùlaiste in 2020, before lockdown, was disturbed by loud laughter and powerful head torches at 11pm. How things have changed. I admit that this mountain is very easy to access and because of this, popular with those who would probably not venture on Bidean on a dark night (there was no moon, just stars).

Equally, emphasising the change, a two-night camp in Coire Gabhail or the Lost Valley, in January 1964 just produced two passing climbers. It is now a very busy place, scarred by incompetent campers' fires, half burnt food and cans. Camping here now would be a public park experience.

Returning to our presence being an intrusion. Three in a small tent leads to plenty of banter and occasional argument and it is surprising how far the human voice carries on a still night – easily several miles on a windless open mountainside. I discovered that cooking smells also travel far in the right

Camp in the corrie of Stob Coire an Lochain, Glen Coe, 2nd January 1965. We never saw a single person despite superb weather, albeit never warmer than -9°C. When we returned in the summer, we discovered we had been camping on one of the shallow lochans. (Norman McNab)

conditions. Camping on the vast space of Braeriach's snow-covered south plateau with my son one March, I had reached the final stages in preparing and dishing an evening curry meal when there was a shout outside the door. It gave us a start. We had seen nobody all day. Our visitor claimed to have smelled the enticing aroma long before he saw our tent in the failing light. He thought he would try his luck, but we had to tell him we had none to spare. 'Would he like a cup of tea instead?' Fortunately, he had the sensitivity to realise that in the freezing cold it was unfair to divert us from our rapidly cooling food and, following some cheery and ironic banter, he departed.

Many in my age group will recall that hill walking and climbing was regarded by many in the general public and the tabloids of the era as irresponsible and slightly eccentric. At social gatherings it was rare to meet someone with a shared love of the hills. Normal people exercised and socialised on the golf course. Now 'Munro bagging' is fashionable and it is relatively unusual at a social gathering not to meet someone with hill walking as part of their recreational activity.

In the early 1960s the only source of quality climbing and camping equipment in Glasgow available to me, was a small Blacks shop – no doubt a situation replicated in other towns and cities. Much gear was 'ex-army'

A typical high camp. The location is the Spainteach top on the Five Sisters in Glen Shiel. On the three days we spent at that spot, one party from the Perth MC passed our tent. Otherwise, we saw nobody. (Norman McNab)

A midnight image taken looking north from a campsite on Doire Leathain with an early digital camera in 2008. The gear has greatly improved. (Norman McNab)

sourced and boots were of doubtful quality – at least those that, as a young man, I could afford. The appearance of Tiso's shop in Edinburgh heralded a revolution. It represented in our minds a mecca which amply justified travelling from Glasgow to inspect its tantalising stock. How different the world is now; the restricting buff Ventile smocks have been replaced by colourful flexible breathing articles of fashion, worn as much by dog walkers in the park, as mountaineers in the Karakorum.

Mountain intelligence came from a gradual self-taught apprenticeship, navigation skills learned as a boy scout, the company of more experienced companions and walking on hills, close to home, in summer, and graduating to the high mountains in winter. Now youngsters are taken, fully and appropriately kitted, by qualified mountain leaders straight onto the Cairngorm winter plateau. All very sensible, but an unknown loss of self-discovery and satisfaction for the youngsters. It is a kind of leitmotif of our age – instant gratification. In it there is a conundrum. The best lessons are learned through our mistakes. Self-taught is a very inefficient and hazardous route to mountain knowledge but perhaps in the end it has advantages that these lessons are never forgotten and a more profound instinct and empathy for the mountain environment is the reward.

I do not suggest that it is not necessary to know how to correctly use equipment, read maps, understand how weather is affected by altitude and recognise unsafe windslab etc. The Mountain Weather Information Service is a superb improvement on the past. There were times in the early days where the long wave Shipping Forecast was an important source. Much like a sailor on the high seas we would listen carefully to weather reports and map in our minds the relevant synoptic situation. On a few occasions a perilous mountain camp was hastily evacuated on reception of an approaching storm and the worst of all situations – a rapidly rising temperature, accompanied by torrential rain. Yes, this did require a radio and reception confined to the 'long-wave'. I wonder what the present generation would make of that in comparison to smart phones.

Another midnight image on Doire Leathain. (Norman McNab)

The early encouragement came from writers like WH Murray and Tom Weir, but it is interesting that at that time the SMC Guides, although full of interest, lacked specific details on access and routes. Poucher's guides were an anomaly, but not necessarily that helpful. A lot of the satisfaction came from planning expeditions. One-inch Ordnance Survey maps would be spread out on the floor and companions would crowd round, interpret the contours, the rivers and burns, woods, and symbols for rocky or boggy ground and plot their own routes and potential camp site. Except for a few places, like Ben Nevis or Ben Lomond, paths, if they existed, were vestigial or mere animal tracks. The One-inch to the mile Ordnance Survey maps of the time were, for the most part, fairly lacking in detail (the Fisherfield area was particularly poorly detailed for example) and photographs, if they existed were generally relatively unhelpful. All this just added to the sense of wilderness and discovery.

Now the situation is entirely changed – an extensive and still growing selection of guidebooks exists, lavishly illustrated with detailed maps and route descriptions, augmented by excellent internet-based resources, and 'outdoor' magazines providing even more access information and advice - the whole energised by social media and smartphone apps which waypoint every step of your GPS-guided adventure. In this context the word adventure is transformed into an oxymoron. Now I admit this is all a bit acerbic and even dishonest since I too indulge in most of these sources of information.

The only certainty is that there is no going back and this huge growth, mirrored in 'Munro Completions', will naturally level off at some future time. It has also delivered an opportunity for commercial exploitation with many individuals and businesses employed in the 'outdoor recreation industry'. This commercial exploitation has created even more growth. The result is that our hills and mountains have become a significant economic asset further fuelling growth. Tourism marketing, aimed at the important objective of employment in the Highlands is also directing attention to climbing 'Scotland's Munros' and encouraging increasing numbers of overseas visitors to 'join the throng'.

In my time I have encountered easy access to hills, blocked by monoculture Sitka plantations, seen them felled and replanted and watched the creeping industrialisation of wind farms erode the wilderness experience. But that is a subject worthy of its own article.

So, is my loss the result of a gain for the many? The answer must be yes, and I cannot argue against it. I have no more right than anyone else to be on the mountain and certainly not to exclusive possession. I am grateful that the freedom of the hills is available to everyone, and a source of satisfaction that so many are now enjoying the same adventures and exercise as I had. Yet there is a conundrum. How do we reconcile the human need for space and freedom to enjoy the 'wilderness experience', if the very promotion of this form of recreation undermines its realisation?

The One that Got Away: Beinn Fhionnlaidh— Charles Murray

One hill that required several attempts was Beinn Fhionnlaidh. Our first attempt in July 1989 was defeated by lack of fitness and poor weather on Carn Eighe. In October 1996 we tried again, but turned back on Màm Sodhail as the weather was against us. Finally, in September 1997, we managed it after climbing over Màm Sodhail and Carn Eighe yet again. We made a movie to celebrate at the cairn. This was one of our longest days on the Munros and we needed a head torch to get back to the car at 9pm in the dark.

LOCHS and LOCHANS

Above – 23rd June 2009, a rest stop above Glas Bheinn's Loch à Choire Dheirg with Quinag in the distance. A prelude to a high summer camp on Glas Bheinn's broad summit plateau.

Below – Early morning passing by the shore of a partially frozen Lochan Fada with Slioch's Sgùrr an Tuill Bhàin top opposite, en route to climb A' Mhaighdean and Ruadh Stac Mòr, 31st March 1986. ***Norman McNab***

Last Waltz

A surging IV 4 finale:
pump up the volume,
the throb of blood in veins.

His back beat
-ing on rock and
roll
-ing on snow-
ice: no black chemistry in
-duced this trip, this hit
of rock,
then roll,
then rock again
(like he never did
in summer).

All the time:
the screaming
feedback from a single
note,
of power
- chords
cut.

A final thrash and
all the lights
go out

forever.

Image: N. McNab

Stuart B. Campbell

Six Decades on the Whaleback

Derek Sime

S een from many angles, Ben Vorlich, above Loch Earn, has the appearance of a giant whaleback. It is the only Munro I can see from my house in Causewayhead, and as a resident of Stirling, I regard it, together with its more craggy but slightly lower neighbour Stùc a' Chroin, as Stirling's hill (although no doubt the good folk of Callander would have at least equal claim). Geologically speaking, these hills comprise Neoproterozoic to Cambrian metamorphosed sandstones and mudstones of the Dalradian Supergroup, mainly mica schists, formed between 600 and 515 million years ago.

Ben Vorlich from Ardvorlich (Derek Sime)

It was in March 1977 when I first set foot on Ben Vorlich (985m), and a couple of years later on Stùc a' Chroin (975m). Living variously in Glasgow, Kirkcaldy and, for the last thirty years in Stirling, these hills were always fairly local and easy to access, and became a favourite, especially in the short days of winter. They have become my most-climbed Munros, and although I can't claim a particularly impressive tally, I have notched up 51 ascents of Stùc a' Chroin and 48 of Vorlich – well short of the impressive four-figure

281

totals of some seasoned hillwalkers on their local hills. Although I can't (yet) claim to have been climbing these hills for 60 years, I have been doing so over six decades, from the seventies to the twenties.

That ascent in the early spring of '77 was in snow, on an outing organised by the Buchanan House Outdoor Club (BHOC for short – an acronym which occasionally caused some merriment); this was the club for railway staff working in British Rail's Scottish Region HQ. We did some ice axe braking practice about 100m below the summit on the way up, on safe slopes below a level section at what might be called the *Frühstückplatz*. In these far-off pre-Gore-Tex days, the well-dressed walker about the hills was to be seen wearing a pair of plus-twos (or maybe even plus-fours with accompanying fore-and-aft) and perhaps a pre-fleece Javelin jacket. One club member even insisted on wearing a collar and tie on the hills. The outer jacket of choice was the all-cotton Ventile, the theory of which was that the cotton fibres soaked up the rainwater which caused them to expand, thereby keeping that rainwater off the wearer, although all that absorbed water probably caused the garment to double in weight. For me, the outer shell was a bomb-proof, indestructible (or so I was told by Nevisport) Helly Hansen rubber-lined nylon affair, which was guaranteed 100% waterproof. Waterproof it may have been, but breathable it certainly was not, resulting in the inside becoming wetter than the outside

The summit of Ben Vorlich on 20th March 1977 – seated left Jimmy Kane; standing centre Jim Bell (Munroist No. 676, sporting a Ventile jacket); standing right Alistair Mowatt; behind, in the red jacket, Tom Hunter (founder of the West Highland Way); others not identified. (Derek Sime)

from condensation. Hypothermia was an ever-present risk.

According to Peter Drummond, in his book *Scottish Hill Names*[1], Stùc a' Chroin most likely means peak of the sheepfold, and Ben Vorlich (Beinn Mhùrlaig) hill of the bay. One of the best views of these hills is to be had from a point south-east of Stirling, when they are seen (preferably when snow covered) rising behind Stirling Castle, although they are also visible from the A9 and the railway line between Stirling and Perth, and from many parts of the Midland Valley. Driving south through Glen Ogle, Vorlich is prominent in the view ahead, but as one descends towards Lochearnhead, Stùc a' Chroin begins to dominate the view as Vorlich gradually slips out of sight. But one of the more striking views of these hills is from the Cultybraggan road a couple of miles north of Braco, as Vorlich almost becomes a Matterhorn lookalike. The two hills also make good landmarks from many parts of the Southern Highlands.

Overlooking Stirling Castle to Stùc a' Chroin and Ben Vorlich (Derek Sime)

As for the views to be had from this group of hills, on a good day with visibility 'excellent or superb' (to quote the MWIS website), the Ochils, the Pentlands, Culter Fell, Tinto, Arran, Ben Lomond, the Arrochar Alps, Stob Binnein, Ben More, the Lawers group and the Grampians can all be seen.

One of the things I like about these hills is the fact that there are five different routes, all with completely different approaches. The most popular is undoubtedly that from Ardvorlich, on the shores of Loch Earn, up the path with its gates and stiles, and even a dog gate, and it gives a fine ascent of the north ridge of Vorlich (Sgiath nam Tarmachan – well named as ptarmigan are often heard hereabouts), particularly in winter, possibly to be followed by a climb of the north-east buttress on Stùc a' Chroin. For the horticulturally minded, Ardvorlich is also a participant in Scotland's Gardens Scheme, with its collection of over 170 varieties of rhododendrons among the oak and birch trees; it is open to the public in May each year.

Another popular route starts from Ardchullarie More, at the bend in the A84 by Loch Lubnaig, a route which is likely to include the Corbett Beinn Each (horse hill, 812m), and the 'knobbly ridge' over Bealach nan Cabar to Stùc a' Chroin. Indeed, a fine traverse over the three hills can be had by starting at Ardvorlich and finishing at Ardchullarie More, provided suitable transport arrangements have been made. This is a route I managed to do in April 2004 on the 'Second TMS Re-visit' (the first having been on Beinn Dorain in November 2003 – these being the forerunners of what became regular thrice-yearly meets). Accompanied by various TMS members as far as Vorlich, only Peter Willimott and I continued over the traverse to Loch Lubnaig, where Peter had a car waiting. (See photo on page 328).

Ben Vorlich from Stùc a' Chroin (Derek Sime)

Much less popular as a starting point these days is Edinample, a couple of miles west of Ardvorlich, not least because of the very limited parking opportunities there – certainly not the ample parking (pun intended) available at Ardvorlich - but I have often used that route for return, descending by Allt a' Choire Fhuadaraich to Glenample Farm and then walking back along the road to Ardvorlich. However, I recall back in December 1979 doing a traverse from Edinample over Vorlich and Stùc a' Chroin to Ardchullarie More with the Dundee-based Grampian Club, transport being afforded by the GC bus, although quite how the bus managed to negotiate the narrow south Loch Earn road I cannot now recall.

A route that I've used a good number of times is that from Braeleny (on earlier maps shown as Thomasgreen) about three miles north of Callander on the road past the golf course and Bracklinn Falls. Walking from there up to the wonderfully named Arivurichardich, a private locked bothy, and then onto the south-east ridge of Stùc a' Chroin, gives a fine approach to the hill, with possibilities to include Vorlich and/or Beinn Each.

Probably the finest approach to these hills however is to start at the car park for Glen Artney Church, for the long walk in. It's undoubtedly the longest approach but walking round into Gleann an Dubh Coirein one then gets a fine panorama of the two Munros – the classic whaleback of Ben Vorlich's south-east ridge on the right, and the craggy profile of Stùc a' Chroin to the left. Once the ruined Dubh Choirein shieling is reached, the south-east ridge of Vorlich makes a fine ascent. This route allows an excellent stravaig over the two hills, or, as an alternative, over Vorlich and the other hill of note in the area – the Corbett Meall na Fearna (alder hill, 809m), although this combination can also be climbed from Ardvorlich. Walk this route in spring and you will have cuckoos, chaffinches, and a cacophony of calling curlews as a soundtrack, and with an early start, you might even hear a black grouse lek – music to the ears. I have also encountered oystercatchers and snipe in the glen. Surprisingly it does not get a mention in the new SMC Munros book[2], although it is cited in the earlier District Guide to the Southern Highlands[3].

Unsurprisingly, over the years I have experienced the whole range of Scottish mountain weather conditions. Although I now tend to choose good-weather days, in earlier times, with work commitments and being confined to weekends, it was often a case of just going anyway, taking whatever the elements had to offer. I have generally favoured the winter half of the year, as out of 70 outings in these hills, 49 have been between October and March, while only 21 were between April and September, with none at all in June. 56 have been solo outings, and 14 accompanied. Snow has featured on many of the days, either on the ground or falling, or both, the critical feature being whether conditions were suitable for a direct ascent of the buttress to the north top of Stùc a' Chroin, where a bit of front pointing can add a little spice to the day. My log of 2nd February 1991 notes 'Would have been a perfect day for crampons. As it was, some step-cutting required', and while it's always good to practice the art of step cutting, it only goes to show the folly of venturing into the hills in February without crampons. (I have since witnessed many a walker struggling precariously up, and down, the steep north ridge of Vorlich in conditions of hard icy snow, with neither ice axe nor crampons, sometimes with a pole or two, and sometimes in trainers – a recipe for disaster.) In recent years however, I have noticed a lamentable lack of snow. The perception is that winters are not what they used to be. Brocken spectres have also featured on six occasions, and inversions on four occasions.

Ben Vorlich summit in winter condition (Derek Sime)

The buttress, Stùc a' Chroin (Derek Sime)

My log of 12th October 2014 states –

Sitting atop Stùc a' Chroin (west cairn) overlooking Lochan a' Chroin as the mist formed, rising up as if from a boiling cauldron, with the rutting stags heard constantly below, all the while with a view of the sun-drenched Carse of Stirling – wonderful.

However, by far the most significant weather event over the last few decades occurred on 18th August 2004, when a thunderstorm sat over Stùc a' Chroin for two hours or more, dropping an enormous quantity of rain, resulting in a 'muckle spate' wreaking devastation in its wake, with a number of bridges washed away. The most significant of these was the bridge on the public road over the Burn of Ample at the Falls of Edinample. This cut off access for the local population for two years, forcing them to travel east via St Fillans, although with a little care it was possible to cross the remains of the bridge on foot. Rumour has it that the delay to reinstatement was due to a disagreement between Stirling and Perth & Kinross Councils as to whose responsibility it was, although current maps show that it is clearly within Stirling Council's area. The bridge was finally reinstated on 10th August 2006. Other bridges which suffered a similar fate included that over the Keltie Water at Arivurichardich, making approaches to the hills from that direction difficult when rivers were running high. This bridge was replaced in 2016 with two bridges (over Alt Breac-nic and the Keltie Water), about which more

The bridge on the South Loch Earn road after the deluge in August 2004 (Derek Sime)

later. In addition to the destruction of the bridges, the storm had also caused new gorges to be formed, and trees to be uprooted up to 3m above the normal water level in the Burn of Edinample.

A more recent notable weather event occurred in early 2021. Drummond Estates had replaced a large section of stock fence at around 450m on the slopes leading up to Meall na h-Iolaire, above Arivurichardich, during 2020. However, a visit in early March 2021 revealed that the brand-new steel fence posts were no match for what was presumably a powerful avalanche, which destroyed a significant length of the fence, sweeping part of it well downslope.

There have been some landscape changes over the years, primarily due to the construction of renewable energy schemes. The most notable of these is the 72MW Braes of Doune windfarm, constructed in 2007, on the southern slopes of Beinn Odhar (616m), which tends to dominate the view to the east, and also those from the nearby Graham, Uamh Bheag (664m). This windfarm is also very prominent when driving north on the A9, welcoming the traveller to the industrialised Highlands! The Daily Mail launched a scathing attack in April 2008 claiming that the turbines had blighted one of Scotland's classic vistas. While the Government clearly regards onshore upland windfarms as a necessary constituent to achieve a carbon neutral future (although where they disturb peat, which they almost invariably do in mountain areas, they are perhaps more brown energy than green when the whole-life CO_2 equation is evaluated), they should surely be sensitively and appropriately sited, and I will let the reader decide whether the siting of the Braes of Doune installation qualifies on that score. Other windfarms can also be seen now in the distance, in the Ochils (two) and Campsies (two), making five in all.

The other significant renewable is of course run-of-river hydro, which has been popping up throughout the Highlands in recent years. That in Glen Vorlich has been so well constructed that one would hardly notice it, with two fairly well concealed intakes high in the glen, and a discreetly sited powerhouse at Ardvorlich, whose presence is only apparent by the sound of the generator on passing it. However, at time of writing, the jury is still out on the recently constructed installation on Allt a' Choire Fhuadaraich, where the once pleasant grassy track down the glen has been replaced by a wide and decidedly ugly bulldozed track for much of its length. I walked down that route in July 2020 (my first post-lockdown Munro day) when this was under construction, with pipes being brought to site by helicopter (something which had not apparently been mentioned in the methodology submitted to the National Park). A third run-of-river scheme has been installed on the Keltie Water, between Arivurichardich and Braeleny, and in fairness, apart from a few minor niggles, this scheme has blended in well, and has greatly benefitted hillwalkers in that, as referenced above, it has provided two bridges replacing the one that was washed away in the great deluge of August 2004.

Another notable change to the landscape is the proliferation of non-native Sitka spruce well above the normal tree line. A veritable forest of dwarf Sitka has grown up at around 850m altitude on the north side of Vorlich, not much more than one metre in height, but altering the landscape irreparably. Presumably the result of seeds from nearby Sitka plantations dropped by birds, this transformation looks set to increase over time, permanently changing the ecosystem. A more positive change however is seen in the recently planted forest in Gleann an Dubh Choirein; this is a mixture of native species as well as commercial Sitka spruce.

The establishment of the Loch Lomond and the Trossachs National Park on 1st July 2002 has, in reality, probably not changed the area to any great extent, although there is certainly a perception that in authorising installations such as run-of-river hydro, while the National Park Authority issues strict planning conditions, enforcement is sometimes less strict. The Park boundary takes in both Munros and Beinn Each, although Meall na Fearna is excluded. Arguably, the creation of the Park, and its attendant publicity, has also led to a 'honeypot' effect, attracting even more people to what was already a popular area.

Path erosion near the summit of Ben Vorlich (Derek Sime)

History has left its mark in the area. I wonder how many people notice the memorial stone by the roadside at Ardvorlich, the inscription on which reads –

> Near this spot we re interred [sic] the bodies of 7 Mcdonalds of Glencoe killed when attempting to harry Ardvorlich Anno Domini 1620.

In more recent times, a memorial stone plaque was cemented into the north top of Stuc a' Chroin in 1958 commemorating Donald Stuart, founder member of Falkirk Mountaineering Club, although weathering over the years has rendered it difficult to read.

Memorial stone at Ardvorlich (Derek Sime)

The church in Glen Artney was built around 1905 by the Willoughby de Eresby family, and is occasionally used for services in the summer months. There is a bench adjacent to the church car park, dedicated to Keith Macpherson (1893-1973), who for many years drove the children of the Glen to school.

The church in Glen Artney (Derek Sime)

The bench bears the following poetic inscription –

> There's folk who like to travel and some foreign lands to see
> Like Spain or sunny Italy or even gay Capri.
> But me I like the hameland so I dinna travel far;
> I go driving up Glen Artney wi my auld Schule car.
> We see the bonnie rowan trees, their flowers the summer's pride
> And then the scarlet berries come and deck the countryside.
> Ye get a great contentment and a pleasure none can mar
> When ye're driving up Glen Artney in the auld Schule car.

Glen Artney is also immortalised in Sir Walter Scott's poem *The Lady of the Lake*.

A somewhat ephemeral marking of a historic moment was noted on 12th March 2005, when my customary lunchtime cheese sandwich was consumed at the summit of Vorlich to the accompaniment of the bagpipes; on enquiry, this was revealed to be a celebration not of another Munro completion, but of the 50th anniversary of the founding of the Ferranti Mountaineering Club.

In earlier times, a popular day outing from the likes of Edinburgh was to take the train to Callander, traverse the two Munros and return from Lochearnhead station, but the railway closed in September 1965, following a landslip in Glen Ogle just a few weeks prior to its planned closure under Dr. Beeching's axe.

Callander Station, 26th July, 1913

(JB Sherlock – John Alsop Collection. Courtesy of the Caledonian Railway Society)

Cycling round these hills, taking in Callander, Lochearnhead, St. Fillans, Comrie and Braco, takes in some off-road sections, including part of the solum of the closed railway between Callander and Lochearnhead, and also the old railway between St. Fillans and Comrie. You could call this the TMV – the Tour du Mont Vorlich – probably not quite Scotland's answer to the *Tour du Mont Blanc*, but at 80 miles and 750m of ascent (almost a Corbett's-worth), it makes a good day out.

On access issues, I recall noting barbed wire and an electric fence deterring access in Glen Artney in July 1993. It would be reasonable to have assumed that the passing of the Land Reform (Scotland) Act in 2003 would have put an end to access issues. However, in August 2004, a notice in Glen Artney proclaimed 'Electric Gate – No Access', a notice which I duly, and legally, ignored. Ironically, it was sited right next to a 'Right of Way' sign indicating the route to Callander via Arivurichardich. By August 2007, the wording had been altered to 'Electric Gate – No Unauthorised Vehicles' – an improvement indeed, and it now simply states 'Estate vehicles only'.

At Arivurichardich, there is a permanent sign worded as follows –

Deer stalking in progress on weekdays from 12th August to 15th February. To minimise disturbance, please keep to recognized routes. Drummond Estates [followed by a phone number],

– although it is assumed that it is for the walker to decide what is, and what is not, a 'recognized route'. Since the construction of the hydro scheme, Drummond Estates have also erected a sign at the junction of the tracks indicating the route to Stùc a' Chroin from Arivurichardich, as, counter-intuitively, it points (correctly) to the right, when the mountain can clearly be seen to the left, which can be confusing to those not familiar with the area.

I have mentioned some of the wildlife, and as well as those species mentioned above, I have also encountered red squirrels, mountain hares, feral goats, field voles, frogs, lizards, red grouse, wheatears, golden plovers, woodpeckers, martins, grey herons, pheasants, lapwings, crows, whinchats, sandpipers, skylarks, meadow pipits, golden eagles, red kites, buzzards, ravens, snow buntings, fieldfares, butterflies and dragonflies. Although grazed by sheep and deer, the area supports a variety of flora, including bog asphodel, foxglove, sundew, butterwort, lousewort, milkwort, wood anemone, wood sorrel, cloudberry, blaeberry, bird's foot trefoil, thyme, cotton grass, lady's mantle, alpine lady's mantle, thistles, willowherb, bluebells, primroses, violets, devil's bit scabious, yarrow, yellow saxifrage, starry saxifrage, heath bedstraw, heath spotted orchid, marsh orchid, tormentil, buttercups, hawkweed, hawksbeard, bell heather, cow wheat, cross leaved heath, lesser celandine and juniper.

All in all, a fine group of hills, which, with all their variety and interest, I can highly recommend.

1 – *Scottish Hill Names*, Peter Drummond; Scottish Mountaineering Trust, 1991. ISBN 978-0-907521-95-2

2 – *The Munros*, Scottish Mountaineering Club Hillwalkers' Guides, 2021. ISBN 978-1-907233-38-8

3 – *The Southern Highlands*, Scottish Mountaineering Trust, First Edition New Series, 1972. SBN 901516 64 3.

'Tis 60 Years Since (Sir Walter Scott)

Charles Murray

The death of Prince Philip, Duke of Edinburgh, on 9th April 2021 reminded me that over 60 years ago, I enrolled in the Duke of Edinburgh Award Scheme. At my secondary school, the geography teacher was very enthusiastic and got us involved. He was assisted by the Principal Teacher of Physical Education who endeavoured to raise our level of fitness to the required standards. My record book starts in April 1960, when I was among the first in Glasgow to take part in the Scheme. To get an award you had to complete A) Rescue and Public Service Training, B) The Expedition, C) Pursuits and Projects, and D) Fitness in the Bronze, Silver and Gold Series.

I will describe here the expeditions, which increased in duration and distance. We did practice trips, but I did not record their details. I had been camping on family holidays and with the Scouts and had access to basic camping equipment. I used my family's smaller 'Bukta' tent with wooden poles, a Kapok sleeping bag and a Primus stove. Food consisted of packet soup, dried mashed potatoes and many heavy tins. I remember hiking up the east side of Loch Lomond from Rowardennan in a blizzard and asking to sleep in a garage at the Inversnaid Hotel because we did not want to camp in the snow. It was not a comfortable night lying on the concrete floor.

The Bronze Expedition in March 1961 was a 24-hour journey covering a minimum of 15 miles across normal country with the night spent in a tent. I was aged 15 and there were three in the party. We caught a bus to Clarkston and set off south on what were then country roads and tracks through what is now a built-up area with housing. We examined a mound marked on the map, before walking south-west to East Moorhouse Farm and round to the head of Bennan Loch where we camped. Looking at this route on the map, I now realise that in recent years, this was a trip I made several times with my two sons on our mountain bikes. From Bennan Loch we climbed over Ballageich Hill (333m) to the Eaglesham road and walked north-east to Eaglesham to catch a bus home.

The Silver Expedition in April 1962 was a three-day expedition including two nights on separate camp sites, covering a minimum of 30 miles across normal country. I was aged 16 and there were four in the party. We started at Brig o' Turk in the Trossachs and walked along the road on the north side of Loch Katrine for six miles before camping. Next day we continued west before climbing north through the hills. As we toiled up beside a burn, we had a drink of cold, clear water, then discovered a dead sheep just upstream. Fortunately, there were no ill-effects and we camped between Loch Doine and

Loch Voil. We then walked the length of Loch Voil to Balquhidder, then south through the hills back to Brig o' Turk. This was before the Glen Finglas dam was constructed and the reservoir formed. This trip of 32 miles involved more cross-country walking on paths and tracks. Not long after this expedition, I attended a course at the Outward Bound Moray Sea School at Burghead. During the course, we walked right across Scotland climbing my first Munros on the way.

The Gold expedition in June 1963 was a four-day journey covering at least 50 miles in wild country. At least three nights were spent on different camp sites. I was aged 17 and there were four of us in the party. We departed from Aberfoyle and headed over the Menteith Hills to Loch Venachar. Was it just by chance we met our Headmaster and his wife having a picnic on the shore of the loch? We continued east to Callander, then north up the valley of the Keltie Water and over the hills to Gleann an Dubh Choireinn where we camped for the first time. Next day we crossed the bealach east of Ben Vorlich at about 600m into Glen Vorlich before contouring round the Ben to Glen Ample. From there we walked across country to the Kingshouse Hotel on the A84 (not the Glencoe one!), then through Balquhidder along the north shore of Loch Voil to our second campsite at Monachyle Tuarach. Next day, we climbed up beside the Invernenty Burn round Beinn Bhreac and down Glen Finglas to Brig o' Turk. We set up our third campsite on the shore of Loch Achray near the Trossachs Hotel. This was rather spoiled by the discovery of a decomposing dead horse near our tent. On our final day we walked over the Duke's Pass back to Aberfoyle and the bus home. I do not have any photographs of these exploits because I did not have a camera then, and our packs were already heavy enough with all our gear and food.

My record book was signed off by the Youth Service Organiser of Glasgow Corporation on 14th June 1963, thus completing the requirements for the Gold Award. I was invited to a reception for the presentation of the Gold Standard in the garden of the Palace of Holyroodhouse on a very cold day in July 1963, and did actually meet the Duke of Edinburgh briefly as he walked round the various groups. My mother was my guest and thought it was a marvellous occasion, but I left Edinburgh as soon as I could to go home.

What was the long-term effect of these Duke of Edinburgh's award expeditions? I think now that these adventurous trips in the sixties were a real eye-opener to us working-class city boys. We discovered that there were wild, beautiful mountains not all that far from home in Glasgow. It certainly sparked a lifelong interest in the hills in me. A few years later, I joined the Moray club and started to climb Munros more frequently. Even so, it took me another 43 years to complete all of them and become Munroist 3,213.

—TMS—

Three Dogs on my Head

Alf Barnard

Introduction

Three dogs were in fact the one and the same, Tess, a Border collie, but on three different hills – the undoubted hero of these tales and many more. She was my first dog that belonged to us, rather than my parents. A great dog. Rescued from Edinburgh Dog & Cat Kennels at Leith, she had a broken leg when taken into the kennels – named Cass (Hop-along-Cassidy) by the kennel girls. Usually adult dogs had only one week before finding an owner, or were put to sleep due to lack of space. Fortunately, the kennel girls liked her a lot, so she had been there a whole month when we found her.

Tess rapidly, and naturally sure of foot, became a superb companion on any terrain. Routes such as the Aonach Eagach, Liathach or An Teallach were taken with aplomb. However, sometimes, even a Border collie needs a helping hand – or even a head.

Ladhar Bheinn

On a Friday evening having driven from North-east Fife, it is a long walk in (10km) from Kinloch Hourn; the path goes up and down and up and .... you get the picture. This is slightly tiring, particularly carrying a tent, food, stove, sleeping bag – and dog food. This was 1984, and I was very keen to visit the fabled Ladhar Bheinn. A friend of Barbara's, and a fellow bell ringer, had regaled me with his account of the 'classic circuit of Coire Dhorrcail' – by far the best route he said. We camped at Barrisdale, which was free in those days; to stay in the estate bothy was an extortionate £1!

The next morning I was up bright (I was only 30) and early. Tess was as keen as ever and took no encouraging to be away. From the campsite, I briefly followed the stalkers' path for a kilometre and then onto the Creag Bheithe ridge. This leads easily and pleasantly towards the steep, imposing, and partially obscured triangle of Stob a' Chearcaill. Due to the clouds moving about it was difficult to spot the best way up; so we just went by 'feel', more or less straight up, with deviations as required. It all seemed to be going well, scrambling up rocky steps and traversing when required, until we came to the awkward bit: this was a much bigger step and seemed to be the only way. The west side to our right fell away very steeply into Coire na Cabaig; the east or left could not be seen due to the cloud. This *mauvais pas* was definitely harder than any other part of the route. It may be, that given better visibility, we could have found an easier way. I got up to assess it, came down and picked

Coire Dhorrcail (Derek Sime)

Tess up and held her on my head – not the most comfortable thing for either of us. I said 'up you go' and pushed her up; she scrambled up then with some ease. The route was cracked and easier ground led to the summit of Stob a' Chearcaill.

Typically enough, the weather improved: the clouds rolled away and the sun came out. From here on, the traverse round Coire na Cabaig was a delight; down to the Bealach Coire Dhorrcail and up Stob Dhorrcail which separates the smaller corrie from the main Coire Dhorrcail. As I ascended, to my amazement I was overtaken by a male runner clad only in very skimpy shorts, armless top, with a tiny rucksack and not much else! Ladhar Bheinn is one of the very best mountains in Scotland, and with only a short distance to go back to the tent, I could savour the traverse around the rim of Coire Dhorrcail up to the summit. The views were tremendous – particularly down over Barrisdale Bay to upper Loch Hourn.

The return was made over the narrow, but easy, Stob a' Choire Odhair ridge, down into Coire Dhorrcail. Looking back, the cirque of the impressive cliffs could be seen from the end of the stalkers' path, which led directly back to the tent at the campsite. The end to a particularly memorable day.

Bidein a' Choire Sheasgaich

This hill was part of a sweep around Loch Monar from the end of Glen Strathfarrar, taking in five Munros and their respective Munro Tops. Unfortunately, there is also in the way (tiresomely as usual) Beinn Tharsuinn, a Corbett, which has to be traversed. This is a Corbett that I have now done

Bidean a' Choire Sheasgaich (Alan Rowan)

quite a few times.

Coming off Beinn Tharsuinn, I thought that I could spot the way up Bidein a' Choire Sheasgaich, either straight up from the bealach, where there appeared to be a breach in the rock band, or a long way across to the right by a grassy ramp. I stopped by the stone dyke at the bealach for a bite to eat and brief relaxation in the sun. Since I am inherently impatient, and an optimist, I thought that I would take the direct ascent.

We went up the first main band of cliffs to where a narrow gully appeared to offer a way through. It looked fairly easy if one was a human, but not for a dog – even a Border collie. There is a nasty corner to the right where a step upwards and round was required. This is quite straightforward (though no jug hold round the corner) if bold. For Tess, easy ground was just out of her reach, without direct help. I called to her to come to my feet and lifted her off the ground onto the slimy gully wall, then with her on my head pushed hard and said 'up you go' – and she did! In reality it was actually quite easy, for a dog.

The second rock band is breached by a left to right slanting steep grassy gully, very easy for a collie, and she was soon at the top waiting impatiently for the slow human.

From the gully it is straightforward, and we were soon on the summit basking in the views all round, and spying our next objective on the round: Lurg Mhòr. I was particularly looking forward to Lurg Mhòr as it has a narrow rocky connecting ridge to its Top, with a *mauvais pas*. Tess made light of this as usual. We were now well on our way back to our starting point back at the Loch Monar dams.

Afterthought: I did this recently for the second time with a dog, some 37 years after the above. Although I had done it again with my son in 2004

Bidean a' Choire Sheasgaich from Lurg Mhòr (Alan Rowan)

my recollection was dim, and as neither of us had found the exposed corner difficult, it had completely faded from memory. This time my dog was Rab: not as experienced as Tess on awkward and difficult ground. He made light of the ascent so far, but with the bad step looming and despite exhortations to wait, he leapt at it, ricocheted off and fell ten metres or so onto exceptionally steep grass. Amazingly he stopped (where a human would have tumbled a long, long way), turned himself round, raced back up to the slimy rock wall that I had helped Tess up, which he bounded up! He was then looking down on me as if saying 'come on'. All this took only a few seconds, so there was no time to worry. Very soon I was joining him and on we went.

The next day he was 'not himself'. He looked 'unthrifty' in agri terms so we went home. The vet (Barbara) said after a thorough examination that he had nothing broken, but was no doubt severely bruised. He received a painkiller. Rab is a long-haired Border collie and no doubt this helped to cushion him to a certain extent.

Beinn Bhàn

This was by far the most difficult of the 'three dogs on my head' occasions. We were staying at Newton Cottage in Torridon, which is very handy for great swathes of the magnificent north-west of Scotland – including Applecross. I hadn't done either of the Corbetts, and was particularly keen to climb Beinn Bhàn. The best 'sporting' route that I could find was to take in a scramble up the precipitous east side via the A' Chioch ridge.

The A' Chioch ridge lies between Coire na Poite (of the pot) and Coire na Feòla (of the flesh), and is a decent scramble, particularly with a dog, even one so adept as Tess (the star of the tales above). The weather was slightly disappointing as the clouds were swirling around, very atmospheric, but leaving everything slightly damp.

The initial ascent onto A' Chioch was easy, as was the descent to a level sandstone pavement. At this point we scrambled down easily to a narrow notch and went right for a short distance before scrambling upwards on loose rock and vegetation. The ridge was regained, and then followed a wonderfully narrow section with sensational views down to the two lochans in Coire na Poite. We trended rightwards and up to reach a narrow gap before the steep final section known as the Upper Connecting Ridge.

This upper section looked steep and potentially awkward. However we set off more or less directly up, choosing the easiest line on some vegetated and at times loose rock. Half way up there was a very steep chimney - wet and slimy. This was going to be difficult. I find that in such circumstances, it is best to get Tess up as high as possible, and then get in behind her and push. To manage this, I had to get her onto my head first, and with both arms push her upwards with all my might – trying to keep in balance at the time. However, it was definitely 'touch-and-go' whether we both overbalanced and fell backwards.

A Border collie is a wonderful dog, and once any purchase, however small and greasy is found, they can scamper up very steep short sections. Up she went at speed. I followed (I was carrying a pack) more sedately. After this, although steep, I could take to the rock, and she worked her way up. Needless to say, she was soon well above me, looking down, and wondering why I was so slow.

Suddenly, the ridge finished and we were on the plateau, and into a stiff wind. From here a 10-minute walk took us to the summit of Beinn Bhàn – in now dense cloud. I had arranged to meet Barbara at the summit carpark, so I was going to have to hurry. Unfortunately, the lure of a second Corbett was too strong and I deviated round to take in Sgùrr a Chaorachain. This meant that when I reached the car I was well overdue, and she was starting to worry – and having to cope with two children, four and six years old.

Tess (Alf Barnard)

299

Summit Nights

Jeremy Fenton

In June 2016 I set off on the 29th ascent of my favourite hill, Liathach. It was late in the afternoon, because for some reason which is not entirely clear to me now, I had decided to spend a night on top. I was not certain that it was possible to lie down anywhere near the summit, which is a huge heap of angular quartzite blocks, so it might be a night sitting rather than lying. I set off up the Coire Dubh Mòr path and turned left to follow the slabs at the east end, and then steep ground with some scrambling to reach the ridge. Time didn't matter — it was midsummer in the north with sunset at 10.20pm — and I dawdled along the crest to the summit, meeting no-one. Then came the moment of truth: I studied every boulder and finally decided that one right next to the summit cairn had just enough space and flatness to lie on: it seemed to be the only possible one, so this may be a one-person-bivouac hill. I was joined there by butterflies and beetles which had climbed the hill more easily, carried up by convection in the warm still air.

Bed for the night on Liathach (Jeremy Fenton)

Evening view of the Am Fasarinen Pinnacles (Jeremy Fenton)

The normally shadowed north side of the Am Fasarinen pinnacle ridge was lit by the evening sun, and the sunset was long and glorious. I took numerous photos of the same views as the light changed, and at sunset I believe that I saw the 'green flash'. It never grew dark and the only 'stars' I saw were three planets. I made my bed with a light air mattress, a light sleeping bag, an unnecessary bivvy bag, and a small pillow, and managed not to fall off my slab. But sleep was intermittent with so much to look at. A ring ouzel down in Coire na Caime chirp-chirp-chirped all night, a rather confused stag roared early in the morning (in June), and a cuckoo started cuckooing in the glen below at 3 o'clock. The last of my many awakenings was when the growing colour on the horizon foretold sunrise, and I watched and waited until the sun suddenly appeared, next to Ben Klibreck 100 kilometres away. Then hill after hill revealed itself as the light grew and another fine day began. At last, I set out and slowly traversed the rest of the ridge, with the pinnacles just a little thought-provoking as I was so alone on the hill, and the first cars on the road a kilometre below. Rather than taking the usual descent after Mullach an Rathain, I continued to the far west end to complete the traverse, found a way down, and took the long weary path round the north side of the hill and back to Coire Dubh Mòr and my car.

That was the inspiration for a project: to spend a night on all the significant hills (Munros, Corbetts and selected Grahams) in my home area (Gairloch). This meant eight hills between Loch Torridon and Loch Maree, five along the north side of Loch Maree, and a lot more in the Great Wilderness and the Coulin area. For the moment I am counting two-Munro hills as one, but that leaves the option of overnighting the second summits of An Teallach, Liathach, Beinn Eighe and Beinn Alligin later; but two of them would be difficult to sleep on! To date, in mid-2021, I have done 23, with perhaps six more to attempt. This does not include A' Mhaighdean, the best viewpoint of them all, but I spent wonderful nights on it in 1974 and 2004 during long walks, well before the present project – but perhaps countable? If not, a third night on it would be no hardship.

Why? I have found several unexpected benefits from this strange habit. It may sound strenuous, but in fact it is a lazy way to climb hills, very different from multi-Munro days or night-time walking. The walk is never hurried: I can take as long as I like over the ascent and the descent, up to a day for each, and follow unusual routes. I can get to know a hill much better by overnighting it, with time to become familiar with it and absorb its character. I see the hill and its neighbours in many different lights: not just the usual broad daylight but the constantly changing colours of evening and morning which are arguably the best times to be on a summit. I get to know the night, which normally we sleep through, the only negative being that I don't get a proper night's sleep; but the compensation may be a sky in which the Milky Way is clearer than can ever be seen from sea level, or a full moon wandering across the sky, or auroral light brightening the northern horizon. And I am more likely to see wildlife because animals like dawn and dusk and there are no other humans around — or not usually: on two hills there was a tent well below me, and on Slioch its occupant, whom I met on the way down, told me that he had visited the top in the night and was surprised to see me lying there in my cocoon.

But there is one thing which can go wrong. The aim is to choose fine settled weather, from April to October, but trusting the forecast is occasionally a mistake. On Meall a' Ghiuthais after a fine evening I awoke to find myself in thick wet cloud and escaped in a hurry. On Beinn Eighe a stubborn pall of cloud hid the view, although oddly a single small lochan far below was lit orange by the hidden sun.

Let me recall some of the better days. Beinn Dearg Mòr up Gruinard River, (with Beag en route), a hill which needs a night out because of its remoteness, but why camp when you can bivouac at the top and spend hours exploring the very fine summit area and admiring the surrounding country? Beinn Alligin (one of the few hills I persuaded a companion to join me on), with a comfortably flat summit, views of the sea and the islands to the west, and the spectacular series of Torridon ridges to the east lit up by the sunset and silhouetted by the sunrise, plus a slow enjoyable descent over the Horns. Slioch, with a wander up the delightful corrie, accompanied only by two golden eagles and a herd of goats, and the best of all sunsets over the Hebrides. Beinn a' Chearcaill with a raven which demanded a share in my sandwich, and the excitement of a temperature inversion in the morning with Beinn Airigh Charr floating on the cloud. Beinn a' Mhùinidh where a pair of goats were noisily clashing horns, the Milky Way was crystal clear, and a long wander in the morning took me down to Lochan Fada and out by the Heights of Kinlochewe track. The steep Torridon Beinn Dearg with evening mist and a Brocken spectre, and a lonely descent of the bad step.

Sail Mhòr with An Teallach's western slopes lit up on one side and the Summer Isles clear on the other, late April snow on the bigger hills, and Ardessie Burn to wander down. On An Teallach I was the only one going uphill as everyone else was going down, leaving me to enjoy the sandstone glowing gold and a high cloud bank underlit by the rising sun. And then there was Sgorr Ruadh with a fine sunset behind Harris, another bright Milky Way with the International Space Station racing past, and waking to a truly remarkable cloud inversion from Ben Klibreck to Ben Nevis, lit by the rising sun; my descent was slow and delightful with many viewpoint stops.

Brocken spectre, Beinn Dearg (Jeremy Fenton)

What kit do I take? The main aim is to reduce the weight to be carried. I usually manage with a 33-litre rucksack, but sometimes need a bigger one to fit a warmer sleeping bag. An unusual problem is the possibility of one's bed blowing away in the night, which can't happen in a tent — and Thermarests and airbeds seem to be designed for tent use. It helps if you do not mind missing a few meals or eating light for a day and not taking a cooker. If you're alone a book is worth taking as another encouragement to stay high: on Beinn Alligin in perfect weather I read most of a novel by stopping to read a chapter at every possible point including each of the Horns. The kit needs to be developed carefully (and sometimes expensively), and I have not yet settled on a regular combination, but this is the approximate list:

– Normal hill-walking clothes, including a fleece; I invariably wear shoes rather than boots.

– Rucksack, lightweight.

– Sleeping bag. This is the most difficult decision. I have a bulky waterproof one for cold or doubtful weather, but normally a light one is enough; down may not be worth risking if dew is possible.

– Mat. I have two airbeds (one very light) and a Thermarest to choose from; two tent pegs and some string can solve the blowing-away problem if the ground isn't rock.

– Bivvy bag. Often not needed, but it can be useful to have bed and mat in a Gore-tex bag in breezy conditions, and it may help in preventing airbed punctures on stony ground (as I found out on Beinn Làir).

– Small inflatable pillow. Essential for a comfortable night, with a folded-up fleece below it.

– Light waterproof jacket and trousers, gloves. Most likely to be needed early and late when it can be cool.

– Food and drink. A lunchbox with cake and sandwiches (and a little to spare for hungry ravens), and chocolate digestives; a water bottle (up to a pint, with orange squash to taste).

– Camera, and binoculars for wildlife, distant hill identification, and star-gazing at night.

– Safety kit: basic first aid, mobile phone, satellite beacon (if you have one).

– Paperback book (optional), map print-out (if needed), and compass (not needed yet).

– Walking poles, if you use them.

You have to make your own rules about what constitutes the 'summit' of the hill. In practice it means the closest point to the summit where you can lie flat: there's no point in torturing yourself by trying to sleep on boulders

The Alligin Horns and Beinn Dearg, evening (Jeremy Fenton)

or narrow ledges. On An Teallach, unless you are very small and thin or can peg yourself to the slope, you have to find the nearest flat sandy ground, a little way below the top. On Beinn Eighe surprisingly there is just enough space for one person to lie beside the cairn. On Beinn a' Chearcaill you can lie anywhere on the 2,000 square metres of the remarkable summit sandstone slab, although the corner with the cairn is the highest. On Sgorr Ruadh and on Meall a' Ghiuthais you have to lie a little way below the cairn. You may want to lie at a distance from a vertical drop: I remember on A' Mhaighdean being woken several times by a nightmare sensation of falling over the edge. Two hills whose summits are impossible to sleep on are Beinn Liath Mhòr and Sgurr Dubh with their rough quartzite scree, but mossy spots some way from the summits give minimal beds.

Another classic bivouac walk: Beinn Làir. I have climbed this remote and wonderful hill many times and by various routes, including North Summit Buttress, but in 2019 I made up my mind to do it justice by a complete traverse and a night on the top. From the Incheril car park I took the Loch Maree path and then threaded Gleann Bianasdail to reach Lochan Fada. A very rough walk along above the loch led me to the beginning of the 3-mile line of crags which are the unique feature of Beinn Làir; I stopped to rest and drink at a burn decorated by water avens. The first part of the cliff-top walk

Beinn Làir sunrise, with An Teallach (Jeremy Fenton)

is varied and interesting, with small crags and bumps, growing views of the spectacular neighbouring hills, and Gleann Tùlacha far below. Then I saw a figure standing on the edge ahead: disappointing, I hoped to be alone. But binoculars soon told me that it was not human: it was a young golden eagle. I swerved to the left to avoid disturbing it, but eventually it took off. Soon after that a family of ptarmigan raced past: I was beginning to feel guilty at disturbing this wild place. Then I put up a pair of goats, which promptly leapt over the edge. The cliff edge became more well-defined, and I followed it up to the summit plateau, skirting Sgùrr Dubh, heading for the large cairn which is in the middle of a plateau, and which was surrounded by red deer. I froze. They were interested, the Vs of their ears all facing my way, but they soon resumed their browsing.

I settled down to watch the colours change on the cliffs of Slioch and A' Mhaighdean and the sunset behind Lewis, accompanied by the wild plaintive calling of golden plovers. The sun rose again behind An Teallach and the light spread to reveal the deer feeding nearby, a cloud inversion inland, a huge cruise ship in the Minch, and a perfect day. I wandered the summit area, then set out along the edge of the crags and down to the Bealach Mhèinnidh (stopping to study the strange anorthosite formations), and so to Letterewe. The long brackened path took me back along Loch Maree, with plenty of time for the wildlife: I counted 31 flower species and timed a grasshopper warbler's non-stop trill at 1 minute 40 seconds.

Evening from Beinn Airigh Charr (Jeremy Fenton)

The best night so far? Difficult to say — they have all been so different. But I might select Beinn Airigh Charr, not just because it is such a fine viewpoint for Fionn Loch, Carnmore and the Great Wilderness, and across Loch Maree to the Torridons, but for the atmospheric conditions that night. The air was calm, but mist was coming and going, and hill and cloud were lit by the lowering sun. The sunrise silhouetted a spectacular cloudscape to the north under a clear sky. In the morning I wandered around that beautiful hilltop, and a golden eagle swept low across the slope just in front of me on its morning hunt. A slow exploratory descent took me over the minor tops overlooking the Loch Maree islands. In the distance Loch Ewe was calm, and in another world a small cruise ship lay off Inverewe Garden.

Evening deer on Beinn Lair (Jeremy Fenton)

APPENDIX 1 – TMS at Twenty

Ten Years On

Derek Sime
(With apologies to William Topaz McGonagall)

(Read at The Munro Society 10th Anniversary Dinner at the Alexandra Hotel, Fort William on 20th October 2012)

In the International Year of the Mountains, a group did meet to see
What could be done to form a club, in the Bonar Hall, Dundee.
Put something back to the hills was the ethos they did agree,
And so it came about – the Munro Society.

With TMS but one year old, they met at Orchy's Bridge,
In mist and rain and wind and snow, but at least no sign of midge.
Beinn Dorain they climbed for sure, but suggesting Beinn an Dothaidh,
Was met resoundingly from all with, 'Absolutely no way!'.

The meets have gone from strength to strength, from Affric o'er to Knoydart.
The varied walks have taken them to Màm Sodhail and to Moidart.
With communal meals, the choicest cuts, a splendid bill of fare,
Then after all that effort, to the pub they oft repair.
They talk about Munros they climbed, and Tops they might have missed,
But when 'Time gentlemen please' is called, they're seldom 'Brahms and Liszt'.

A matter of some concern was the extent of path erosion.
Some members got together and put a plan into motion.
A group set off to the Glenquoich Estate equipped with pick and spade
And to the path on Gleouraich, many a repair was made.

With Irvine Butterfield at the helm, in October 2004,
A picture display was mounted, showing many Munros, and more.
With great aplomb and minimum fuss and never any hassle,
Amidst the palatial surroundings of the rooms in Blair Castle.

When Robin told the committee of Munro One Hundred Fifty,
They acted fast and quick and keen, and really rather swiftly.
Great interest and fervour they certainly did unleash,
They even climbed a hill and pitched a tent on top of Driesh.

Unsuspecting walkers made a tribute for all to see,
And when they'd done, they wished them well, and even made them tea.
To celebrate the day, young Stewart, his spirit rousing,
Joined in to climb the hill which was for him Munro three thousand.
And with the hard work done, they retreated to take cover
In the luxury on offer at the hostelry in Glen Clova.

To run the Society smoothly, they have a committee.
A secretary, a treasurer and a VP,
Six ordinary members keep them right and stop them roamin',
Six Presidents past and present, four gents and then two women.
To stop the meetings rambling on into a proverbial rabble,
From wood of Lindertis was made a Presidential gavel.

The Newsletter's sent to members by our very own Anne Marie.
No longer twice a year though – now she's made it three.
And furthermore, with the discipline of British Army colonels
They set about producing two rather splendid Journals.

To follow that this year though, for which please no apology,
All Munros are to be climbed, to make up the Anthology.
As well as all this printed stuff, and all those jolly fine writings,
They have a group whose task is clear, to ascertain the Heightings.

The wind blows strong, it's hard to stop the GPS entering orbit,
And when the number crunching's done, it's just another Corbett.
The weather's wild and wet, often raining, often pouring,
And all that hard work does is to produce another lowering.

After all that effort on lonely Beinn a' Chlaidheimh
At last, the SMC concedes it's now the Fisherfield Five.
So if the trend continues, from Lomond up to Wyvis,
There'll only be one left, and that's sure to be Ben Nevis.

They have another mission; ours is not to reason why.
O'er the sea to the Hebrides, and the misty Isle of Skye,
Where no doubt after breakfast, with a tea or caffè latte,
They'll set off up the ridge once more, to measure Sgùrr a' Mhadaidh.

The MQIs are, of course, another red-hot topic,
With information taken down, in detail microscopic.
Spring's near done and summer too, and autumn's at a canter.
It's just a shame they can't get round the northern hills in winter.

The website's just been revamped, for purpose it's now fitter,
And maybe someday soon they'll say, 'Follow us on Twitter'.

They were keen to get into movies, a new field in which to encroach,
But not with Steven Spielberg, nor even the great Ken Loach.
Instead they looked around, and were not at a loss,
When with his video camera, in stepped Mr Closs.

From the List of Compleators, they interviewed a few
Who climbed them all in days of yore, before both me and you.
Sales were brisk and healthy, and now the many fans
May hope to see the films on show at the festival in Cannes.

The Annual Dinner's been around, from Blair Atholl to Strathpeffer
One year in a gale, a storm, a tempest, not a zephyr.
They all meet up and eat and chat and maybe have a port,
And o'er the years the favourite place has been right here – the Fort.

The starter, then the main course, a sweet of cream and peaches.
And after that, the special guest, and all those memorable speeches.
And when the eating's done, the wine all drunk, well almost,
The President will rise to speak, and then propose a toast.
And after all that eating, a drink and so much talk,
To work off the excess next day, they join the President's walk.

And so it seems in TMS, activities are a-plenty,
To keep the Society in good form, until it reaches twenty.

The Following Ten Years

Ed Smeik
(With even more apologies to WTM)

To get the membership higher
Catching those who might be missed
For compleations a brand-new flyer
To be sent by the Clerk of the List.

To encourage more member participation
Was also an aim of their mission
So at Annual Dinners an innovation
A nice new photo competition.

The Heightings they carried on for a while
More accuracy they did seek
On Skye they surveyed with great style
So Top no more was Knight's Peak.

The AGM has moved around
From Birnam to Dewars as well
But then in 2019 it found
A home at the AK Bell.

But future plans proved just academic
In the sudden impending doom
Caught up in a global pandemic
They found themselves on Zoom.

With social media now all the rage
They began to feel left out
So they started up a Facebook page
To tell folk what they're about.

With effort, sweat and tears it took
The committee working days and nights
And so they went and published a book
They called it *Scaling the Heights*.

To mark the passing of Munro
An Exhibition was mounted
The exhibits formed a logical flow
And many visitors were counted.

It started off on the banks of the Tay
In Perth at the AK Bell
And then it went on a nationwide tour
And several books did it sell.

The meets they've moved around a bit
To places too many to mention
And with our members they're quite a hit
Of that there is no contention.

'Tis true to say for TMS
In spring, summer or fall
The weather's not always been the best
But Galloway sure beat them all.

On an antiques show on the BBC
Was our President, but not for long
Proudly kilted and showing a knee
He sold his sporran for a song.

At Kirriemuir a plaque unveiled
To Munro and all his good works
But not a word of the speeches was heard
Thanks to the noisy roadworks.

With German TV in on the Heightings game
A film crew descended en mass
To the top of Ben Lawers was their aim
But they didn't even reach Beinn Ghlas.

The MQI project was ended
With write-ups on every Munro
With procedures all now amended
Mountain Reports are the new status quo.

The annual sub's been upped but one time
In 2008 when it went to pounds twenty
But despite higher costs it remains just fine
And still deemed that twenty's plenty. [1]

The Newsletter goes from strength to strength
And since 2014 with all-colour pics
It grew to 32 pages in length
But since last year it's been 36.

The Journals numbers 3, 4 and 5
With articles quite a mix
You'll see, dear reader, it still survives
As we're now at Journal number 6.

So what's in store for TMS
For the next twenty years and more
It's bound to be of the very best
To keep the Society to the fore.

[1] Correct at time of writing

APPENDIX 2 – 2002–2022; The First Twenty Years

The next 15 pages comprise a photo-montage of the activities of The Munro Society since its inception in 2002 to the present day, both on the hill and off it. The Editorial Team is grateful for all the photographs received and wishes to thank all the photographers, and also Gary Duncan for painstakingly assembling the photographs in an attractive 'photo-album' format.

The Munro Society
2002—2022: The First 20 Years

Iain Robertson's 50th anniversary Munro completion,
Beinn Eighe, August 2013

Guard of honour for David Batty's
Grahams and Full House completion,
Carnan Cruithneachd, October 2015

Colin Walter's third Munro completion on
Ben Chonzie

Anne Butler's Full House completion,
Fiarach, September 2018

John Green at summit cairn of Carn Eighe
on his Anthology walk, April 2012

The Munro Society
2002—2022: The First 20 Years

Arran enjoys the company of Michaela Strachan, Annual Dinner 2019

Honorary member Ralph struggles to hide his disappointment at the absence of actual bones in the Bone Caves

Keep it Wild at the Scottish Parliament ... David Batty, Derek Sime and Stewart Logan

An injured Barn Owl gatecrashed the Aultguish meet, 2018

The Munro Society
2002—2022: The First 20 Years

Fred Ward, Elsa Yates, Glen Breaden,
Crianlarich meet 2018

Suilven ... five of the six summitteers with a
combined age of 425, Inchnadamph meet 2019

Robin Corlett, Galloway meet 2017

Peter eating his Willimott Hill
Sandwich at Lochivraon

Alan Brook, Robin Corlett and John Green,
Glen Feshie meet, July 2019

The Munro Society
2002—2022: The First 20 Years

Debate on Sir Hugh Munro at the Scottish Parliament attended by TMS members Alan Watt, William Munro, Stewart Logan, Bill Taylor, Bill Wheeler and Liz Smith MSP

Stewart Logan is interviewed by STV at the opening of the MLE

Eleanore Hunter, Derek Sime, Glen Breaden and Walter McArthur, AGM 2008

The Munro Society

2002—2022: The First 20 Years

Alan Hawarth on the summit ridge of
Beinn Dearg Mòr

150th Anniversary, Driesh ... Eleanore Hunter,
Charles Murray and Bill Taylor

Alan Hinchcliffe, Alan Brook and Maggie
Kift on Clach Leathad

Alan Hinchcliffe's completion of Munro's
Original List with Charles Murray and Ralph

The Munro Society
2002—2022: The First 20 Years

Alan Brook and Oliver Bartrum .. social distancing, Inchnadamph, September 2020

Iain Robertson and Nan Rae, President's Walk 2016

Hear no Evil, Speak no Evil, See no Evil. Stewart Logan, David Batty, Keith Williams, Knoydart, May 2017

Heather Morning, David Whalley and Di Gilbert on Fiarach, 2018

Bill Taylor, Derek Sime, David Batty and Peter Willimott, Carleatheran, August 2016

Alan Rowan and John Speakman, Fiarach, September 2018

The Munro Society
2002—2022: The First 20 Years

Maggie Kift, Oliver Bartrum, Catherine Bartrum and John Green, Braemar 2016

Fred Ward, Irene Leckie, Elsa Yates

TMS First Revisit, Beinn Dorain, November 2003

Roderick Manson, Sàil Mhòr 2019

Alan Brook's Deleted Tops completion

The Munro Society

2002—2022: The First 20 Years

Charles Murray and Lancaster Wheel, Beinn Eighe, Torridon meet, May 2015

Alan Brook abseils off the Inaccessible Pinnacle in style, May 2017

John Rogerson, knackered on the Beinn Bhreac heighting

Mark Gibson loses the will to live on Blackcraig Hill. Galloway meet 2017

Walter McArthur, Beinn Teallach 2009

The Munro Society
2002—2022: The First 20 Years

Charles Murray arrives home after fracturing his ankle at the Torridon meet 2011

Colin Walter takes the hard way, Kintail 2015

Fred Ward and Bill Taylor, 2007

Alastair Milner, Beinn Teallach, 2009

Peter Willimott on Beinn Bhreac heighting

The Munro Society
2002—2022: The First 20 Years

The masses gather for Anne Butler's Full House completion, Fiarach 2018

Iain Robertson's Graham completion on Carn Salachaidh

Alistair Milner, June 2011

Alan Rowan's Graham completion, Beinn Fhada, Mull 2019

Charles Murray and Alan Hinchcliffe

The Munro Society
2002—2022: The First 20 Years

First Continuous Munroists. Kathy Murgatroyd, Hamish Brown, AGM 2019

Anne Marie Foot and Robert H MacDonald

Chris Townsend and Alan Haworth, Annual Dinner 2014

Iain Robertson, Chris Smith and Fred Ward

Nan Rae and Ina Morris, Annual Dinner 2016

Michael Cowen and Robert MacDonald, Annual Dinner 2010

The Munro Society

2002—2022: The First 20 Years

David Batty, Jim Robertson and David Gibson on Fiarach 2018

Bone Caves gang ... Top - Alan Brook, Mary Coventry, Eleanore Hunter, John Rogerson, John Green, Irene Leckie. Bottom - Gill Nunn, Marley, Anne Butler, Elsa Yates

All smiles ... Frank and Liz Johnstone

Norman Wares and Colin Walter, September 2018

Frank Johnstone and Bill Taylor, Crianlarich meet 2018

The Munro Society

2002—2022: The First 20 Years

Robert MacDonald, Hamish Brown Peter Willimott, David Gibson, Annual Dinner 2012

Alan Watt and Bill Taylor dressing the mannequins at the MLE, Perth 2019

Sir Hugh Munro enjoys a dram at the 2006 Annual Dinner

The Munro Society
2002—2022: The First 20 Years

Glen Feshie meet 2019

Maggie Kift and Irene Leckie,
Crianlarich meet 2018

Anne Butler and Oliver Bartrum, Fiarach

Kintail meet 2015

The Munro Society
2002—2022: The First 20 Years

The second Munro revisit on Ben Vorlich in April 2004 with four future Presidents
(John Burdin, Iain Robertson, Peter Willimott and Eleanore Hunter)
along with Angus Campbell and John Ross.

David Batty and Norman McNab,
Stùc a' Chroin, January 2017.

Completion of David Batty's Munro and Tops round,
Ben Vorlich North Top, June 2019